THE
PERFECT
NAZI

THE PERFECT NAZI

Uncovering My
Grandfather's Secret Past

MARTIN DAVIDSON

G. P. PUTNAM'S SONS
New York

PUTNAM

G. P. PUTNAM'S SONS
Publishers Since 1838
Published by the Penguin Group
Penguin Group (USA) Inc., 375 Hudson Street, New York, New York 10014, USA •
Penguin Group (Canada), 90 Eglinton Avenue East, Suite 700, Toronto, Ontario M4P 2Y3,
Canada (a division of Pearson Penguin Canada Inc.) • Penguin Books Ltd, 80 Strand,
London WC2R 0RL, England • Penguin Ireland, 25 St Stephen's Green, Dublin 2, Ireland
(a division of Penguin Books Ltd) • Penguin Group (Australia), 250 Camberwell Road,
Camberwell, Victoria 3124, Australia (a division of Pearson Australia Group Pty Ltd) •
Penguin Books India Pvt Ltd, 11 Community Centre, Panchsheel Park, New Delhi–110 017,
India • Penguin Group (NZ), 67 Apollo Drive, Rosedale, North Shore 0632, New Zealand
(a division of Pearson New Zealand Ltd) • Penguin Books (South Africa) (Pty) Ltd,
24 Sturdee Avenue, Rosebank, Johannesburg 2196, South Africa

Penguin Books Ltd, Registered Offices: 80 Strand, London WC2R 0RL, England

Library of Congress Cataloging-in-Publication Data

Davidson, Martin P. (Martin Peter), date.
The perfect Nazi : uncovering my grandfather's secret past / Martin Davidson.
p.   cm.
ISBN 978-0-399-15701-1
1. Langbehn, Bruno, 1906–1992. 2. Nazis—Biography. 3. National socialism—History.
4. Germany—History—1918–1933. 5. Germany—History—1933–1945.
6. Davidson, Martin P. (Martin Peter)—Family.   I. Title.
DD247.L248D39   2011   2010029596
943.086092—dc22
[B]

Printed in the United States of America
1   3   5   7   9   10   8   6   4   2

Book design by Michelle McMillian

While the author has made every effort to provide accurate telephone numbers and Internet addresses
at the time of publication, neither the publisher nor the author assumes any responsibility for errors, or
for changes that occur after publication. Further, the publisher does not have any control over and does
not assume any responsibility for author or third-party websites or their content.

*Penguin is committed to publishing works of quality and integrity.
In that spirit, we are proud to offer this book to our readers;
however, the story, the experiences, and the words
are the author's alone.*

FOR ALEXANDER AND LOUIS

Ma la notte risurge, e oramai
è da partir, chè tutto avem veduto.

But once again night is rising, and now
it's time to leave, for we have seen everything.
                    —DANTE, *INFERNO*, CANTO XXXIV

Contents

Acknowledgments

A personal book as enmeshed with the lives of so many in my family—none of whom I wish to discomfort, embarrass, or expose to scrutiny—could have been undertaken only with their collective blessing, even if it was sometimes hard for them to express. First, I would like to toast my main collaborator, my sister, Vanessa. We conceived the book together and shared much of the research, and I looked to her throughout for support, reality checks, and her sureness of touch, navigating where family and history collided. I held the steering wheel, but it was she who held the maps. I have to thank my mother, Frauke, not least for enduring the anguish that dredging up all this caused her, but above all for bowing to the pressure of what must have looked like a strange and personal obsession on my part, and not standing in its way. To my father, Ian, my huge appreciation for sharing with me his own family recollections, and for responding so positively to an early draft, as many of his suspicions about this father-in-law took on worrying form. Thanks also go to Gudrun and Georg, my aunt and uncle in Berlin, who watched nervously from the sidelines; and to my German cousins, Stella and Bakis, who were infectiously curious about what we might uncover.

Friends and colleagues read various drafts and gave invaluable suggestions; Michael Jackson in New York and Tim Kirby and Denys Blakeway in London were just three of them. All were kind enough to insist that, in a world heaving with books about the Nazis, there was indeed room for this one. My editor, the redoubtable Eleo Gordon, earned my gratitude for seizing on the story's potential right from the start, but especially for her stoic patience in the face of the (many) months it took me to adapt the art of writing for television to that of the printed page. Ben Brusey helped steer the project through its key stages with great tenacity and skill. In America, Kathryn Davis provided much-needed acumen, while George Lucas was the source of endless diplomacy and encouragement. Peter Robinson, agent and friend, wielded his editing pruning knife with the élan of a samurai, proving time and time again that less is always more.

I benefited from the help of a number of academics and re-searchers who illuminated the parts of Bruno's story that were otherwise inaccessible to me. Early on, Professor Michael Wildt, the world's expert on the SD, steered me in some very helpful directions, not least toward a research student of his acquain-tance, Anna Hájková, an authority on wartime Czechoslovakia, who is writing a Ph.D. dissertation on Theresienstadt; her forays into the Prague archives were invaluable. Jaroslav Čvančara was also kind enough both to share his enormous expertise on Prague in the shadow of the swastika and to lend me immensely valu-able primary materials. The Terezín Initiative Institute provided me with both guides to wartime Prague and valuable background information. In London and Washington, D.C., I was particularly fortunate to work with Dr. Nick Terry, whose insights—and formidable organizational skills—were indispensable. His forensic grasp of the inner workings of the SS formed the basis for some riveting conversations. In Berlin, Dr. Martin Schuster guided me through the dark underworld of the Charlottenburg storm troopers of the Berlin SA—and much more besides. The team at the London Library furnished me, as they do so many writers, with the wherewithal to complete huge swaths of my research. My old BBC colleague Tilman Remme pointed me toward a number of other experts, in Ludwigsburg, Berlin, and London, all of whom dealt with specific inquiries with exemplary patience and knowledge. Any errors, lapses, or outrageous extrapolations should, of course, be laid at my door, not theirs.

Two debts, however, tower above them all: First, to my boys, Alexander and Louis, who, for about as long as they can remember, have had to pick their way around mountains of their dad's "Hitler books" on the way to the family computer. And last, to the person who not only shared the trawl through family darkness at first hand, but also directed the rigor of her peerless mind toward my attempts to make sense of it, merciless on what should go, yet even more important, on what should stay: my wife, Janice Hadlow. Truly my *trina luce* . . . *'n unica stella scintillando*—triple light dazzling in a single star, muse, confidante, love of my life.

PREFACE

For thirty-five years of my life, my sister and I lived in the shadow of an unanswered question: What had Bruno Langbehn, our German grandfather, done during the war? When we were young, we didn't know *how* to ask it. But even as we grew older, and understood better, we still couldn't broach it. We knew it was there, but, like the rest of the family, tiptoed round it. It became a taboo.

The answer, when it came in the early 1990s, proved that, in a world full of dark family secrets, ours had lost none of its power to appall. For the next ten years, it burrowed its way deep inside me, until I could bear it no longer. I had to know everything. I was driven by curiosity. But trepidation, too. What would I find out? Did I *really* want to know? Having once embarked, there was no turning back. I was determined, once and for all, to know the truth about my Nazi grandfather.

Bruno may not have been a participant in the darkest of Nazi atrocities; there were many Nazis more heinous than he. Neither a camp *Kommandant* nor an architect of the Holocaust, neither a Höss nor an Eichmann, he was nevertheless an enabler of evil, one of its indispensable, and very active, minions.

Men like Bruno propelled the Nazi movement from the fanatic fringes into the mainstream. Their support gave it life long after it should have fizzled out in the Munich beer cellars of its birth; they made sure it took root in the minds of more than just a handful of madmen. Bruno and fellow early joiners provided the energy, the determination—and the violence—that overcame all obstacles to power. They formed the backbone of the apparatus of terror that ensured compliance in the new Third Reich and they were in the front line, fighting the war that erupted six years later, regarding it as the final great expression of Nazi values and its most important project.

As a self-declared Nazi militant, Bruno did none of this out of coercion, or even convenience, but from deeply held, long-term conviction. His commitment to National Socialism never wavered. He remained true to its world vision until the bitter end. He had no reservations about Hitler's genius or its consequences for the people of Europe. Only self-preservation eventually forced him to renounce it.

No account of Bruno's life could therefore be complete that did not confront his beliefs or interrogate the values that he found so inspiring, values that he was prepared not just to support but also to help realize, even to the point of war. The Nazi movement set out to destroy all that was liberal, decent, and humane, which they regarded as weakness and corruption, and they came close to doing it. Bruno proudly wore uniforms that he felt embodied a truth that was superior, stronger, and more heroic than what were, in his mind, the outmoded values held by the rest of the civilized world.

He was a very particular kind of Nazi, but one whose story rarely gets told. We know lots about the top-level henchmen, and even about the wider German population who may, or may not, have been seduced by Hitler's message. It's the willing agents, the factotums, the managers—like Bruno—who are taken for granted, who function as unthinking givens. They were there at the beginning, were crucial at every juncture, and were there at the end—and beyond. The Nazi story is inconceivable without them. Bruno's ambition was to become as respected and trusted a Nazi as he could, and in this, at least, he succeeded.

It's not hard to see why those of us who came after Bruno would prefer caginess to confrontation. Who wants to be touched by a secret as toxic as this, especially when it is lodged deep in the heart of the family? It has been a difficult book to write, with a story I find hard to come to terms with. But it is an important one, and I have learned much while doing it.

Bruno was never a repentant man. Everyone acquainted with him could see that he felt he had nothing to answer for. His cause had lost, but he was quite prepared to move on and enjoy the compensatory benefits of a postwar German economy. Nor did he see any reason to explain what had happened, far less offer any contrition. Why would he? There had been no sacrifice, certainly no sanctions, and he got to live to the fine old age of eighty-five—old enough to see the Berlin Wall come down and the dissolution of the USSR. There was no final reckoning, beyond having to forfeit the right to boast about what an important man the Third Reich had made him—at least to those outside the circle of his fellow *Kriegskameraden*.

This book is therefore intended to redress Bruno's well-insulated sense of non-accountability, to probe, if only post-humously, his apparent circumvention of any material or moral consequences of a long and embattled Nazi career. In writing it, I have been driven to ask not just what he did, but why. What motivated him? Why did he believe these things as fanatically as he did? What was it about National Socialism that spoke to him so loudly and irresistibly? What kind of man regards Adolf Hitler as the answer to his political dreams? Insofar as Bruno's life contains a "warning from history," then it is here; not just in specific crimes, but in his mind-set, which spurred him to join the movement and compelled him to work tirelessly on its behalf.

That is why this book is neither a conventional biography nor a case study. In researching it, I was forced to reassess everything I thought I knew about the Nazi system and Bruno's place within it. I have extrapolated where I needed to, joining the gaps in his story as well as the dots, tracking his Nazi career over a quarter of a century, trying to understand what drove each key stage. The events of his Nazi career betray an underlying pattern, which I have used in combination with my residual memory of his personality to help reconstruct his journey from teenage fanatic to Third Reich perpetrator.

It helped that Bruno was neither a reticent nor an enigmatic figure. What views about the world he had he wore on his sleeve. Some of this was the bravado of an egotistical old man, but some of it represented the afterglow of the biggest adventure of his life—his years as a Nazi activist. He had spent decades convinced he was in possession of a great and transcendent truth, and the habit never entirely left him.

In a period when family history has burgeoned on television

and in books and magazines, I realize that I belong to a generation who see themselves as custodians of their grandparents' lives. We are voluble and emotional about their experiences, where they were modest and reticent. Usually, the result is a kind of retrospective pride, a greater recognition of achievements than they received during their own lifetime. In my case, of course, there is none of that. There can be no self-satisfaction here: only the sobering realization that barely fifty-four years separate our respective dates of birth, though, mercifully, our worlds could not be more different.

Of course, Bruno was *forced* to be tight-lipped about his past—to his very considerable chagrin. It wasn't the result of natural modesty, but of a powerful postwar embargo, motivated at first by the need to avoid exposure and arrest, then later as part of a much more widespread national reticence that chose to turn a blind eye to the past. This, then, is as much of his archetypal Nazi career—and the path of a generation of Germans born in the early years of the last century—as I have been able to piece back together. Some, at least, of Bruno's story is now out in the open, where it should be.

One

FUNERAL IN BERLIN

Edinburgh and Berlin, 1960–1984

It's such a sweet picture. That's me, chuckling away, my pudgy little arms waving about in delight. Behind lies the gentle curve of a Scottish beach an hour's drive east of Edinburgh, where I was born and grew up. It's sunny and warm, the perfect day for a drive to the shore, armed with a brand-new home movie camera. Holding me to his shoulder is a man in his mid-fifties, smiling, only too happy to play his part in this little family moment. In fact, he is my German grandfather, and he seems very proud of his first grandson. He has a distinctive face, with close-cropped hair, large ears, bulbous nose, fixed eye line, and slightly serrated smile. Beyond that, he appears perfectly benign, a little stern maybe, but open-faced, and unembarrassed to have his cheek pawed by a gurgly baby. It's August 1961, and I am nine months old.

For the next thirty years, like anyone who has at least one German parent, I was taught to remember that there was so much more to Germany than just the Nazis. The world's obsession with Hitler, and with the Second World War, was just a vast distraction from the rest of German history. Even though it was a struggle to get terribly excited about the court of Frederick the Great, or the premiership of Willy Brandt, I did my bit and tried hard to avoid simply collapsing the entire meaning of the word *Germany* into a synonym for the Third Reich. And then, in 1992, I realized I had no choice.

Bruno Langbehn, my grandfather, the man in the home movie footage, had died at the age of eighty-five. Only in the weeks after his death did I discover that "Papa," as my mother always called him, hadn't been just a German dentist who had happened to live through the tumultuous decades of the Nazi nightmare. Nothing of the sort, in fact.

I had always had my suspicions, of course, and as the years went past I had chipped away at the protective carapace that had been erected around his early career. I had tried to prize information out of my mother, but it was only with him dead that my mother felt able, finally, to tell me the truth—or at least one tiny bit of it.

I had never met my other, Scottish, grandfather. I knew he had been marched off to the trenches of the First World War with the Seaforth Highlanders and, against the odds, had managed to survive, unlike many of his friends, or indeed his older brother. Returning from France, he had decided what he most wanted to do with his life was to fish for salmon and drive down his golf handicap, each and every day. To do so he needed a job that didn't take him away from his rods or his clubs, so he opened a cinema in his Highland hometown of Dingwall, in Ross-shire. He never needed to work during daylight hours again. My father grew up in its shadow, collecting the posters, loitering in the projector room, in his wartime Cinema MacParadiso. But all that standing up to his thighs in ice-cold Highland water ruined my Scottish grandfather's health, and he died many years before I was even born. I would never know more about him than what my father could tell me. I had no idea even what he looked like, how he spoke, no sense at all of his personality beyond family anecdote.

The relationship my sister, Vanessa, and I had with Bruno, however, was more complex, and more immediate. Our lives *did* overlap, and we grew up with a very clear impression of what kind of man we thought he was. To this day I can call to mind his appearance, a sense of his personality and presence. And yet despite my vivid recollections of him, much about Bruno remained unknown. The mystery didn't arise from simple distance, and the inevitable haziness of memory. The obscurity that enveloped him always felt deliberately constructed, a smoke screen and not just generational amnesia.

It wasn't hard to see why this might be so. Simply knowing where and when he was born—Prussia, 1906—had ominous significance. It was impossible for him not to have come to adulthood in the heart of Nazi darkness. And, as for all Germans of his generation, it raised a mass of implied questions. What had he done? What had he been? What did he know? Bruno's behavior did nothing to dispel such questions; on the contrary, it positively invited them. Of all my German relatives, he was the least apologetic, the least self-effacing. Even in his seventies he bristled with views about life, about politics and human nature, about the follies of the world, which he expressed with uncompromising force, and the vigor of someone whose whole life had been one long argument. In this regard he always struck me as being the most explicitly belligerent German, the one whose convictions about the present most provoked you into *daring* to think about his past.

But thinking about it was as far as we were ever allowed to get. Talking about it—or even asking questions about it—was *not* encouraged in our home. My mother would refuse point-blank to be drawn into our speculations, deflecting and evading them whenever they surfaced. We were children, indulging in subjects we couldn't possibly understand. The subject was closed. The result was that we grew up with huge and tantalizing gaps in our knowledge of him. These made him only more mysterious, as did the defensiveness with which my other relatives had encircled him. He was a no-go area.

If, as a child, I hadn't been curious about my older German relatives, everyone else around me certainly was. The culture of Britain in the 1960s and 1970s was dominated by the long shadow of the Second World War, which had ended only fifteen years before my birth. Like everyone else of my generation, I may not have known much about their historical reality, but the "Nazis" were as vivid to me as the Daleks on *Dr. Who*. I thought I knew what they looked like, what they sounded like, how they behaved. Defeating them had been the greatest achievement of the twentieth century.

They were tall and blond; they often had scars; they clicked their heels and held their cigarettes with sadistic precision. They didn't talk, they barked, though sometimes they issued their threats in quiet, determined tones, choosing their every word carefully, and with cruel, menacing deliberation. More usually they shouted, especially when enraged, which they seemed always to be, at which point they would scream into phones, or bring their fist crashing down on desks. They were oleaginous in their behavior toward attractive women, who would recoil and squirm when their hands were kissed. I knew all this because not a week went by without some kind of war film on television, whose basic grammar was replicated wildly in comics and playground games. I watched them all avidly, as did everyone my age. We all loved imagining what it must have been like to have been a Spitfire pilot, a jungle commando, or a cocoa-supping officer on the bridge of an Atlantic destroyer. I may have been half German, but I wasn't the slightest bit confused about who the heroes were. Every Messerschmitt shot down, every German battleship sunk, every defeated Wehrmacht soldier was a triumph to cheer. Above all, Nazis were *them*, separated from *us* (not just the British, but the entire human race) by an uncrossable divide. And yet I still stopped short of seeing my grandfather reflected in these depictions.

There was no question that my German relatives, especially my grandfather, had been on the wrong side, and yet even as a child I couldn't fully equate him with the grimly robotic "krauts" and "squareheads" whose walk-on parts were so unvarying— there to display the arrogance and cruelty that would be tamed by Tommy bravado. He would have had to have been unutterably evil to have been *one of them*. Surely the truth was less melodramatic than that. The movies appeared to bear me out. As I grew older, a new generation of Second World War Germans were depicted in a much less one-dimensionally unpalatable way. They had stopped being either morons or psychopaths and had become, instead, conflicted officers usually alienated from, and deeply disillusioned by, the Nazi regime. Most ambiguous of all was *Das Boot*, which featured in the character of the captain played by Jürgen Prochnow the ultimate example of a man with no love for the politics that had triggered the war, anxious only to do his duty and get his men out alive. Perhaps *that* was what my grandfather had been like? Needless to say, my mother felt much more comfortable with these more complex and ambiguous portraits of Germans at war. So it appeared possible to wear a German uniform without necessarily being a fanatical Nazi.

But as a twelve-year-old I felt residual self-consciousness about having a German mother. It still chafed a little. When I talked to the parents of school friends, my heart would always beat a little faster when explaining how Berlin was our favorite holiday destination. Nobody ever said anything, but I knew what they were thinking. Of course, far less reticent were my school friends. For them it was all too obvious. They would taunt me with their playground *Sieg heils*, giggling as they decided my mysterious German relatives must all have been Nazi soldiers who knew Hitler personally. It was embarrassing, though I don't recall finding any of this especially traumatic. I was big, I was good at sports, and therefore not a natural public-school victim. Anyway, it wasn't as if I had an overtly German name. But they only had to come and visit our house to see with their own eyes, I wasn't, finally, a hundred percent British. Anyone meeting my mother could see, and hear, in an instant, that she was German.

She had come to Edinburgh in 1958, to learn English, had met my Scottish father, gotten married, and stayed there ever since. But she never concealed, or even camouflaged, her roots. She has always kept her German passport and maintained her ties with Germany through frequent trips and a network of family and friends. Later she became a brilliant German teacher at the school I had attended, introducing her pupils to a vast array of subjects that weren't just the Third Reich.

Of course, the experience of the Second World War might just be the stuff of movies for me, but it wasn't for her. She had lived through it as a child far younger even than I was. Every now and again she would drop hints about what it had been like, and then even as a naive schoolboy I would sit up, dumbfounded. There were memories of times spent shivering in Berlin air-raid shelters as night after night the RAF pounded the city. The rubble, the sirens, the casualties. And then there had been Prague, where she had been at the end of the war, where she witnessed and experienced at first hand the nightmare of the collapsing eastern front, and the spasms of revenge and bloodshed that greeted German capitulation; the summary executions, the bodies littering the streets, the terrible acts of physical retribution. These were not things to stir up lightly. The more she squirmed at talking about it, the harder it was to dampen our sense that it was simply impossible for an entire family to have lived through those years and not have something to hide.

Every year till my late teens, we would visit the part of Germany that wore its history in the most open-scarred and still-threatening way, staying there for up to five weeks at a time. It became the regular and most glamorous experience of our year. Compared with Edinburgh, Berlin was huge, modern, and in the front line of world current affairs.

The simple business of getting there was so fraught with Cold

War drama that it was hard not to feel we too were plunging down the throat of history. We almost always drove, down to Harwich, and then by overnight ferry to the Hook of Holland, before plowing across the Netherlands and into West Germany. After we reached Hannover, though, a heavy silence gradually fell as tensions mounted. My mother would light up her first, and only, cigarette of the whole trip, because ahead of us lay the dreaded border.

The "zone," as it was called then, involved a four-hour piece of Cold War purgatory, crossing at Helmstedt from West Germany into the GDR. Endless, countless passport checks, full car searches, East German conscripts with terrible skin who stuck their heads into the car and assailed us with a list of weapons they demanded to know if we were smuggling: revolvers, rifles, semiautomatics, machine guns, grenades, and so on. It was heart-pounding stuff. Behind the one-way mirrors, the dogs, and the barbed wire lay the tangible sense that the price for any irregularity or anomaly could be really serious. It was my first encounter with genuine enmity. These people didn't like us and they didn't want us visiting that thorn in East Germany's flesh, West Berlin. But our unease was nothing compared with my mother's. She would retreat into frown-lined silence, her body rigid behind a shell that refused to be violated by these Soviet-sector East German faces and their East German accents, even when her posture so clearly provoked them. I could tell there lay behind this spectacular disdain a real fear that had its origins long before my time, in experiences I didn't comprehend.

After the border, West Berlin was a further four hours' drive. We experienced the frisson of knowing that the road we were traveling on had been one of Hitler's great autobahns, and still

had its original 1930s road surface. It was a very physical reminder of what kind of city we were entering. And then, at the
outskirts of the city itself, another "zone," reprising the unpleas-
antness and apprehensions of the earlier one.

But once through that, we were at last back in the safe embrace
of Western Europe, in the Allied sector of what soon became West
Berlin. All that remained to do was thunder along the old AVUS
racetrack, join the Messedamm, and pass the Funkturm (Berlin's
mini–Eiffel Tower) on our left, before reaching our destination—
the Kaiserdamm, the great east-west axial boulevard that bisects
Berlin. A quick left turn at the lights, find a parking spot, pour out
of the car, march up to a familiar gray door, and we had arrived.
For the next month or so this would be our home, the flat that
Thusnelda (or *Mutti*, as my sister and I called her), our grandmother, shared with her fox terrier, Pippi.

She greeted us at her flat's front door, beaming and hug-
ging us, as we slithered out of the inevitable kiss like eels. Within
hours we were back in a warm and familiar groove, which started
with raiding the mirrored cabinet in the living room that contained its irresistible booty of marzipan animals and bars of
Kinder Schokolade. Breakfast meant *Brötchen*, the rolls we bought
every day from a bakery on the other side of the Kaiserdamm
and drenched in cherry jam. We were sent out to the cigarette
machine to walk the dog and returned with endless packs of
Milde Sorte cigarettes, which my grandmother chain-smoked all
her life.

I loved not only West Berlin's sheer scale and cosmopolitan
excitement, but also the unmistakable, slightly ominous rumble
that lay just below the surface. Everything about Berlin reeked not
just of the Cold War, but of the war that had preceded it. Even

when we were this age, our familiarity and ghoulish relish for the Wall, Checkpoint Charlie, the "*Sie verlassen jetzt die amerikanische Sektor*" signs, and all the rest served to underline the fact that, whatever else our German family had done, they had certainly lived through interesting times.

Nowhere was that more discernible than in the other fabulous old-world Berlin apartment we regularly visited. This was owned by the oldest of our living relatives, my great-grandmother, Bruno's mother-in-law, who, like him, was a dentist, and was still practicing in her seventies. Her name was Ida Pahnke-Lietzner, and she was as formidable as her name, a matriarch, and Prussian to her core. Her flat was a thirty-second walk from where my grandmother lived, but felt as if it were separated by decades. If the city provided us with only distant murmurs of its hidden past, then Ida's flat turned these echoes into a shout.

It was the kind of apartment you can get only in metropolitan Europe. Reached via a marbled vestibule, with infinitely receding opposing mirrors, and an elevator with clunking metal gates, it was up on the first floor. A heavy door would open, and we would be drawn into a large hallway, with a deep, dark corridor penetrating the main salons. This doubled up as her dentist's waiting room, which guarded her fully functioning surgery, complete with rows of specimen dentures and magazines to soothe the nerves of waiting patients.

By now, all outside sounds had been banished, muffled by thick walls overlaid with dozens of Persian rugs, too many for the floor alone. And around them were hung the fruits of her other great passion—oil painting. Taking pride of place was the great battleship *Graf Spee*. The creaking parquet floor, the dark wooden panels, and the great double windows looking out onto the breadth of the Kaiserdamm outside made it clear how we were supposed to behave: *very* formally, and *very* politely. We would make our way to the heart of the flat, the great sliding doors behind which was located the *Herrenzimmer*. Now we would have our audience with her.

As we sat nervously in this throwback to an earlier era, the Biedermeier vitrine, with its myriad wines and liqueurs, and flutes and other glasses, and the dark leather and velvet sofas power-fully evoked an earlier era of Berlin life. It wasn't the flat she had lived in before or during the war, that was a few miles to the west, but it might as well have been. The most unsettling part of any visit was the way she would make patients wait until she had finished her conversation with us before she would see them. The look of fraught concentration on my mother's face told me that her grandmother was not somebody to be trifled with. I suspected it was a lesson she had learned early in life.

So even if you didn't go rooting around after it, and despite Berlin's feverishly modern urban cladding, its shops, and neon, its signature modern buildings, its past history remained con-spicuously part of its DNA. There was the Russian T-34 tank on a plinth down near the Brandenburg Gate. There were bullet-hole pockmarks on the side of older buildings. There was Teufels-berg, an entirely artificial hill built out of bomb rubble, and wildly rumored to be home to all sorts of British spook activities. And above all was the Death Zone, the widest area covered by the Wall separating East and West Berlin, a strip of wasteland that only the guard dogs could now roam, but which had once been the most important real estate in Nazi Berlin, home to Hitler's Chancellery and its underground bunker, visible now only as a small mound in the earth. (It was finally flattened when the Wall came down in 1989.) So alongside the beautiful Grünewald lakes, the outstanding architecture of Mies van der Rohe's New National Gallery and the seductive expanse of the KaDeWe department store, all of which made our Berlin holidays so exciting, there was also, undeniably, a darker character. Even as children we knew it.

Berlin contained other family traces, the names of people whom, though they were still alive, we never met. There was my mother's uncle Ewald (Bruno's brother-in-law), who had been banished as the family black sheep after getting a housemaid pregnant. Great-grandmother Ida was clearly a woman unstoppable in her pursuit of family success and not very forgiving in the face of weakness or fallibility. Much more frequently—and warmly—talked about, though, was *der alte Herr*, the old gentleman, her second husband (her first had been killed in the First World War). He had been a professional soldier his whole life, ending up a major at the end of the Second World War, an officer of the old school, with the reputation for having fought a decent war. My mother would always speak fondly of him, with palpable and infectious respect—not something she ever did about her own far more abrasive father.

But none of these family members could compete with Bruno for notoriety and mystique. This was reinforced by his sudden absence; one year, he simply wasn't there anymore. Only later did we discover the real reason. My grandmother had divorced him, after he had left her and moved in with her onetime best friend. It was a grim reward for all her years of keeping the family together. My mother squarely sided with my grandmother, and he retaliated by severing all contact with the rest us. One consequence of this rift was that, when we *did* later resume contact, his visits assumed the proportions (and complexities) of major diplomatic events, fraught with tension. There was no chance he could simply sidle in and out of our lives as of old; from now on, our encounters with him would be especially tough for my mother, still bristling at his treatment of my grandmother.

He came to see us in the long, hot summer of 1976, when I was fifteen. It was the first time we had seen him properly since the divorce. I knew it was going to be a chance to gauge for myself what kind of person he really was. It could not have been more different from our previous meeting, nearly ten years earlier, in Berlin. This time, the setting was the utterly incongruous one of a school cricket match. I suspect the scene amused him, too. The gap between the world of my upbringing and that of my German mother was starkly visible as I strode across the outfield in my white flannels to greet him. My first impression was how physically changed he was. When I had last seen him he had been tall, even rather gangly (as I was myself). But the man walking next to my mother was very clearly an old man, walking slowly with the aid of a stick, his legs bowed, his face dominated by a formidable double chin. I was a lot more nervous about the encounter than he appeared to be. He clapped me around the shoulders and beamed, exclaiming how much I had grown. The bravado in his manner took me aback. Any nervousness about the intervening ten years was simply cast aside by his hale and infectious gusto.

Nor did it let up over the following few days. He wasn't a man to waste time with pleasantries and small talk. I remember being swept up into his bon vivant gregariousness. Within minutes of our first greeting him, he was regaling my sister and me with stories about his recent trip to the States, full of anecdotes underpinned by the fact that his single visit had turned him into an unimpeachable expert on all things American. (I later realized this must have meant he had filled in a visa application form. How, I wonder now, had he dealt with the question "Have you ever been a member of the Nazi Party or the SS?"—a question that is *still* there.) Above all, he was delighted by his capacity to remain unimpressed by things; they had flown a light plane over the Grand Canyon, but he had slept through it all, he exclaimed, enjoying the disbelief this created in my sister and me, who were unable to understand that anyone could be so nonchalant.

What I found most striking about his manner wasn't his urge to perform, or his eccentric candor, it was the last thing I had expected of him, namely how unburdened by secrets he appeared to be. There was *nothing* retiring or self-effacing about him. He was a big man in every sense—though no longer over six feet tall, thanks to a large girth and an old man's stoop—and his florid, determined face, vibrant shock of white hair, and garish cravats made him impossible to ignore. He was a Technicolor character, whose unapologetic flamboyance and gallantry seemed all the brighter when set against the staid monochrome of life in 1970s Edinburgh. He never sought to blend in, to pass himself off, and to go unnoticed. He was charismatic and knew it, and I have to admit to finding his persona, if not appealing, certainly magnetic. But that, as it turned out, was his greatest act of concealment.

That evening, he took Vanessa and me out for supper at his hotel and proceeded to make us drink our way across an entire shelf of spirits and liqueurs, with all too predictable results. By the time we got home we were completely inebriated, which earned him a tirade from my mother. He was gloriously unrepentant. We could tell how much he relished making trouble, mocking her indignation at the state we were in. It was an act of brazen hypocrisy, however, when compared with how he had brought her up as a teenager—with iron inflexibility, full of prohibitions—against jazz on the radio, against meeting boys from school, against wearing anything fashionable, let alone risqué.

There were other times, though, when the bravado that had protected him all his life almost got the better of him, times when he wanted to do more than just be the center of attention. These were the moments when he would start to play a rather more dangerous game, moments when I realized we had strayed into forbidden territory, and he started to talk more openly about the past. Not to reflect on it, and certainly never to repent—that wasn't his way—but to tantalize, tease, and boast about it. When I was in my early twenties, he would sit me down with a large brandy and an even larger cigar and drop a succession of ever more pointed hints, allusions, and cryptic remarks that I now realize were actually a kind of bait.

He would take a large and deliberate puff and lean over. *"Mahteen,"* he would mutter, the clipped German pronunciation of my name, promising an instant semi-conspiratorial intimacy, and then it would start. Some of his taunts were historical ones: "You know, all we wanted was an empire, too, like your Churchill's." It was the first time I had encountered what is now quite a familiar piece of German post-rationalization—that the quest for *Lebensraum* ("living space") had grown out of the same impulse that had helped plant the Union Jack over so much of the eighteenth- and nineteenth-century globe. Other allusions he made were far more opaque; they seemed prosaic, straightforward remarks, but they had the whiff of something darker behind them. He gave me a recording of Liszt's *Hungarian Rhapsodies*. Only later did I discover that one of these was the favorite fanfare used at the start of all major Nazi newsreels and wireless announcements. He loved Hungarian culture, he told me, thought it was wonderful. His favorite. Only later did I start thinking—and when the hell were *you* in Hungary?

He then described what he did for fun. He enjoyed watching football, he said, but best of all was meeting his *Kriegskameraden* (his wartime buddies), around a regular *Stammtisch*, the table that many German pubs have, reserved for use by customers wanting a regular meeting place, perfect for eating, drinking, and reminiscing. The word *Krieg*—war—lay quivering there in front of me, and it hadn't even been me who had mentioned it.

For years I had been taught to be circumspect, coded, discreet—and now the man who had motivated all that secrecy was fixing me with this skewerlike explicitness. Was he suggesting that the subject was now no longer off-limits? He rounded off the effect by giving me another gift, this time 1,000 DMs, to help me on my way. "We all need help starting our lives," he said. "I, too, got help when I had to start again." Start again? You mean, like you did in 1945? But instead of picking up the gauntlet, I just sat there, dazed by the alcohol and the smoke and said . . . nothing. I never rose; I never reached up to swallow the tidbits of provocation he held out to me. Instead I hemmed and hawed my way back onto safer ground.

Why had I found it *so* difficult to just ask him questions? I wasn't stupid. Even then I could see what he was doing, that at some level he was desperate for me to start a conversation. Had I done what he wanted, I'm sure he would have told me everything—at least his version of it. The whole lot. Where he'd been. What he'd seen. What he'd done. What an important man he had been. But I didn't, because deep down I don't think I wanted to know. For one thing, I knew he wasn't trying to recruit me as some kind of genuine confidant—I was being groomed as a foil against which to do some historical jousting. How he would have loved turning my limp liberal disquiet inside out, demolishing all my protestations and disapproval. I would have been such easy meat, and I had no desire to get sucked into whatever game it was he was playing.

But there was a deeper reason. What would I *do* with the knowledge, once he'd shared it with me? What would it make me feel, not just about him, but more important, about myself? It's one thing to encounter one of the great evils of the twentieth century, through the testimony of others, in novels and pictures and films. It's quite another thing to accept that a little bit of that malign phenomenon has taken up residence within the confines of your own family, that presiding silently over everything is a terrible secret, a secret that involves not the universal small sins of infidelity, bankruptcy, or drink but something that speaks to the true heart of darkness. Well, I couldn't handle it, so I nodded and kept quiet, storing away what I thought Bruno was trying to tell me until I could work out what to make of it all. It was the closest I had come to discovering, from his own mouth, who and what he had been twenty years before my birth. Was I ever going to find out?

Berlin, New York, and London, 1992–1993

And then came the inevitable moment when everything about him finally came to a head. He was dying. This man who had come in and out of our young lives was about to leave it for good. It was spring 1992, and my mother, sister, and I were driving through central Berlin on our way to visit him. He was now eighty-five, and riddled with cancer. I was shocked to realize that it had been six years since I had last seen him. I wondered if there would be another six. We arrived at his flat only to find he wasn't there. Gisela, his wheelchair-bound common-law wife, explained to my mother that his condition had deteriorated and that he was now in a hospice. So we sat down in the flat that had been his home and chatted with her. She had always been a sweet-natured woman, and it was almost possible beneath the pleasantries to forget that he wouldn't ever be returning.

The following day, my mother went to visit him in hospital. He was indeed dying, she told us. Would we be able to visit him? She told us no. He had expressly asked her not to bring us on any future visits. We were rather taken aback. That sounded rather dramatic. Why not? He didn't feel up to it, my mother explained. It hardly seemed the appropriate moment to protest, so we accepted it, probably a little relieved to be spared some ghastly scene in a hospital ward. But it gave me pause for thought, as I realized the extent of what he would be certainly taking to the grave. I would never get the full disclosure to which I rather selfishly felt I was entitled, even though it had been years since we had last spoken to him. With him gone, all that would remain would be a series of maddeningly incomplete snippets: of wartime experiences that I had heard of from my mother, first in Berlin, and then in Czechoslovakia, where they were all captured by the Soviets. There were other bits and pieces of the puzzle that were added later on. Bruno, we were told, never drove across the GDR, but only flew, "to avoid being arrested by the Communists." Gisela, we learned, had been one of the dancing gymnasts performing at the opening ceremony of the 1936 Berlin Olympics. Beyond that, it was all white noise.

A week after Bruno's death, I was on the phone to my mother. She was in a reflective mood. We started talking about Bruno, and soon she was recounting her wartime memories. I had heard these all many times before, but on this occasion she was reliving them with unusual intensity. I picked up the pace still further, asking her more and more about her days in Berlin, and in Prague, about what she had seen, what it had felt like, what she thought about it now. And still she kept on talking, long after our normal conversations on the subject would have been discreetly wrapped up. And so, finally, out of nowhere, I simply blurted it out, the question that had welled up in me and which would finally breach the dam of silence that had surrounded my grandfather. "What kind of soldier takes his family with him to foreign postings? Why were you with him in Prague at all?" She didn't answer. "Come on," I said, "it doesn't make any sense. He couldn't have been a civilian, not that late in the war, when they were calling up teenagers and old men. And if he was an ordinary soldier, why would he have had you and your sisters there with him—families stay at home, they don't travel with the army. What was he *doing* there?" She paused, and I carried on: "He wasn't in the army, was he?" And then, unburdened by his presence at last, she made the fateful admission: "No, you're right, he wasn't, he was in the SS."

For all my dispassionate bluster, nothing had prepared me for the echoing hiss of two tiny letters, whispered over the telephone line. The SS. Bruno Langbehn, my grandfather, the retired Berlin dentist, the man who had hoisted me on his shoulders as a toddler; lavished watches, cameras, and cigars on me as a teenager; and embroiled me in combative conversation as a young adult, had been an officer in the *SS*. It was a fact that had been assiduously kept from us for all those years, but now, finally, I *knew*. I had probed and pestered, and now I had my answer.

It made sense of all my foreboding that there must be more to his past than met the eye. It had simply *never* occurred to me, for all my suspicions about this aggressive, reactionary man, that he had been in the SS. "All I can remember," she told me next, "was he was a *Hauptsturmführer*. And he had nothing to do with the camps, I know that." I put the phone down, my heart thumping. All I could hear were these two phrases: "a *Hauptsturmführer*" and "nothing to do with the camps." I had no idea what a *Hauptsturm-führer* was, but it was my mother's desperate certainty about what he had *not* done that most struck me. Well, I thought to myself, you sound very sure about that. I really hope you are right.

Solving the first of these two mysteries was easy enough. The following day, I found a list of SS ranks in the appendix of a history book and ran my finger down it till it came to rest on the right one. A *Hauptsturmführer* was the equivalent in rank to a captain. It didn't sound very senior, certainly not "policy-making" senior. But as I had no idea how rank and seniority worked in the SS, it remained an open question just how much comfort there was to be derived from his apparently modest place in the hierarchy. It was the second mystery that I knew, with some dread, would take a lot more investigation to solve, one way or the other. What *kind* of SS officer had he been? What had he actually done? I was just allowing this all to sink in when I suffered another pointed awakening.

Oxford, 2005

I got older, and I suppose Bruno and the untold story of his SS career might slowly have receded into the hazy landscape of the past. I brooded over it in the months after learning the truth, but with him dead, there didn't seem anything more I would be able to find out. I realized, too, just how little I really understood about the system that had created him, and men like him. I became a documentary maker for the BBC and made a series of films about the Nazis, particularly those who had wrestled after the war with the meaning of their infatuation with the regime: one on Hitler's friend and architect, Albert Speer, and the other on the talented but deeply flawed Leni Riefenstahl. What drew me to them was that both had managed to reinvent themselves and had all but succeeded in making their intellectual and moral complicity with the regime appear at worst merely ambiguous and at best simple human fallibility. Guilt and responsibility in all their complex manifestations fascinated me—as did the historians and writers who had made them their subject, and with whom I was now collaborating, such as Gitta Sereny, Ian Buruma, and Hugh Trevor-Roper, all of them authors of major works exploring these and related topics. And inevitably I thought about Bruno.

The names of the architects of Nazism acquired a kind of horrible familiarity during the 1946 Nuremberg trials, or fifteen years later with the capture of Adolf Eichmann. But the stories of the anonymous men who actually made the mechanics of the system turn, whose malign perseverance in their allotted tasks turned Nazism from rhetoric into action, remain largely hidden from history. We know they were there—and gradually scholarship is revealing more and more about what they actually did—

but we still don't know much about who they were or what they felt or why they did what they did.

The story of the choices Bruno made from early adulthood right up to 1945 is therefore about much more than an episode from one family's past. It illuminates a crossroads in the life of a whole nation. The decisions that transformed him from a young, newly fledged Berlin dentist into an ambitious, committed flag waver for the Nazi regime were mirrored all over Germany.

There's a photograph of Bruno dated 1931. It shows him tall, gangly, too young yet to have filled out into the commanding figure he later became. His wife stands next to him. They both look into the sun, slightly uncertain, wishing to please. He is a Monsieur Hulot figure, on his way to play that famous game of tennis. This is not, you feel, the man whose sheer force of personality later announced itself the minute he entered a room. Compare it with the family portrait taken in July 1941. These were among the few prewar and wartime photographs owned by my mother, and kept in a large, heavy German photo album, each page separated by a sheet of heavy tissue paper. My sister and I had been very familiar with most of these as children, and I later realized with a shock that I *had* seen this particular photograph many times but had never identified the uniform. As it was neither black nor sporting the SS symbol, I had always assumed it was just a generic army uniform. Now I knew differently.

But even if Bruno's uniform is hard to identify, the way he wears it is not. He exudes the conviction of the true believer. His wife gazes into the middle distance with eyes lit up, her blond hair gleaming in soft, tight Valkyrie waves. She no longer remotely resembles the rather frumpy figure of ten years before, but it is Bruno who has been most strikingly transformed. Not a hint of diffidence; no trace of doubt, ambiguity, or hesitance. This is a man who could quell you with a glance; he radiates cold command. Tomorrow—and the day after—you feel, really does belong to him.

What did they do for the rest of that July day on which the picture was taken, at that point in 1941, with Europe at Germany's feet? What kind of party did they make, leaving the studio, walking down whichever Berlin thoroughfare it was located on? Had the two girls (my mother and aunt) overcome their very apparent ill ease, thankful that they hadn't spoiled the picture? Did fellow pedestrians stand to one side on the pavement, unconsciously even, to let them by, this man with the cascade of SS pips on his collar, his wife beaming imperiously on the arm of one of the regime's undisputed winners? Did he slip off back to the office? Did she get home feeling that things just couldn't get any better? Beautiful, healthy girls; a husband involved in the most important state work; and a homeland on the march to unimagined greatness?

Ten years separate the two photographs, just one decade that turned the gaunt, rather gauche newlyweds into the chilly, beaming poster couple for the thousand-year Reich. One German had irrevocably become another, as surely as the nation itself had turned into something different. I knew I had to find out who this man and his wife really were.

But the question still haunted me: Did we want to know more? Of course, we didn't have the faintest clue what he actually did. My mother said she had no idea, and we believed her. She had been far too young during the war to be entrusted with that kind of knowledge, and after the war had done everything in her power to avoid it.

There is a stark and shocking brutality to the phrase "SS"; it has no ambiguity, no obvious possibility of extenuation. It opens up a plague of possibilities that start with the merely criminal and proceed from there. It might mean *anything*, from simple bureaucratic handling of some of the most pernicious memos ever committed to paper all the way through to actions that are unimaginable. I had swallowed that naive canard, that the SS contained only psychopaths and sadists, but now I realized that the truth was more upsetting. People like my grandfather had joined the SS, educated middle-class professionals—people like *me*, in other words. I also realized how little I really knew about the SS, and the rise of Nazi Germany, beyond the framework of dates and generalizations. It would have to be a dual exploration.

I was particularly interested in the story of the years that created him. I wanted to put a career to a face by discovering what it was my grandfather did in the SS. In the process I also wanted to do the opposite, to put a face to a career, by finding out more about the SS in general. What kind of men did it attract? How did they join? Was Bruno typical? What role did he and men like him play in the larger trajectory from ideology and careerism to genocide?

The story of Bruno's SS career might shed light on the last century's most horrifying questions: Why had these people done it, and why were so few of them *sorry*? There is a further personal element to this too, of course. The German part of me has to face the question: What would I have done? I asked my mother once if she thought he slept well at night. Oh, yes, she said. He wasn't the sort of man to have nightmares.

For the rest of us, things were different. Strangely enough, it was we, his relatives, who had become the true keepers of Bruno's secrets. It was we, not Bruno, who left thoughts unspoken. And, in doing so, we had become unwittingly complicit in his secrets. To break the hold his powerful personality still exerted, a decade after his death, I would have to discover the truth. Only by breaking the shell of silence that had grown, little by little, to obscure his life would we ever, finally, be free of him.

Two

SS CURRICULUM VITAE

T hanks to an often cited and rather gruesome family story, I knew how Bruno's war had ended. It was a chilling business. He had spent the final year of the war stationed in Prague. When the city fell, he had been one of a group of around a dozen German men who had been rounded up by vengeful Czechs. They were dragged out of a cellar and made to kneel on the curb outside. A Czech partisan pulled out a revolver and shot the first of them in the back of the head. And then the second, and then the third.

I had always interpreted this story as a ghastly instance of the arbitrary terror of the war's descent into anarchy and retribution. My grandfather was simply in the wrong place at the wrong time, a casualty of an uncontrollable maelstrom of violence. But that was when I had thought of him as a civilian, or as nothing more than a conscripted soldier. For an SS officer, though, waiting for the bullet in the back of the head, the scene played rather differently. Now it represented a kind of more understandable, if savage, justice.

It should all have ended for him there and then, but something extraordinary happened. With only Bruno and one other German left, a Soviet officer intervened and ordered the vigilante executioner to stop: "No more shooting, no more blood," he had shouted. And the shooting stopped. The two remaining Germans, which included my grandfather, were hauled back to their feet and led away past the line of corpses, reeling and stupefied, but still alive. For ten of those men, their Nazi stories had stopped right there, but not Bruno's. He had been spectacularly and remarkably lucky. As a result, he would get to live out his remaining forty-seven years, unmolested by any particularly troubling consequences of the first thirty-nine.

My mother had very little to add to the snippets she had already told me. She had been far too young to have absorbed any real detail—and after the war had been far too traumatized to have had the slightest desire for greater acquaintance with her father's life as a Nazi. She jealously guarded her ignorance, only too happy to know nothing. As for the question of *why* he had joined, she could do no more than we could, and offer an educated guess. He had certainly never discussed it with her.

If we were ever going to find out more about Bruno, it was clear what our first, most important step would need to be. We had to find, and then follow, whatever paper trail still existed in the official records, assuming any had survived. There was no point even thinking about living witnesses. Any contemporary of his would by now have to be more than a hundred years old. We would need to work it all out for ourselves; there would be no shortcuts. We were counting on the fact that the Germans had been meticulous record keepers. Though they managed to burn and shred huge mountains of material in the dying days of the war, the great majority of SS personnel records had survived. I knew Bruno's date and place of birth: July 27, 1906, in Perleberg, a town ninety miles to the northwest of Berlin. I also knew what his final rank had been: a *Hauptsturmführer*, or captain. Beyond that I knew nothing. But it was a start.

The main archive is located in Berlin, the so-called Document Center, part of the enormous Bundesarchiv, or Federal Archive. From 1945 to 1992 it was run by the Americans, who ensured that none of its incriminating contents would fall victim to any postwar shredding. The archives had provided vital evidence for the many postwar trials conducted in Germany, including the hearings at Nuremberg. Later, as the judicial activity fizzled out, the archive became an invaluable resource for historians. After nearly half a century of American administration, and as one of the consequences of the Wall coming down in 1989, the archives were handed back to the Germans. There is a sister archive in Maryland just outside Washington that contains microfiche duplicates of the Berlin Document Center's entire collection of papers, which would keep these records accessible and safe from German privacy laws. So we wrote to them with our details and steeled ourselves to anything they might find.

Most important, we wanted to know whether there was any documentation to indicate that a Bruno Langbehn had really belonged to the SS and, if so, to which department he was attached. It took only a couple of phone calls before we had our answer. An archivist promised to look Bruno up in what is called

the *Dienstalterliste*, or admissions roll, a Who's Who of SS officers. The SS published it at regular intervals between 1934 and
the end of the war, and it included names and dates of birth, as
well as awards, dates, service numbers, and departments. He duly
looked him up, and sure enough it confirmed in clear Gothic
script that Bruno Langbehn, born in Perleberg on July 27, 1906,
had indeed been a member of the SS.

We had now tracked down Bruno's Nazi Party number, his SS
number, and the date he had been made an officer—September
11, 1937 (just a few days, in fact, before my mother was born).
But there was more, he added. The *Dienstalterliste* showed that
Bruno had won two key Nazi Party awards. The first was the so-
called Gold Honor Party Badge (Goldenes Parteiabzeichen), the
most prestigious token given to the Party's most valued supporters, Party members with numbers *below* 100,000—very early
joiners, in other words, like Bruno, who had become a member
many years before. He had been a Nazi convert from the very
start. We could see, on closer inspection, that he was wearing his
Gold Honor badge in the SS family picture; it's the small, round
pin with a swastika on his forward-facing breast pocket. I had
always imagined that Bruno had been no more connected to the
regime than millions of other Germans, but this notion felt increasingly remote from the figure now emerging, that of a man
whose commitment to the Party had been long, deep, and therefore utterly heartfelt.

Another symbol in his personal entry told us that the badge
wasn't Bruno's only Nazi award. He had later been presented
with an even more ominous seal of Third Reich approval, this
time, the sole preserve of SS officers. This was the so-called

Totenkopfring, or Death's Head Ring, which was decorated with carved skulls and other runic devices. No artifact, short of Himmler's personal SS dagger or Heydrich's Luger, arouses the same degree of craving and lust among Internet hoarders of Nazi paraphernalia. It was a token personally bestowed by Himmler, the head of the SS.

The most important piece of information, though, was kept till last: the identity of which SS division Bruno had served in. This would be central to all our future inquiries and decisive in helping us form a view of who he had been. The SS was no monolith, but an organization that comprised a bewildering variety of activities, some military, some not. It drew a range of men into its embrace, from those who ran its concentration camps to those whose sole interest in putting on the uniform was to join one of its mounted cavalry divisions and pursue their love of riding. Bruno's attachment, however, turned out to be a very specific one: neither camp nor cavalry regiment, but to the SD-Hauptamt, the head office of the SD, the Sicherheitsdienst, or Security Service. An SS veteran my sister managed to track down warned us to be very careful how we then proceeded: *"Ach, die SD, die waren sehr böse Buben"*—"The SD, those were the really bad boys."

A week later a photocopy of the relevant page from the *Dienstalterliste* arrived, sent to me by the archive, so that I could see it for myself. It is a glossary of the state within a state that constituted the SS. That much was clear from the frontispiece proudly announcing that the SS had only one *Führer*, Adolf Hitler. There is a list at the front of all the main German SS regional offices and their geographic abbreviations. There is even a helpful glossary for all the tiny icons delineating the awards that the SS men had been awarded; these ranged from sports medals to military Iron Crosses (three classes) to various early Party medals given, such as the Gold Honor badge.

And then we got to the names of the men themselves. The list consists of eight columns. Here was Bruno fixed in Gothic typeface. My eye wandered down the page. I was curious about all the other names, and the dates of birth, concentrated mostly in the first decade of the century, but some going back to the late nineteenth.

The details confirmed everything we had been told. He had become a commissioned SS lieutenant (*Untersturmführer*) in September 1937. We had his party number, too—there were two columns: those in the left were reserved for numbers below 1.8 million, those on the right for those above. Bruno had by far the lowest party number on the entire page, so low it even merited being printed in bold: 36,931. Several tens of thousands, even hundreds of thousands, lower than most of the others. The lower the number, of course, the earlier they had joined; a number this small must have meant a joining date long before 1933, when Hitler became chancellor. Bruno himself must have been barely twenty or twenty-one years old. Far from being some kind of later aberration, his SS career had in fact been the climax to many long years of Nazi activism. His membership dated back to the years of the fragile Weimar Republic, a moment in his country's history that had clearly inspired only anger and loathing. As he grew older, these emotions had seemingly intensified into ever more radical forms, culminating in his membership of not just the SS, but the SD, its most elite department. The man staring out of the photograph at us, with his tonsured hair and a constellation of pips on his collar, was a man at the halfway point of a career played out at the very heart of the Nazi web.

Normal mitigating factors didn't apply to Bruno. He wasn't young (he was in his thirties at the outbreak of war, perfectly old enough to form mature judgments); he wasn't conscripted, but had actively chosen the toughest selection procedure available; at no point had he ever been merely a willing passenger, but the very model of a long-term committed activist, a man with the deepest conviction, if those awards were anything to go by. All of this made it seem even more important that we unearth his full personnel records from the Bundesarchiv. The archive in Maryland had further documentation, much more than the single page of the *Dienstalterliste*. It comprised over twenty-five pages—but most of it had been very badly burned (either deliberately or, more likely, from bomb damage) and was virtually illegible. Our only recourse was to go back to their original source, the Berlin Document Center, and hope that photocopies of documents (rather than blurrier microfiche) might just be easier to read. A few weeks later, a second envelope arrived, and this time, to our huge relief, their contents were indeed much clearer. What was more, included in this collection of papers were miscellaneous records that hadn't made their way to the American archive. Though there was still evidence of the fire that had come so close to turning the whole lot to ashes, spread out before us was the correspondence that over the course of around six months in 1937 had seen Bruno win his coveted place in the SS.

The bundle of forms included appraisals, questionnaires, records, affidavits, and references, all connected to Bruno's application to join the SS. For fifty years the facts about Bruno's early life had been kept hidden, yet here they were, restored once more to daylight, in fading black-and-white. They were especially fascinating because they weren't retrospective accounts written after the event. Bruno had had no opportunity to doctor them, to filter and color them for a postwar, post-Nazi audience. These *were* his Nazi career. These documents had been assembled and completed expressly to win him a place in the Nazi inner circle. This was Bruno as he most wanted to be judged, by other Nazis, *back* in 1937.

But there was one particular document I wanted to see more than any other: Bruno's *Lebenslauf* (or curriculum vitae). All SS applicants wrote them, in their own handwriting, spelling out the key moments of their upbringing, while seeking to persuade the SS to take them on. What made them particularly insightful was the form they took. These weren't single-word answers to pro forma questions, but extended pieces of prose designed not only to convey information, but to make a case. I had never read one before, though I had heard of them. I was terrified that it might have been the one document to have gotten lost in the lottery of fire and decay that any wartime archive is subject to. But there it was, safe and sound.

Consisting of two sides of A4, it was covered in the spidery handwritten script of a thirty-year-old German dentist making the most momentous decision of his professional and ideological life, justifying why the SS should accept him into its ranks. Eventually, we were able to recover about eighty percent of what it contained. It was an extraordinary document to read, not just because it cut through the "cloud of unknowing" in which his life had been shrouded ever since the war, but also because it allowed me to infer what thought processes were required when trying to join the SS.

On first inspection, however, its tone and content appear disappointingly neutral. Even when Bruno describes his own life, the effect is rather impersonal. Of course, as it is an application letter rather than a political testimony, there are no expressions of attitude, or even of political sloganeering (beyond the final *"Heil Hitler"* sign-off). Bruno clearly felt no need to express support for Nazi ideals in any explicit or ostentatious way. There is nothing of the overwrought, rather hysterical special pleading of the so-called Abel testimonies, for example.[1] Bruno had worked hard to strike a particular tone, that of a man determined to be taken seriously, convinced he has the right qualifications to offer, for which straightforward exposition remains the most appropriate idiom. The facts of his life and his obvious commitment to the movement will, he clearly hopes, speak for themselves. But beneath the officialese, there *are* some deeper signs that indicate this is no normal job application, some hints about what the SS was looking for in its aspiring applicants, and how clearly Bruno understood what those were.

To begin with, he offers some family background—invaluable, given how little other members of the family appeared to know about their own relatives—including even their names; "I am the son of Justice Inspector Max Langbehn, and his deceased wife, Hedwig, née Röhl—born on July 27, 1906, in Perleberg, in the Westprignitz district." This was our first indication of what his father's job had been; obviously some kind of magistrate, civil servant, or legal functionary, and thus no stranger to issues of law and order. Hedwig, Bruno's mother, had died in the early 1930s. He then goes on to describe himself, and his immediate family, quick to underline how racially immaculate they all were: "My wife and I are German, of Aryan descent, Protestant, unimpeachable, and of sound inheritance; we are citizens of the German Reich. We have a one-year-old daughter."

The simple matter of nationality has a Nazi rubric all its own. The word *German* was not enough. He had to be the right kind of German—Aryan, and deeply Aryan at that, the product of generations, and *unbescholten*, "unimpeachable." It wasn't just a box to be ticked, but something one had to plead—guilty until proven innocent. The equal weight given to his religious denomination and the bathos of announcing his one-year-old daughter suggest this type of reasoning had become completely normal for him—a source of pride, too, rather than just passive accommodation.

The next paragraphs are much less loaded, as Bruno goes from school to first job: "My school career was completed by reaching . . . [text indecipherable] at the Leibniz Senior School in Charlottenburg. After a short spell as a clerk I started the winter term 1925/26 at dentistry. I finished in the summer term of 1928. I passed the practical exam with 'good' and the dental exam with 'very good.'"

In prewar Germany there was an important distinction between being a *Dentist* and a *Zahnarzt*. The latter was a full medical qualification, requiring a university degree; a *Dentist* was more a vocational qualification, its training shorter, and more practical in orientation, its status less exalted. For lack of either money or academic wherewithal, Bruno had opted for the lesser of the two routes, the one that later had him rubbing shoulders with less well educated but nevertheless ambitious and practical-minded colleagues. His journey through training and into the world of work seems to have been relatively smooth—working as an apprentice or assistant during the tumultuous years that culminated in the election of Hitler as Germany's new chancellor. He had begun his training in the Weimar Republic and completed it in Hitler's new *Reich*. What could have been more intoxicating for a young, ambitious Nazi than feeling that he and the regime had achieved maturity together?

Till this point, it seemed we were merely reading the CV of an eager young dentist rather than an aspiring SS officer: "After four years as an assistant I passed my state exams in Feb. 1934 and have been running my own practice since 1.04.1934 [April 1] in Charlottenburg. I am licensed to treat patients from many different health insurance schemes and charities." Apart from his racial disclosures (which would have been compulsory in any case), there had been nothing so far to alert anyone stumbling on this document that it belonged to a die-hard Nazi. The next section, however, becomes more explicit, as Bruno describes his political background: "For approximately one month I was a member of the German Youth Union—but this did not fulfill me. Later I joined the German Freedom Party, but it was only in 1924 with the Charlottenburg Frontbann that I really felt that my expectations were being fulfilled. I remained with the Frontbann, Charlottenburg, until I joined the NSDAP and SA on 17.05.1926 [May 17]. During the *Kampfzeit* [time of struggle] I was once seriously injured and slightly hurt on several occasions. I was never convicted."

He was clearly no stranger to the association between politics and violence. On a separate affidavit dated March 6, 1932, a full description is given of one such incident, in which Bruno was set upon by three Communists brandishing heavy sticks, who inflicted a blow to the head and some minor injuries to his upper body. Not that Bruno appeared to have let all this brawling interfere with his career. He completed his studies and embarked on a four-year apprenticeship, all the while attending to his SA activities, combining both strands of his life when he was promoted to *Banndentist*, or regimental dentist. By 1934, with the Party now in complete control of Germany, he was ready to make his next step: on April 8, "SA Obergruppenführer von Jagow nominated me into the SA *Ehrengericht* [Honor Court]."

After this, there was no stopping him, as a torrent of Nazi qualifications and achievements attest. First, there were his two awards, gold and silver, the most prized attributes of the early joiner: "I hold the Gold Honor Party Badge, with a membership number of 36,931 and the silver *Gau* Honor Badge, number 33."[2] Party affairs also spilled into his leisure time; he seemed motivated by a desire for the company of other men as well as by personal conviction. "Before the seizure of power, I joined the NS professional tourist association with several other Party and professional comrades."

Bruno the dentist moreover was working hard to insinuate his way into as many professional and state bodies as possible. Clearly the world of the private surgery was too constricting for him. There was scarcely a health insurance or dental administration department that he wasn't seconded to. "In February 1935 the head of Reich dentists, SS colonel and Party member Schäffter, appointed me to the Honor Court of Welfare Insurance Adjusters; additionally, on 1 October that same year I was appointed deputy to the regional service director in the Guild of Reich Dentists, in the regional main office, Berlin, becoming an honorary member of the association. Furthermore, I was entrusted with the following offices: a member of the main claims office at the head insurance office, Berlin; deputy to the department head of the Reich Health Insurance Service; DAF regional manager; manager in arbitration department for disputes over payments for dental services; adviser to the Berlin head office of the People's Health Bureau."

Through his dentistry, too, Bruno was becoming ever more deeply ensconced in the very distinctive bureaucracy of the Third Reich, with its tangle of jargon-laden titles and hydra-headed organizations, a man deeply at home in the world of currying favor with professional patrons and also able to make the best of a not very promising situation—in his case, being only a *Dentist* rather than the more highly respected *Zahnarzt*.

April 1935 marked another great leap forward when Bruno was finally commissioned an officer—a lieutenant, or *Sturmführer*, which would have put him in charge of between twenty and thirty men. Maybe he would have been promoted earlier and more quickly had he been older, though he would never achieve an especially high military rank. But he was catching the eyes of his superiors (SA General Dietrich von Jagow, who inducted him into the SA honor court, was a hugely senior SA figure in Berlin; it must have been a real coup for Bruno to have won his support, which explains why he mentioned the general in his *Lebenslauf*). The result was that, by his late twenties, Bruno had established himself in the key professional networks of the early Third Reich, manning a wilderness of Nazi outposts along one of its most important front lines—where medicine met politics in the forging of a new Third Reich. He finishes by rounding off two pages of self-promotion with the hardy perennial of all CVs, of all ages, in all societies—the fact that he has a clean driving license: *"Ich besitze Führerschein I und III Klasse."*

Bruno appears to have taken the more standard parts of the vetting process in stride. His intelligence was *"überdurchschnitt"*—above average. He was energized and *"zielbewusst,"* focused on his goals. His racial profile, too, provided few wrinkles: *"vorwiegend nordisch"*—predominantly Nordic. He was characterized as *"offen, ehrlich und aufrecht"*—open, honest, and upright, free of any obvious defects, and objective in his *Lebensauffassung*, his view of life. These attributes, combined with the length and stead-fastness of his commitment to the movement and his lack of ra-cial or political "blemish," were all evidence that Bruno was more than an "old fighter" in name only, but a perfect match for the SS ideal of character and propriety. As an organization for which there was no higher virtue than being able to fulfill the tasks demanded of it, no matter how unpleasant, they were evidently reassured that Bruno had the ability to get the job done.

Although he was only in his mid-twenties, his early joining date made Bruno an *alter Kämpfer*—a veteran fighter, a badge laden with sentimental Nazi prestige, bestowing real cachet. On its own, this wouldn't have been enough, however; the SS prided itself on recruiting people clearly useful to it, rather than just rewarding long service. But it did Bruno no harm—in the words of one SS *Oberführer* reviewing his first promotion, in November 1939, from second to first lieutenant (*Unter-* to *Obersturm-führer*): "A promotion for SS 2nd Lt Langbehn is approved, in view of his long years of active involvement with the movement, and his duties hitherto performed for the SD."

But the real measure of Bruno's suitability for membership

in the SS lay in what he could offer *them*. He had little trouble convincing them that he was a more than usually strong candidate. Again and again, his political views are commended for being *überzeugt*—persuaded, a convinced Nazi. The word that crops up, though, isn't *ideology*, or even *politics*. It's the much bigger one, *Weltanschauung*, or worldview, something much broader and deeper than just a particular political manifesto. This goes far beyond simple agenda, or even a body of opinions; National Socialism was an ideology that sought to embrace every aspect of German life, from its views about humanity all the way to justifying its future empire. His Nazi assessors weren't just probing him for evidence of political reliability; they were testing him to see how well he would contribute to the SD's main purpose, which was to take that worldview and use it as the model from which to build the new Germany.

This sheaf of scarred, frayed documents from 1937 represented the culmination of a long and sustained apprenticeship in the politics of the Third Reich, of which so much of the detail remained obscured—and deliberately so. The next generation, my mother and her sisters, played their allotted part in this process of dissimulation and denial. They knew better than to ask impertinent questions, and it was drummed into them that they couldn't possibly understand what had been at stake. By and large, they fell into line. Mostly, it was done out of shame. Not just for what he may or may not have done. It went deeper than that. It was a reaction against the most obvious fact about Bruno's past, revulsion for the fact that he and thousands like him had seemingly adored being Nazis and had appeared to relish every part of it, including the anti-Semitism that fueled it. I once asked my mother,

"Did you *feel* like you were living in an important family?" "Oh, yes," she replied. "Papa was an important man."

National Socialism was a politics designed to gratify inner longings and frustrations, and it had clearly formed, sharpened, and justified every one of Bruno's most important opinions. His induction into Nazism had been a long and complicated process, beginning as a response to the catastrophe of the First World War and continuing to evolve all the way to 1945. Fighting for it had been the greatest privilege of his career. That was what the family had so wanted to avoid being reminded of. They were right. They had spent *years* dismantling, and dismissing, Bruno's active life as a Nazi. Now I was going to re-Nazify him, and it wasn't going to be an easy experience.

All I had to go on was a clutch of papers, names, dates, and forms, which together produced the bare bones of a Nazi career. The two eras covered by his CV—the early pre-Nazi world of the early joiners and later that of the SS, the ideologically driven executors of Hitler's plan—represented as comprehensive a Nazi experience as was possible to imagine, one that touched on virtually every major juncture and watershed in the story of the Third Reich, from its earliest days to its last. There was scarcely a Nazi institution Bruno did not at one point or other experience: the Party itself; the Jungbund, the Frontbann, the SA, the SS, the SD, the DAF, the world of Nazi medicine, the Nazi Tourist Association, Nazi civil administration, the Wehrmacht. In these capacities, he was drawn into every dimension of Nazi policy—from ideology, to welfare, to race (especially the "Jewish Question"), culminating in war, from the early heady days of easy triumphs to the last-ditch battles of the collapsing eastern front.

Over a single career, he wore three entirely different uniforms—SA brown, SS black, and Wehrmacht field gray. Over that time he was involved in dentistry, soldiering, espionage, policy implementation, and political agitation—all in the service of the Third Reich. It also lasted pretty much the maximum period of time possible. Very few others his age could point to twenty-two-year careers so actively engaged with the movement, and across so broad a front. He had been a storm trooper, street brawler, ideologue, policy intellectual, biological warrior, acolyte, soldier, snitch, spook, bureaucrat, arbiter of social policy—in short, *the perfect Nazi.*

Fleshing out Bruno's Nazi career would involve more than just arranging bits of personal biography. We needed to place it all in context. The Third Reich was a very particular kind of enterprise, characterized by highly specific individual actions perpetrated against a vast and mobilized common background. It was impossible to understand one without the other. Everywhere I looked I could see that there were three main constants in Bruno's perfect Nazi career, profoundly dictating its shape.

The first was Hitler himself. As the pole star of his obsessive devotion, as well as author and instigator of the Third Reich, Hitler's presence, of course, loomed large over Bruno. From the very beginning, Bruno identified himself with Hitler's struggle to take first Germany, then the whole of Europe, by storm, both militarily and racially. The second was the Nazi *Weltanschauung,* the worldview, or body of doctrine far beyond mere fascist dictatorship, which would lay the groundwork for crimes beyond comprehension. And the third was the movement's core of zealots, people like Bruno, men (and some women) who, from the start, provided the ballast for the organizations of Third Reich terror, the SA, the SS, the Gestapo, and the SD. They were the active Nazis, around whom the rest of the regime would later form.

These were the threads that wove their way through his career. Hitler was driven relentlessly forward by his worldview, as Hitler in turn drove his fellow fanatics, while they, for their part, propelled the wider movement. Between them they created a perpetual-motion machine of dynamism and hatred. And powering that machine was an unquenchable sense of entitlement for future German greatness and a hatred of the Jews, which became two sides of the same coin. The background to Bruno's story was one part Hitler, one part ideology, and one part individual fanaticism. From these sprang the multiplicity of evils that defined the Third Reich.

I began to realize that discovering more about my grandfather would mean finding out more about the Third Reich. Understand him, and I knew I might understand it. I now had a paper trail, and it was time to see where it might lead.

Three

FATHERS AND SONS

1906–1922

could now see that Bruno hadn't just ended up a Nazi fanatic; he had started off adult life as one. He was no "March violet," as those late-joining pragmatists were known, who flooded into the Party after 1933, when Nazism looked like a calculated career opportunity for an ambitious man on the make; he was an ideologue from the very beginning. Bruno's rise mirrored that of the Party itself, ending only when the Third Reich lay in ruins. The roots of such loyalty had clearly been planted deep, and in his case, they had been planted early. I became convinced that Bruno's formative years were perhaps the single most important key in the struggle to make sense of the choices he made. His childhood and adolescence mattered because they created not just Bruno the man, but Bruno the Nazi.

This wasn't just the case for Bruno; his entire generation may be said to have been formed by the experiences endured in youth. From among men of his age had emerged nearly all those who later became the most passionate advocates of National Socialism. Their undiluted fervor led historians to dub them "the unconditional generation."[1] Their number includes Joseph Goebbels (born in 1897); SS leaders Heinrich Himmler (born in 1900) and Reinhard Heydrich (born in 1904); Hitler's architect, Albert Speer (born in 1905); and Adolf Eichmann, one of the leading architects of the Final Solution (born in 1906).[2] Leni Riefenstahl, whose films captured and codified the malign glamour of Nazism, was born in 1902. Almost every well-known name associated with the triumph of Nazi will was born in the ten years around the end of the nineteenth century, and Bruno, born in 1906, was no exception.

Establishing the hard facts about Bruno's early years turned out to be a hard task. His CV identified his parents as Max and Hedwig Langbehn, but beyond that, I could discover very little. Bruno's daughters were adamant that they could not help. "We never met them, and Papa never, ever mentioned them," insisted both my mother and my aunt, who were vehement that, even as very young children, their grandparents had played no part in their lives. With no family anecdotes to rely upon, the SS *Lebenslauf* was yet again our only reliable source of information. That told us that Bruno had been born in Perleberg, a small Prussian town in northeastern Germany, and that Bruno's father, Max Langbehn, had been employed in the civil service, or perhaps even the police force, as a justice inspector (*Justiz Inspekteur*). It also made clear that Bruno had been an only child.

Until then, I had never heard of Perleberg. No one knew anything about what Bruno and his parents had done there, or how they had lived. A map showed that it had been absorbed into East Germany after 1945, thus making it impossible to visit, adding political inaccessibility to the sense of psychological distance the family seemed so keen to preserve. But things were different now; Vanessa and I could visit the town for ourselves. No sooner had we booked our tickets than something quite extraordinary happened. An unexpected letter dropped through my mother's mailbox.

It came from Perleberg and was sent to my mother, as a surviving descendant of Bruno Langbehn. Unbeknownst to his daughters, it appeared that, after the fall of the Berlin Wall, Bruno had written to his old hometown to inquire about the status of the house his parents had once owned there. After the reunification of Germany in 1990, he was one of many thousands of Germans who saw a chance to reclaim property they had regarded as lost forever, immured behind the Wall. It had taken a number of years to investigate the case, the letter explained, using careful legal terms, but it was unequivocal in its final declaration. We were owed nothing; the old Langbehn home now belonged to the present inhabitants, and the matter was considered closed.

Indifferent to the disappearance of our hitherto unknown inheritance, Vanessa and I were far more excited about something else: the entirely unexpected information that the letter yielded up. To substantiate his claim, Bruno had been obliged to provide family details—dates, names, and even professions—going back two generations, which went far beyond what we had been able to discover about his early life. It gave us a birth date of February 13, 1881, for the shadowy Max Langbehn, which meant he had been twenty-five at the time of Bruno's birth. But the document also included his job title at the time of the war, years before he became a justice inspector, allowing us to piece together some impressions of the world into which Bruno had been born. It could not have been more illuminating. During Bruno's childhood Max had been a *Kasernen Wachtmeister,* a hybrid military and police rank. It literally means "barracks supervisor."[3]

I had never had an inkling that the young Bruno had anything to do with the army, far less actually grown up surrounded by it. We had to go to Perleberg and find these mysterious barracks. It is a midsized place, with a charming enough central square, whose buildings have the gables and windows typical of a prosperous northern Hanseatic League town. Dating back to the thirteenth century, and bearing the scars of the Thirty Years' War, Perleberg has only one claim to wider national acclaim: its most celebrated daughter, the soprano Lotte Lehmann. Yet not even that could really compensate for the drab anonymity of the town, set well back from the Hamburg-to-Berlin autobahn. This was a remote and rather austere place. But having gotten this far, we were still determined to locate the address of what had been the old Langbehn family home.

We finally tracked it down on the town's outer edge. The street name was the same, as were the house numbers, but the building itself had long gone. The Langbehn residence had been turned into a small block of flats, still gleaming from a lick of post-GDR paint. The building itself may have changed with later modifications, but it was easy to make out what it must once have been—the gatehouse to a vast complex of gargantuan, now deserted, red- and yellow-brick buildings. Vanessa and I walked through the open gateway and began wandering through the warehouselike structures, forlorn and melancholy, but with their imposing mass still intact. It was entirely silent apart from the cawing of wintry crows, high up in their trees. *These* must be the barracks alluded to in the letter. We crossed over a wilderness of drill squares, past stables, dormitories, and what must once have been the regimental headquarters. Impressions and echoes spilled off the walls. So this was where the Langbehns had lived and worked, and where my grandfather had spent his formative years. We had found the first link in the chain.

The town's tourist information office provided further details. The barracks really had been a major military establishment, with a long and virtually unbroken history. They had been in use until as recently as the mid-1990s, and for just over two centuries had housed German soldiers: from Prussian hussars to the Reichswehr (the pre–Nazi era German army), the Wehrmacht (the Nazi-era German army), East German—even Soviet—forces after the war, and most recently, Bundeswehr NATO troops. Every major wave of twentieth-century German history had passed through these buildings, and each had left its mark, though none as indelibly as in the years surrounding the First World War.

Most important, this had been Bruno's father's workplace, where he had discharged his duties as *Kasernen Wachtmeister*. It had clearly been a key job. Barracks of this scale were a symbol of national pride, for both the community in which they were placed and those connected with their administration. Max would never have been entrusted with his supervisory role had he not been profoundly committed to the Prussian military ideal. His family occupied the former gatehouse to the barracks complex, as befitted his role as a privileged and important member of the garrison community.

In 1906 it must have seemed to Max Langbehn that everything in his life was coming to fruition. In that year a massive new building program doubled the size of the already huge barracks complex to accommodate the rapidly increasing size of Kaiser Wilhelm's army. And in July his only child, Bruno, was born, a son, into whose head he would one day drill all his closely held views about the army, its ethos, and its importance to Germany.

Like most Prussian boys, Bruno would have loved playing soldiers—but unlike them he got to grow up surrounded by the biggest, most exciting war chest imaginable. Every day many hundreds of Germany's finest troops assembled, marched, and conducted their military exercises—right on his doorstep. As an only child, Bruno grew up with a regiment of young recruits instead of brothers and sisters. This was a boyhood that reverberated to the echoes of thundering boots, marching columns, screaming sergeant majors, and endless drill.

The drama played out in front of Bruno carried deep and important lessons, too, not just visual excitement. Perleberg's barracks may have been geographically remote, but in terms of Prussian traditions they could not have been more central; they were the perfect place in which to indoctrinate a young and aggressive mind with ideas of the holiness of war and the men who fight it. Part of Max's role as a *Wachtmeister* was to instill key Prussian values into the men, an experience I doubt Bruno was spared, back in the house. The result was an unsentimental education steeped in an ethos of swagger, sacrifice, and male camaraderie that appeared to have stuck with Bruno for the rest of his life.

Soldiering had always been what Prussia did best, ever since Frederick the Great had launched its transformation from tiny northern European duchy to an aspiring Continental power. From that moment on, Prussia had become synonymous with the greatest standing army anywhere in Europe, and its quest to use that army to win parity with its greater imperial rivals, Austria-

Hungary, France, and even England. The spirit of militarism ran through Prussian veins, for which the Iron Cross would later become the most powerful symbol. It made the French philosopher Voltaire quip, "Where some states have an army, the Prussian army has a state."

Bruno's formal schooling, too, was dominated by lessons drawn from Prussia's military past. German teachers in this period were notoriously jingoistic. Military victories, first in the Napoleonic Wars (including Waterloo) and later over France in the Franco-Prussian War, had helped create modern Germany itself in 1871. It had been the army that had presided over the birth of the German nation. The next thirty years, first under Bismarck, then under the much more volatile militarism of Kaiser Wilhelm II, saw the emergence of an economic and industrial giant, able to underpin German military ambitions with coal, steel, and armaments produced in quantities outstripping those of Britain, France, and even America. Each time the Prussian army had departed its barracks to wage war, it had returned to a state more powerful than the one it had left. These barracks were a staging post in Germany's most important aspiration, its growth into a European superpower.

Even on the day we visited, the power of the place still lingered. We had been curious to see Perleberg, but nothing prepared us for how clearly it would evoke a part of Bruno's life that had hitherto been such a completely closed book.

Though neither my mother nor my aunt could shed any light on what kind of people Max and Hedwig had been, it wasn't completely true that we knew absolutely nothing about them. One person who had been rather better informed about Bruno's parents and childhood was Gisela, his common-law wife. She bequeathed to us what few photos we have of Bruno's parents. They date from the late 1920s, but they are particularly vivid. In one, Max and Hedwig are seated in a Berlin meadow, relaxed and pastoral; they exude a kind of haughtiness, not aloofness exactly, but they seem unmistakably sure of themselves. You would never guess that Hedwig, every inch the grande dame, was in fact the daughter of a roof tiler. Max's career, first in the army and later in the field of law and order, allowed them to claw their way out of their modest origins, and they wear it proudly. Max looks every inch the autocrat, with a taste for impressive cravats, and the posture and demeanor of an opinionated man unaccustomed to being disagreed with.

Even more tantalizingly, Gisela would occasionally divulge the odd throwaway remark about Bruno's past. Max, she confided to Vanessa, had been a forbidding and dictatorial paterfamilias; but it was Bruno's relationship to his mother that had troubled Gisela most. His grim and unindulgent mother had refused him any physical contact, which Gisela firmly believed had cauterized his emotional development. Bruno had thus absorbed his father's authoritarian certainty and his mother's distant steeliness. Their inflexible parenting habits and infatuation with military prestige took their toll, but it was what happened next that played an even more significant role in making Bruno into an embryonic Nazi. That event was the First World War, the single most dominant episode not just in his young life, but for his whole generation.

However, with the exception of one rather striking gift (of which more later), there was nothing left to indicate what Bruno's reactions to the war must have been. No diaries, no letters, no retrospective comments. We have no records at all of what

Bruno thought or did during these early years of his life. I would have to work it out as best I could from his later actions, often identical to those of virtually every other early joiner, for whom the First World War and its revolutionary aftermath were repeatedly cited as the main reasons for their later politics. Helping me to break through his veil of silence were those contemporary testimonies, especially from the Abel collection, written by men close to Bruno's age, which provided an echo chamber for the tumult that must surely have raged in Bruno's head, too.

Some historians have argued that these men, even more than the actual veterans of the trenches, later provided Nazism with its most radical advocates. As the journalist and Nazi exile Sebastian Haffner sardonically observed on the eve of the Second World War, "[Nazism's] roots lie here: in the experience of war—not by German soldiers at the front, but by German schoolboys at home. . . . That is easy to understand. Men who have experienced the reality of war tend to view it differently. . . . The truly Nazi generation was formed by those born in the decade from 1900 to 1910, who experienced war as a great game and were untouched by its realities."[4] It's so evident in Nazi reminiscences: the war remains *the* seminal experience in their journey to the right. Bruno was clearly one of them.

But as a twelve- or thirteen-year-old, whose war was Bruno experiencing? Who was based here in Perleberg? What regiment did his father belong to, and what kind of war did they fight? Perleberg's local archivist gave us the information that we needed, including the regiment's formal history, written in 1923 by one Hans Rosenthal.[5] The barracks did indeed date back to the eighteenth century—1772, to be precise. In 1899 they became home to Feldartillerie-Regiment Nr. 39 (mounted artillery, FAR 39)—Max's regiment.

So even before war broke out, the eight-year-old Bruno found himself exposed to a rising tide of feverish expectation and patriotic fervor, as the whole of Europe prepared itself for war. On August 1, 1914, at 5:45 p.m., the mobilization order arrived. For Bruno, perhaps it felt as if it had been laid on entirely for the benefit of the wide-eyed solitary child, growing up on the edge of the great military compound. The excitement was visceral: the bands playing, the speeches, the processions, the adults buzzing with anticipation. What's the use of soldiers who just march up and down, polishing their boots and oiling their rifles? By early morning on August 3, the first detachments had boarded their trains and were heading west in a large convoy of horses, men, and artillery pieces. Early in the morning of August 4, the first transport reached Aachen, on the Belgian border, joined the 11th Infantry Brigade under Generalmajor von Wachter, and moved toward Verviers, across the border.

Little Bruno would have had to have been a very unusual German eight-year-old not to have been gripped by war fever—the great majority of his age clearly were. As a Nazi born in 1905 later described it, "A terrific time began for us boys. Everyone turned soldier and we plundered kitchen and cellar in order to give presents to the departing troops. Then came the first victories. One victory celebration followed another."[6] Along with his regimental colleagues, Max would have regarded this as Germany's most decisive moment.

First, there was the elation of 1914, to be replaced by a more somber mood as the war got bogged down in the quagmire of the trenches: "Gradually things calmed down. Young as we were, we realized this was not a game of soldiers." By the spring of 1915, Max's regiment had been well blooded, having fought engagements at Tirlemont, Mons, Andecy, Montceaux, Vailly, and Arras before transferring to Serbia at the end of the year. In 1916, they were sent back to France, where they took part in the battle of Verdun. After a brief period of respite near Reims, between June 25 and August 8, the regiment fought on the Somme.

The boys at home, however, soon had new heroes to idolize, a new kind of German warrior—General Ludendorff's storm troopers. These were elite units of soldiers, handpicked for their courage, aggression, and initiative. Their tactics were highly unconventional; instead of waging a campaign from long range, with artillery barrages and walls of indiscriminate machine-gun fire, the storm troopers fought up close and personal, leaping into enemy trenches and fighting hand-to-hand. Nothing could have been more stirring to a schoolboy's imagination than accounts of these crack formations of mobile units, armed with carbines and grenades, wearing distinctive steel helmets. It was the start of a German love affair, which turned the storm trooper into a potent icon for decades to come. And it appeared to work. Storm troopers struck fast and decisively, blowing holes in the Allied lines, leaving it to the infantry to mop up behind them.

The following year, 1917, gave Bruno and his companions in the playground an even bigger treat—German success in the east. He didn't need to know the intricacies of the Treaty of Brest-Litovsk.[7] All that mattered was that great swaths of the east, including Poland and most of the Ukraine, now belonged to Germany's all-conquering eastern armies. Many in Regiment 39 knew the eastern front well, having fought for months in Romania. The endgame in the west could play itself out, and the war would be over. Germany would have taken possession of an imperial landmass of vast scale, and the Kaiser's Second Reich could take its place at the head of the great European superpowers. They were unstoppable. The Germans—and not just the children—allowed themselves to believe this was a direct precursor of final victory.

For Max, too, 1917 was to prove a thrilling and watershed year. He had been considered too old to go to the front at the beginning of the war, but that all changed with the casualty rate, making it vital to find reinforcements. Now the regiment's older men were on the march, and it was finally Max's turn to board the troop train and be waved off by wife and son, no doubt crying tears of pride and apprehension. Regiment 39 had fought in Belgium, France, and Serbia as part of the 3rd Army Corps until September 1916, when it was amalgamated with the 187th Infantry Division, fighting in Romania. Then, in early 1917, the regiment became part of the 228th Infantry Division, once again operating in France—and this time, Max fought alongside them. A week or so after leaving Perleberg, he reached his destination, an army base near Verdun, where he joined the rest of his regiment and prepared for active service.

The year 1918 began with three great assaults against the Allies, led by storm troopers. They appeared so successful that Bruno, like every other schoolchild in Germany, was given a special "victory" holiday on March 23.[8] But a tactic that had worked so brilliantly in short, explosive bursts was not powerful or sustained enough to counter the hundreds of thousands of newly arrived American soldiers pouring off the troopships. With the United States officially in the war, the balance of power began to swing inexorably toward the Allies.

Bruno and his war-gaming pals had no idea that everything was about to come crashing down. The end, when it came, arrived with terrible swiftness, like a tidal wave of chaos and disaster engulfing the home front, Perleberg included, before there was any time to react. In one fell swoop, every one of their most deeply held fantasies was destroyed.

In the autumn of 1918 the entire German war machine began to collapse; Max and the rest of Regiment 39, though still stationed in France, were about to be overrun. For all their faith in individual heroics, the decisive factor of the war had been logistics, technology, and sheer numbers, and by November there was only one possible outcome. The German army had been beaten, dumbstruck from the blow inflicted by their defeat.

All that early, vicarious triumphalism had turned to ash; throughout Germany, families reacted to the news. As the son of a grocer, born in 1908, put it: "I shall never forget the day when my father came home with the horrible news. . . . The big, strong man was in tears. This was the one and only time I ever saw him cry. We children felt helpless in the face of his emotional outbreak."[9] Perleberg, like the rest of Germany, was now in a state of traumatized mourning, those of Bruno's age very much among them; "then came the collapse. For us boys who had been soldiers in body and soul, a great deal collapsed."[10]

Bruno was finally reunited with Max on December 15, after his father had endured a long and complicated homeward journey from France; the last leg alone had slowly snaked its way through Bebra, Eisenach, Erfurt, Sangerhausen, Magdeburg,

Stendal, Wittenberg, and finally Perleberg. The disembarking troops were greeted by hundreds of civilians and members of the city council at Perleberg railway station with "grateful love and admiration." At three p.m. the two batteries, led by their commanders, Leutnant Helferich and Oberleutnant Wackerzapp, marched through the city back to their old barracks. They were accompanied by local dignitaries and increasing numbers of civilians, as well as the band of the Perleberg reserve detachment.

But there was a shock in store for them. The city councillors who greeted them as they disembarked their train had been stripped of their powers; Perleberg's local government was now run by a workers' and soldiers' council. Even worse, the reception committee that had formed to greet the last battery platoons closed their speeches by calling for three cheers, not for the Reich, but for "the new German republic." The regiment band retaliated by playing the "Preußenlied," the Prussian national anthem, as loudly as they could. The senior officer present, Major Niemann, thanked the mayor for his speech but very conspicuously turned his back on the town's new revolutionary council, closing instead with a defiant toast to "the old, dear city of Perleberg."

If losing a war wasn't bad enough, what awaited many soldiers returning to Germany appeared even worse. In a matter of days the old imperial Reich that had marched so confidently to war in 1914 collapsed under the weight of defeat. First to go was the Kaiser himself, forced to abdicate and flee to the Netherlands, taking the entire monarchist system, and its supporting aristocracy, down with him.

That was quickly followed by the creation of an unprecedented kind of German government to take the place of the old monarchy—a democracy. The new republic took its name from the town where its new constitution was ratified, Weimar, chosen because it was a healthy distance away from Berlin's rioters. Left-leaning, modern and liberal in its outlook, the republic was supposed to offer a redeeming contrast to Bismarck's Prussia. Observers such as the diplomat Count Harry Kessler were stunned: "So closes this first day of revolution which has witnessed in a few hours the downfall of the Hohenzollerns, the dissolution of the German army, and the end of the old order of society in Germany. One of the most memorable and dreadful days in German history."[11]

It was a revolution that had few friends, however. The new Weimar Republic was loathed by both the extreme left and right. For hard-core Bolsheviks, it was a bourgeois sellout, and they vowed to overthrow it. They were supported by many tens of thousands of disillusioned troops, convinced the war had been for nothing. As far as they were concerned, the artillery shells and machine-gun fire had turned proud individual warriors into a proletariat of death. Among many drawn from Germany's huge and highly radicalized working class, the result was a savage backlash against everything the war had stood for.

A wave of mutinies and uprisings threatened to bring the Russian Revolution of 1917 to Germany. As early as November 6, 1918, Harry Kessler recorded his alarm at the rising tide of militancy threatening to engulf a vulnerable postwar Germany: "We were told that the naval mutineers have seized Hamburg, Lübeck, and Cuxhaven, as well as Kiel. At Hamburg the soldiers have joined the sailors, forming a red government. Reds are streaming with every train from Hamburg to Berlin. An uprising is expected here tonight."[12] A few weeks later, the Spartacists (precursors of Germany's Communists) were openly planning an entire Soviet-style "council republic," or *Räterepublik*, to the consternation of their horrified opponents.

Even more ominously, this swing to the extreme left provoked an equal and opposite reaction on the right, which took Germany to the brink of civil war. The specter of *both* a democratic Weimar government and, worse, armed soviet councils in cities like Munich was for nationalist veterans, and their young acolytes like Bruno, utter anathema. Dismay turned into rage among men who could not bear to see their once mighty country brought to its knees: "A disgusting sight met our eyes," wrote one shattered veteran, describing the trauma of his return from the front. "Beardless boys, dissolute deserters, and whores tore off the shoulder bands of our frontline fighters, and spat upon their field gray uniforms; who had never seen a battlefield, who had never heard the whine of a bullet . . . or actually fought themselves."[13]

Theodore Abel's testimonies are full of tales of injured virtue among veterans for whom the experience of defeat had left deep and indelible scars: "On November 15, 1918, I was on the way from the hospital at Bad Nauheim to my garrison. . . . As I was limping along with the aid of my cane at the Potsdam Station in Berlin, a band of uniformed men, sporting red armbands, stopped me and demanded that I surrender my shoulder bands and insignia."[14] Anecdotes like these, with their Grand Guignol levels of self-pity, would provide the later Nazis with one of their most important founding myths: "I still thank my stars for sparing me the experience of witnessing the humiliation inflicted . . . upon wounded comrades by these subhuman animals. . . . We screamed with rage. For this kind of Germany we had sacrificed our blood and our health, and braved all the torments of hell."[15]

For aggrieved right-wingers including the Langbehns, father and son, who were unshaken in their belief that the war had been noble and righteous, there remained one burning question. What exactly had *happened* in November 1918? Whose fault was it? Their answer was simple. Pro-Moscow Bolsheviks hadn't just profited from Germany's defeat, they had actively caused it. The army hadn't lost the war, they had been "stabbed in the back,"[16] betrayed by "ruthless elements [who] had long prepared to undermine this iron front, to rob it of its faith in the fatherland, and to make it tired of the war. . . . Thus we returned humiliated but undefeated." The newspapers, too, were soon trumpeting this slogan of defiance and turning it into a national myth: "Bring in your banners, you brave soldiers! You were not defeated by the enemy, but by the crumbling home front. The most tragic feature of the present situation is the realization that Germans have fought against Germans."[17]

Though only a teenager, Bruno must have absorbed endless variations of this kind of invective and accusation, for which an army town like Perleberg was the perfect breeding ground. For the moment, though, they were still the preserve of right-wing extremists whom the great majority could ignore. But all that changed in June 1919, when the victorious powers served Germany their final peace terms, the Treaty of Versailles.[18] At a stroke, nationalist paranoia exploded into the mainstream of respectable opinion, as 70 million Germans rose up in indignation against being declared a pariah state, blackballed from the club of acceptable nations. It remained an utterly toxic subject for the next twenty years—for Nazis and non-Nazis alike.[19]

For the revolutionary left, the treaty served as an even greater impetus to seize control of Germany. But by late 1919 the Weimar government itself was growing alarmed at increasing Bolshe-vik agitation. They decided to act, even if it meant entering into an alliance with the nationalist right, even though they had no love for the new republic, either. For the time being, all that mattered was that the government should respond.

The Weimar Republic agreed to pay German soldiers still in uniform, to help bring Germany back to heel. Many exulted at the prospect of yet more fighting. Armed formations sprang up in military bases and garrisons across the country, built around the authority of individual charismatic officers, becoming the so-called Freikorps. More than just mercenaries, they were free-booting soldiers who turned their experience of the trenches into a new kind of nationalist solidarity. Civilian life was just going to have to wait.[20]

Once again, Bruno's Perleberg barracks provided him with the perfect front-row seat from which to observe it all happen, as the garrison was converted into a major Freikorps base. On April 5, 1919, a "Detachment Stillfried" of the Freikorps Hülsen (named after its commanding officer, Lieutenant General Bern-hard von Hülsen) moved into the barracks. The detachment had been formed in Berlin in December 1918 and had fought against Communist insurgents there around Christmas 1918 and in Jan-uary 1919. Von Hülsen's force numbered over 11,000 men, until it was dissolved on May 15, 1919, and replaced by a second Stillfried Freikorps detachment that, according to the records, was greeted "very warmly" in Perleberg. This detachment con-sisted of four companies and a machine-gun platoon, with mor-tars and artillery.

The great buildings that surrounded Bruno's home echoed yet again to the shouts of drill sergeants, weapons training, and the thundering crunch of marching boots—only this time these soldiers would be fighting on the streets of German cities, not in the fields of France or eastern Europe. Their first task was to pull down the red flag flying over Perleberg's town hall, "to the joy of the population." They then organized an open-air concert in the town's main square and hoisted the nationalist black-white-and-red banner instead. After a few weeks, their job done, the Freikorps left Perleberg. Once they had gone, a civil defense unit was set up by Perleberg citizens—almost certainly including Bruno's father—to fill the gap.

These battles had simply swapped one battlefield for another, an old enemy for a new one—streets instead of trenches, Commies instead of Tommies.[21] The Freikorps were street-rampaging vigilantes, marching under nationalist banners, death's-head insignia, and, increasingly, the hooked cross, or swastika, which was fast becoming their most popular symbol. And for over two years they swooped on any red threat, real or imagined. This was Bruno's first introduction to the idea of the paramilitary life and its heady satisfactions.[22] The thirteen-year-old soaked it up like a sponge.

By late 1920, the Faustian pact between the Socialist government and right-wing Freikorps had appeared to pay off, as the last of the mutinies and the workers' councils finally capitulated. Their "purification by thunderstorm," as they called it, had appeared to avert Bolshevik revolution.[23]

For Germany's angry right wing, crushing the Spartacists was only the beginning. Their country's greatness could be restored solely by a complete purge of all that they considered alien and weak. This wasn't the old-fashioned jingoism of 1914. This nationalism was far more aggressive than the Prussian militarism it had grown out of. Fired by tribal fervor, and the dream of national redemption, its flames burned hottest around the concept of Germany's ethnic essence, not only its men in uniform. Where the Bolsheviks had class, postwar German nationalists built their edifice of myth and resentment on the idea of the *Volk*, the "people." Bruno the Nazi would have found this idea both electrifying and deeply consoling.

But the *Volk* was in no condition yet to take on its mighty nationalist mantle. As far as the grieving nationalists were concerned, the war's appalling outcome proved that Germany had been conquered from *within*; it had suffered not just military defeat, but a *complete failure of nationhood*. Only an act of national salvation could make Germany rise from the ashes once more. The nationalists pledged themselves to make this happen.

There was, of course, one major obstacle they faced in this— the small matter of the First World War. Everything that victory would have offered—national prestige, military power, and continental domination—lay in ruins. For Bruno's generation it was imperative, therefore, that they rescue the war's sacred significance from the reality of its disastrous result and eradicate the stigma of 1918. The national soul was at stake, and it would need the help of Germany's most powerful imagination to be able to restore it.

Fortunately for the nationalists, one such man existed, in the shape of an ex–infantry officer, Ernst Jünger—an author who had captivated the fifteen-year-old Bruno, already an avid reader with an appetite for nationalist literature. In the mid-1980s, Bruno had presented me with a German edition of Jünger's most famous novel, *Storm of Steel*. Read this, Bruno told me. It was the book he and his *Kriegskameraden* admired most, the best book ever written about war, he explained. One bit of me could see that it was indeed a genuinely thrilling book. But it would be years later before I really understood its wider resonances.

Jünger was a fascinating and ambiguous figure. He had been a storm trooper in the war, of the sort that Bruno had so grown to admire as a child. He was wounded many times, and just as frequently decorated (winning the highest German medal of all, the Pour le Mérite, or Blue Max). He had translated his still vibrant memories of the front into an astonishing first novel a few months after the end of war and published it to huge acclaim as early as 1920. It is a raw, vivid classic of war literature, which still has the capacity to shock. For those of us brought up on British, French, or even American memoirs, diaries, novels, and poems about the war, the contrast is stark.[24] The great majority of these Allied representations paint a picture of futile waste, needless sacrifice, and political folly. They are laden with elegy and pathos, a melancholy rebuke to the excesses of nationalism and militarism run amok. This was a war that should have been avoided; a tragic mistake, ill conceived and criminally badly run.

All of this was reinforced by an extraordinary diary I inherited, written by my Scottish great-uncle, Algy Davidson, who had served in the trenches as a second lieutenant with the Seaforth Highlanders, alongside his brother Don, my grandfather. It chronicled his many months on the front and was full of reflections about why he was there and what the fighting was for. Full of patriotic stoicism, the war was something that had to be fought and won, if only to allow them all to get home again and never have to fight another war like it. Serving in the army was a source of pride, of professionalism, and of comradeship, but the cost in suffering and sacrifice never allowed him to indulge in the fantasy that any of this was somehow *pleasurable.* There isn't a hint in any of the diary's curled, yellowing pages, with their light pencil script, of combat being exciting, or fulfilling needs that peace never could: "Saturday 7th April, 1917. The weather is dull and overcast and rain falls. After lunch we go to Head-quarters and are given some parting advice by the CO and Ad-jutant. They appear confident of success. I am suffering from an abscess which is very irritating but I must carry on as cheerfully as possible. I give 'bon chance' to Capt. Will and other officers proceeding up the line. Ken Ross hears that his cousin from Tain has been killed. He is a good soldier and will be greatly missed. God help his sorrowing mother. In the evening we attend to our platoons. There is much airplane activity, the sky being clear for good observation. At night we write some parting letters to friends. Tomorrow we proceed up the line and take up our posi-tion. God help us in the fight and grant us Victory." It was his final entry; three days later, he was killed, shot through the head by a sniper while returning to a dressing station.[25.] For Algy the real meaning of life was not to be found on the battlefield; it was back home waiting for those fortunate enough to survive. Though it was their duty to fight, war was an aberration, an experience of hell to be endured so that the next generation would be spared it.

But not for Jünger, or his ardent first readers. It's impossi-ble not to be struck by his refusal to shed crocodile tears over the physical cruelty of war, or by his infatuation with the adren-aline of killing—a sobering honesty of sorts, but one that couldn't be further away from the world of Wilfred Owen or Robert

Graves. Where they had pity, Jünger has pitilessness; instead of elegy, ecstasy; instead of flesh and blood, iron and steel; instead of the dead, whose memories haunt and chasten, Jünger has the fallen, whose sacrifice will one day be consummated in revenge; instead of mud and rats, soil made holy by blood. Jünger's storm trooper never feels more alive than when surrounded by men he has just killed. But his intense evocations of combat become something rather more ominous—a celebration of war itself. It was a way of talking about the war that many veterans (and later Nazis) found both powerful and arresting and would become one of the founding myths of the Third Reich.[26] No wonder Bruno so enjoyed giving Jünger's book to me; it was yet another one of his presents laden with ulterior purpose.

And yet, for all its violent sublime, *Storm of Steel* doesn't ever mention politics—or nationalism. Jünger's picture of war says nothing about the attraction of empires or the need to invade and dominate foreign countries; for him, war's only role was to give its participants the most challenging experiences open to mortal man. For Bruno and his ilk, that was not enough, as exhilarating as they found his prose. They were *very* interested in nationalism and politics, empires and conquest, and they could see that Jünger wasn't (at least not yet—that would change in time). For the moment, they would have to go elsewhere for their role models.

For some, there was, of course, the example offered by the Freikorps, whose suppression of Communist unrest had been so ruthless. But there were limitations here too. For the new German nationalists like Bruno, shooting Spartacists and cudgeling mutineers to the ground, as the Freikorps had done, was gratifying to watch, but not enough to build their future on. Jünger's literary style was too Olympian to mobilize the masses, while the Freikorps were too nihilistic, too damaged, too besotted with the short-term addiction to street violence. Neither alone could save Germany.

What Bruno was starting to look for was *politics*: not just literary excitement or action for its own sake, but a program of values around which an eventual government could emerge and one day take over running the country. Ideally it would combine the tenacity and activism of the Freikorps with Jünger's adoration of the German fighting man, but it wouldn't be limited to these.

All over Germany, in isolated pockets, something akin to what Bruno was seeking was beginning to emerge. All those grievances and resentments, born of defeat and revolution, were slowly starting to cohere, not simply in vicious opposition to Weimar, but offering a blueprint for a completely new kind of Germany. During 1919 and 1920, tiny, impoverished factions and sects congregated on the right-wing margins of German politics. There were Anton Drexler's German Workers' Party (later called the National Socialist German Workers' Party) in the south, and Erich Ludendorff's German People's Freedom Party in the north. Their new nationalist manifestos were the insistent tribal backbeat to Bruno's late adolescence.[27] With an outer coating of ethnic idealism and an inner core of pure vindictiveness, they would come to dominate the years to come.

Their appeal lay in the extremism with which they expressed their loathing not only for rival political parties, but for the whole of Weimar politics per se. What was much harder to determine was what they would do with power if they ever won it. What would a *völkisch* nationalist government be like? Nobody knew.

The ferocity of their message and the depth of their nationalist fervor felt entirely without precedent. But all that was about to change. German extremists may have been languishing a long way from power, but not so in Italy. Europe had a new state in its midst, which gave the world its first long, hard look at Bolshevism's counterpart on the right. Fascism—the only political system invented in the twentieth century[28]—would have much to teach the fledgling German nationalists, not least how best to achieve "a frankly anti-democratic and imperialist form of rule . . . [which] in a certain sense is comparable (in the opposite direction) to Lenin's."[29]

There were many values that both German nationalists and Italian fascists venerated as defining their memories of the trenches. Camaraderie was one; duty, obedience, and courage were the others. But they all paled against what for many remained the pinnacle of their experience of combat, the *violence*. Violence was what tempered a soldier into a man of steel.[30] Violence was also what made a political system dynamic and virile, the opposite of all that is craven or impotent. That was why it became the principal ingredient in a new political religion.[31]

But whom was this violence to be directed *against*? This was still a world seething with scores to be settled. The idea of an "enemy within" took hold after 1918 with savage consequences. The Communists seemed the obvious answer. They were the ones enthralled to a foreign power and its alien ideology, and it was they who had taken to the streets with their red banners and preached national insurrection. But could a few Bolsheviks, so easily routed by the Freikorps, really have brought the might of the German Reich to its knees? Bolshevism was too recent and too disorganized to have been capable of such an act of sabotage. The rot must lie elsewhere.

Who had had most to profit from German humiliation? Who had had the influence, the organization, and above all the motivation to undermine the Reich? Who among their population could be accused of being the enemies of German nationhood? Who deserved to take the blame? For those Germans who had no intention of accepting that they had been outgunned and outmanned by an Allied army, there was a much more satisfying explanation for their misfortune, one that could draw upon a theory about the world that had first formally been named by the German writer Wilhelm Marr in the late nineteenth century: anti-Semitism. Extreme nationalists now had their "explanation": the German army had been undermined by the Jew.

For many of the returning veterans, it was a "truth" that they claimed hit them between the eyes. From the moment they first got home from the war, they found a landscape full of sexual insult, squeamish revulsion, and the obscenity of social inequality, behind which, they were convinced, lurked the specter combining all these horrors in a single form, that of the Jew.[32] Blaming the Jews was such an easy way to lash out against the self-loathing triggered by defeat. Once unleashed, this new, virulent anti-Semitism escalated rapidly, and violently, through three major falsehoods, each an extension of the other, before finally taking on a life all of its own.

The issue that first explicitly linked the "Jewish Question," as it would come to be known, to the war itself was money. This offered a vicious little twist to the "stab in the back" theory so beloved of Germany's smarting military generals. It began in conspiratorial whispers and ended up as a malignant article of faith: Jews had shirked doing their fair share of the fighting—and had done so in order to stay at home and get rich out of the war. General Ludendorff was simply the grandest (and not the last) in a long line of German notables to take refuge in anti-Semitic cliché when he wrote: "The war profiteers were first of all essentially Jews. They acquired a dominant influence in the war corporations . . . which gave them the occasion to enrich themselves at the expense of the German people and to take possession of the German economy, in order to achieve one of the power goals of the Jewish people."[33] Of course it was a palpable lie—tens of thousands of Jews had fought alongside Corporal Hitler, and Captain Jüngers, and been decorated for it. But few Germans were listening. The picture of the nonfighting Jew who not only made money out of the war while safely ensconced at home but, worse, carried on profiting from the poverty and despair of the immediate postwar years lingered in German folk memory for many, many decades to come. It was a pernicious caricature that Bruno later instilled in his daughters. My mother remembers being repeatedly told as a girl that no Jews had fought in the German army in the First World War. In fact 100,000 of them had—the same number as later constituted the entire post-Versailles German army.

But this was only the first of the three great malignant slanders laid at the feet of Germany's tiny, and highly assimilated, Jewish population—two more were quick to follow. First there was politics. Jews were simultaneously top-hat-wearing plutocrats *and* agents of the red menace, their numbers disproportionately represented both in the major private banks of the world (the Rothschilds, the Warburgs, the Simons, and the Weinbergs, for example) and among the ranks of the Socialist and Communist movements in Germany and Bolshevik Russia (not least the figure of Karl Marx himself).[34]

These utterly contradictory caricatures "proved" that Jews sought to deliver Germany to the mercy of all that was most terrifying about the modern world and destroy them with it. As one put it, "The first official to meet me at home was a Jew who talked very fast and praised the blessings of the revolution. I replied with hard and bitter words but was not yet completely aware of the role of the Jews. Years of observation and, at last, reading my Führer's book, *Mein Kampf*, fully opened my understanding of the fateful molelike activity of these corrupters of the earth."[35] He was one of many for whom their years of study were "rewarded" with the fatal insight (which Marxism could not give) that every one of the world's contemporary ills could be laid at the feet of the Jews.

To anti-Semites like these, there was no contradiction in the Jews' ability to be both capitalist and communist because both the world's banking system and its (apparent) opposite in communism were themselves merely the outward guise of what the Jews really were—and here they delivered themselves of the third and final mantra of Jew-hating paranoia—a global conspiracy with the aim of controlling the world's economies and dictating its politics unseen—as such, the perfect scapegoat for all of Germany's ills. The result was a terrifying eruption of paranoid fantasy that saw *all* of history as little more than the operation of a secret cabal of Jews, Masons, and other illuminati, hell-bent on bringing the world to heel. It was the world's profoundest, most arcane secret, and according to later Nazi dogma, it would take the world's bravest and subtlest minds to bring it to light.

Out of this trilogy of anti-Semitic slanders—that the Jews were financial predators, left-wing revolutionaries, and above all global conspirators—the Nazis would create the "Jewish Problem." It was their ultimate shibboleth, one that they would spend the next twenty years documenting, elaborating, and finally, of course, "solving," the bedrock for the later Nazi worldview, right up until the moment of its final destruction. No ardent Nazi could deviate from it, or question its all-encompassing validity. For an early joiner like my grandfather, a hatred for Jews was the major pillar of his nationalist beliefs, an entirely non-negotiable theory about the world. Having once blamed them for the war and made them synonymous with all the consequences and the miseries of defeat, the Nazis felt fully justified persecuting Europe's Jews, while simultaneously making them the subjects of far-reaching racial and scientific "research," in which Bruno would himself, as an SS officer, later become both zealot and expert.

On the day that the Treaty of Versailles was finally signed, Count Kessler confided to his diary: "Sat 10 Jan 1920: A terrible era begins for Europe, like the gathering of clouds before a storm, and it will end in an explosion probably still more terrible than that of the world war." The First World War was never simply going to fade in their memories; its legacy would be long and disastrous. What had begun as despair had mutated into something much worse. As Bruno grew from late adolescence into early adulthood, he and thousands like him greedily consumed a fantasy that was paranoid *and* self-aggrandizing. In an instant they could flip on its head all that most oppressed them about life in Weimar Germany. In a reversal of the normal order, from nemesis had emerged hubris. The nationalists had completely transformed the meaning of the First World War, and Germany's future prospects, too.

But the "nationalism" that Bruno was increasingly drawn to fed on emotions far more destructive than just thwarted patriotism. Instead of being chastened and tamed by the nightmare of the 1914–1918 conflict—the heartlessness of mass industrialized warfare—later Nazi war veterans would seize on it as the unavoidable price for future German greatness, and its most important model. Many would even come to venerate the nature and the scale of the war's carnage, regarding them as indispensable ingredients of future German politics. The war's most destructive consequence was a mind-set of destruction and vengeance, from which to build a new world, whatever the cost, as Kessler could see: "Berlin has become a witches' cauldron in which opposing forces and ideas are being brewed together. Today history is in the making and the issue is not only whether Germany shall continue to exist in the shape of the Reich or the democratic re-public, but whether East or West, war or peace, an exhilarating vision of Utopia or the humdrum everyday world shall have the upper hand. Not since the great days of the French Revolution has humanity depended so much on the outcome."[36]

The legacy of the First World War and its revolutionary aftermath left Bruno with a fierce, personal ambition—one day he would join that "street fighting in a single city," but not as an army soldier. All he had seen and experienced between 1914 and 1922, everything he had grown up with, had ended in abject failure. He would never now invest, as his father had done, in the kind of Prussian militarism represented by all those men who had marched away from Perleberg back in 1914. Bruno wanted a template for the future, not the past.

The search was on for a politics that could fuse the courage of the trenches with the power of German mythology, and an ideology powerful enough to lead the assault against a world of political enemies, especially on the left. It would combine Jünger's love affair with the world of soldiering, extreme nationalism, and Freikorps brutality. All Bruno needed was a party—and a leader— that could combine all three. He was not alone in his search, or the only one for whom the circumstances of his early life proved decisive in shaping his later decisions. "The experiences of war, revolution, and inflation tell you all you need to know. We were spared nothing. We were rudely expelled from our childhood and never shown the right path. Misery, shame, hatred, lies, and civil war imprinted themselves on our souls and made us grow up fast. So we searched for, and we found, Adolf Hitler. What attracted us like a magnet was precisely the fact that he only made demands of us and promised us nothing. He required only our total commitment to him, and to Germany."[37] Thus wrote a clerk, born in 1911. It was a magnet that would very soon also have Bruno firmly in its pull.

Four

FULFILLMENT!

1922–1926

Until the age of sixteen, Bruno experienced the world vicariously and remotely. But in 1922 that all changed, as the family swapped the backwater of Perleberg for the drama of Berlin, Germany's largest and most volatile city. With the dismantling of the Freikorps in late 1920, the Perleberg barracks had no more need for its *Wachtmeister*, so it was the perfect time for Max to take up his career in law and order once again. Bruno must have been ecstatic when he discovered the family was heading for the great imperial capital itself. The young provincial nobody was going to become a *Berliner*. The city of Frederick the Great, and of Otto von Bismarck, was just waiting to swallow him up.

Even in the impoverished years of the early twenties, Berlin was one of the world's great capitals, bursting with history. For a boy as entranced with the idea of German power as Bruno, neither Munich nor Hamburg could compare with Berlin. Behind the splendor, however, it was a very different story. If Bruno had wanted to see for himself just how deep were the fault lines that ran across the face of the Weimar Republic, he had come to the right place. Berlin was Germany at its rawest, rife with chaos and poverty. Outside the central government area, with its ministries, embassies, museums, and statues, lay the industrial areas of the north and east, blighted by the largest, most overcrowded slums in the whole of Europe. To the south and the west lay lush green suburbs, whose great villas nestled between woods and rivers, a stark contrast to the maze of back streets and five-story tenements, called *Hinterhöfe* or *Mietkasernen* (rental barracks), built around squalid central courtyards in which lived Berlin's teeming population. These were raging breeding grounds for extremism of both left and right.[1]

The German Communist Party, or KPD, still commanded fierce loyalty in the city, even if the Freikorps had averted outright Bolshevik revolution. The city had more than earned its nickname "Red Berlin," because it could boast the second-largest Communist population outside Moscow. Presiding over all of it was the Weimar parliament, or Reichstag, desperately trying to control political anarchy with its permanently unstable coalitions.

The Langbehns were fortunate, however. As befitted the family of a justice inspector, their new home was in smart and comfortable Charlottenburg, a district to the immediate west of downtown Berlin, linked to the heart of the city by the great east-west axis (the six-lane boulevard that links the Brandenburg Gate to the city's western fringe). Neither full of slums nor cushioned by suburban detachment, it lay only a short ride on Berlin's fast-modernizing public-transport system from the downtown areas around the Unter den Linden and Potsdamer Platz, as well as the flashier west end of the Kurfürstendamm.

It is doubtful whether Bruno had the time or inclination to enjoy the scenery. These were angry, turbulent times in Berlin. Even if he had wanted to avoid sectarian politics, it was impossible. In fact, he was actively seeking them out. Every movement across the political spectrum had a toehold here, mounting endless rallies, mass demonstrations, and marches. The city was heaving with paramilitary formations. The Communists had both their Marxist ideology and their Roter Frontkämpferbund (RFK). Even the centrist SPD had its Reichsbanner organization. Simply to walk a Berlin pavement was to find yourself sucked into an argument, surrounded by a cacophony of ever more strident posters and headlines, which together "transformed the street into a vertically spread newspaper."[2] As the Nazis later claimed, "Who conquers the streets conquers the masses, and he who conquers the masses conquers the state."

For Expressionist painters such as Otto Dix and George Grosz, who flocked to Berlin, there was no other way to depict its street scenes than as a razor-edged vortex of anxiety and potential violence. Old-style courtesy politics were long dead; all that remained was fragmented, angry chaos.[3]

Even the schools were hotbeds of political activism, including the Leibniz Senior School, where Bruno was finishing the last two years of his education. As émigré journalist and author Sebastian Haffner recollected from his own Berlin school days, it was the teenage fanatics in the classroom (people like Bruno) who succeeded in keeping the torch of hatred and agitation alight, when everyone else only wanted things to calm down:

After [1920 or so], interest in politics flagged among us boys. All parties had been compromised and the entire topic lost its attraction. . . . Many of us sought new interests: stamp collecting, for example, piano playing, or the theater. Only a few remained true to politics, and it struck me for the first time that, strangely enough, those were the more stupid, coarse, and unpleasant among my school fellows. They proceeded to enter the "right sort" of leagues: the German National Youth Association or the Bismarck League . . . and soon they showed off knuckledusters, truncheons and even coshes in school. They boasted of dangerous nocturnal poster-pasting or poster-removing expeditions and began to speak a certain jargon which distinguished them from the rest of us. They also began to behave in an unfriendly way toward the Jewish boys.[4]

Even among boys as young as this, there was a hard core forming, one that grew even more radical in the years to come; Bruno's later record proves that he was very much one of them.

The nationalist dream that had erupted all over Germany seduced its followers with more than just naked aggression. As powerful as brass knuckles or truncheons were the pamphlets, booklets, tracts, and propaganda of the *völkisch* movement that were pouring off the presses. Their combination of stirring hymns to the German race and vicious caricatures of Germany's racial opponents found an avid audience and excited young men such as Bruno, greedy for the kind of certainty and uplift that they promised. Reading the literature on which Nazism built its political credentials proved as mobilizing as the thrill of combat in the streets: "That day I saw my first nationalist [demonstrators] with a bloodred swastika banner and a picture of Hitler with pine branches round it. Their courage and flair cast a spell on

me. . . . I began to read *völkisch* literature and particularly Theodor Fritsch's *Handbook of the Jewish Question*. Then I joined their
ranks, and thus the wonderful and bitter hours began in my life
which I would never have wanted to miss."[5]

Bruno had found others his own age who, like him, had been
torn apart by hatred for the Weimar Republic, inconsolable frustration at the loss of not just a war, but a world war, and loathing
for the Communists and the Jews they blamed for both. They
began dabbling with fashionable nihilism, which grew to be defined by searing scorn and exaggerated disgust, and it bound
them together as a generation. What began as adolescent posturing was on its way to becoming deeply held conviction. Their
bleak indulgence in these attitudes was destructive enough. But
even more dangerous was the dream of national awakening
spawned by their rage and resentment, which appears to have
ensnared both Bruno and a large number of his fellow disillusioned nationalists.

But as compelling as this was, Bruno the schoolboy had to
face up to the most pressing question: What career was he going
to choose? Germany in the 1920s was no time to leave school
unemployed—not that his parents would ever have allowed him
to neglect his future prospects. He had a quick mind and was
drawn toward a career that combined scientific understanding with physical dexterity—dentistry. As he had neither the
financial wherewithal nor perhaps the patience to go to university, medicine was out. But dentistry was the ideal compromise—
especially in the vocational non-university form then available in
Germany. It was a shrewd choice. Dentists were immune to the
vicissitudes of the economy (everybody gets a toothache), and
they commanded respect without being locked away in ivory

towers. He applied for a place in a nearby Charlottenburg technical college and was accepted.

But Bruno was not allowed to forget politics for long. In 1923, Weimar Germany was struck by two disasters, a godsend for the angry right, who looked on with malicious glee as the government's legitimacy was sorely tested. First, early in January 1923, the detested French army marched into Germany's industrial heart, the Ruhr Valley, and defiantly occupied it.[6] This violation of Germany's borders—compounded by the use of colonial soldiers—was met with rage and shame.[7] As a German historian later wrote: "German public opinion was only united all the more in an orgy of nationalistic frenzy. . . . A flood of propaganda was let loose . . . charging the French with carrying out a policy of terror, brutality, rape, destruction, abuse of justice, sadism, and willful creation of starvation and disease."[8]

Before having had a chance to redress the French emergency, Germany was brought to its knees again—this time by money. Just when Bruno's generation might have been lured away from their radical politics by the prospect of a strengthening currency and a rise in living standards, the entire economy was detonated from within by hyperinflation. The Germans had been printing money overzealously since 1919 to help pay their postwar debts—with alarmingly predictable results. Before 1914, the dollar had been worth around four German marks, but "in August 1923 the dollar reached a million. We read it with a slight gasp, as if it were the announcement of some spectacular record. A fortnight later, that had become insignificant. For, as if it had drawn new energy at the million mark, the dollar increased its pace tenfold, and began to mount by a hundred million and [billions] at a time. In September, a million marks no longer had any practical value, and a [billion] became the unit of payment."[9]

By November 1923 a dollar was "worth" four *trillion* marks; ordinary shopping trips now had to be undertaken pushing prams laden with worthless notes, zeroes were added to the cost of goods by the minute—the cup of coffee you drank tripling in cost before you had finished it. "My parents' house, which had been worth 38,000 marks, was sold for what had become the price of a pound of butter. Bank savings disintegrated to almost nothing. What my parents had owned all their lives was now in the hands of foreigners, and they were tossed out on the street. Losing everything that they had worked for their whole lives put my parents into an early grave. They simply couldn't conceive how a pile of banknotes could be literally worthless."[10] It wasn't hard to predict where the finger of blame would be pointed; "Bavarians, who preferred to barter agricultural produce, sneered at money as 'Jew confetti from Berlin.'"[11]

Both these traumatic events pushed Bruno deeper into the clutches of the extreme nationalists. Any ambitions he might have had about going to university were well and truly dashed. Though his parents were as insulated as anyone could be (at least Max's *Justiz Inspekteur* job appears to have been safe), the family savings were wiped out. But the damage went much deeper than this, creating not just destitution, but disillusion of the most corrosive kind. What had seemed solid was exposed as hollow and fraudulent; the solidity of money had been turned into a worthless mirage. My grandmother Thusnelda frequently used to describe to us the horror that hyperinflation had caused, and how proud her generation of Germans had later been of the monumental stability of the postwar Deutschmark. During the 1970s, when Britain was ravaged by widespread strikes, inflation, and protracted power cuts, she sent us food parcels, emergency supplies of sugar and butter, convinced she was protecting us from the kind of poverty Germany had endured during the early 1920s.

The moral damage inflicted by invasion and then inflation was even more serious because it appeared to embody every accusation made against Weimar by Germany's rabid nationalists. Their invective against Germany's political weakness grew more shrill, its language less temperate; Germany was broken, impotent, the plaything of malicious foreign powers, they screamed. Just open your eyes and look around you! This wasn't just angry polemic but, increasingly, a call to arms. Just when normality might have stepped in to defuse the power of the extremists, the French army and hyperinflation had blown it all away. For Bruno, the political lesson was stark: any value not rooted in the eternal *Volk* was at the mercy of forces that could destroy the country at will. Weimar could never redeem itself; it didn't have the strength of vision to reverse Germany's hemorrhaging national honor. For Bruno and so many like him, this was the moment they began to hanker for a solution that lay beyond conventional politics, in the miraculous form of "a man who might succeed in uniting all Germans who still had some regard for honor."[12]

And suddenly in November 1923, as though through breaking storm clouds, Bruno was rewarded with his first, intoxicating glimpse of what the future he so yearned for might look like— thanks to astonishing news from Munich. The headlines could hardly have been more dramatic. The army had thwarted an attempted military coup d'état. Bavarian right-wingers, led by their acid-tongued orator, Adolf Hitler, with First World War veterans General Ludendorff, Ernst Röhm, and Hermann Göring (among others), had tried to seize key buildings in Munich, in their bid to overturn the government. Since 1920, these so-called Nazis, with their distinctive swastika banners, had been a Bavarian sensation, the noisiest, angriest, and most militant of southern Germany's *völkisch* agitators. But even by their shocking standards, this was extraordinary—an armed insurrection against the state, deliberately designed to trigger a right-wing revolution.[13] Bruno was thunderstruck. As for many later Nazis, this was a decisive moment: "I felt electrified as the word went abroad in the newspapers in 1923 that down in Munich a man by the name of Adolf Hitler, aided by a little band of followers, had tried, in an excess of patriotic zeal, to shake off red rule and restore its honor to the German people."[14]

It wasn't the black farce of the coup itself that made the real impact, but the voice from the dock in the subsequent trial, a voice that echoed and amplified every thought Bruno had ever had about national salvation and the forces that stood opposed to it. For twenty-four days in February and March 1924, Adolf Hitler took the stand in what was political theater of the most scandalous and thrilling kind. Day after day Hitler weighed in against the "November criminals," justifying his would-be rebellion as the ultimate act of patriotic conscience. He turned the dock into a national soapbox. Here was a man who combined the brutal directness of both words and actions, who crystallized nationalist frustrations in military bravado and the rousing rhetoric of a supremely nationalist "J'Accuse." Millions of Germans were horrified, but for some the result was an epiphany. Inside the courtroom, too many were enthralled by his performance, not least the judge.[15] He couldn't save Hitler from a prison term, but he ensured the sentence was a derisory five years.

It had been an intoxicating moment, but with the Nazi Party and its paramilitary auxiliaries banned, it appeared to be over before it had even started. But something *had* changed. Munich showed Bruno that his search for "fulfillment" was not just a lonely indulgence; it was shared by like-minded Germans across the country. Their numbers were low, but they were uncompromising in their fervor and prepared to undertake any sacrifice in pursuit of their grievances. Bruno could do no less. The setback of Hitler's imprisonment and the banning of both Party and armed militias did not deter him. He spurned soft options and sought political maturity in its most extreme nationalist form, even as the *völkisch* movement faltered. That was why, as he made clear in his *Lebens-lauf*, he had dismissed the Jungbund (Youth Federation) as insufficiently militant. Its wholesome walks in the German woods, swimming, sailing, and singing anthems of worship to all things Teutonic were simply not revolutionary enough. Campfires were one thing, but Bruno wanted fully mobilized *Kampf*. He had outgrown these childish things; he wanted to join a party and play with the grown-ups.

Living in Berlin, Bruno was drawn to a breakaway splinter group, the "Freedom Party."[16] It was small, angry, and explicitly anti-Semitic.[17] For both Langbehns, father and son, its greatest asset was its principal figurehead, long a hero in their Perleberg barracks household, the First World War general Erich Ludendorff. The closer to the geographical center of German national power Bruno had gotten, the further he had been propelled to its most extreme political periphery.

Not even this appeared to fulfill Bruno for long, according to his later CV. The Freedom Party's rhetoric was angry enough, but that was all it remained—rhetoric. What Bruno lusted for was the chance to take up arms, join a marching column, wear a uniform, and seize Germany by the throat, to make up for having been too young to fight in the real war. It looked as if politics alone was not enough. Perhaps fulfillment existed only *outside* politics, somewhere more explicitly committed to counterrevolutionary action, rather than just speeches and committee resolutions. If it was impossible to find a politics that could embrace violence, Bruno decided he would be better served finding violence that embraced politics. But from where?

In 1924, as he neared the end of his first year as a dental student, Bruno got his answer, thanks to one of Hitler's key Munich coup accomplices, a First World War veteran and ex–Freikorps leader named Ernst Röhm, a bald and pugnacious parade-ground martinet who looked like a crude (and scarred) version of Bruno's father. But under the porcine exterior, Röhm was an organizational dynamo, a passionate nationalist loath to scrape the First World War mud from his army jackboots. He had been a close associate of Hitler's since the earliest days of the Nazi Party, and he chose the moment of his mentor's imprisonment to put into action a plan long brewing in his mind—to form a paramilitary organization based on the model of the now banned SA, but with even greater armed muscle and organized on a national basis. He called it the Frontbann (Front Regiment), a name that could not have been more synonymous with the First World War and the years of revolutionary turmoil that had followed. Its mission was to mobilize Germany's extreme nationalists and turn them into a force to be reckoned with, operating at the very edges of the law.

Bruno joined the uncompromising and formidable Frontbann as soon as he could. Here at last was the thrilling shortcut to active confrontation with Weimar he had been seeking for so long. All thoughts of Freedom Parties and Youth Movements fell by the wayside in favor of radical, disciplined activism. Everything about the Frontbann was modeled on the real army: its uniform, its ethos, and even its structure, with its regiments, battalions, and platoons (*Standarten, Stürme, Truppen*), all powerful echoes of Bruno's youth.

Bruno was one of 30,000 men Röhm managed to recruit to his new organization, many of whom later recognized the Frontbann as their initiation to the National Socialist Party. They wasted little time putting their beliefs into action, and in doing so provided an ominous foretaste of things to come—a self-righteous campaign of retaliation and shoot-to-kill that lasted for years. "I was there," wrote a messenger boy, born a year after Bruno in 1907, "when one of our first victims in Berlin . . . was shot to death by a Jew on the Kurfürstendamm."[18]

Till this point, I was painfully aware of how much I missed having any pictures of the young Bruno. Whatever family albums might once have existed had long disappeared. I had all but given up hope of ever finding any image at all of a Weimar-era Bruno, much less one of him actually in uniform. And then I found a book the Nazis had published in the mid-1930s that had celebrated their early paramilitaries.[19] It was exactly what I had expected: a raucous homily to the men in brown who had first hoisted the banners and pounded the streets of Germany in their National Socialist insignia. The book was full of endless pictures of SA men marching along cobbled streets, gathered in front of tents in the woods or lining the pavement, reaching out ecstatically to a passing Adolf Hitler.

But one image was of particular interest: a group shot of the Charlottenburg Frontbann members, in uniform, taken in Potsdam in August 1925. There are around a hundred or so men (and boys) in the picture, symmetrically organized for the camera: those at the front reclining, with the rest either kneeling or standing at the back. Some are smiling, some are frowning. There are lots of walking sticks, rucksacks, and even a drum, the detritus of an organization built half around marching and half around hiking in the woods. They are in uniforms, of sorts, but many of them look scruffy and improvised. If it wasn't for the large swastika banner in the middle, or the smaller ones on their armbands, it would be no different from a thousand other such shots from the period—of scouts, ramblers' associations, the league of young foresters.

It took a few minutes with a magnifying glass to find him, but there he was—second-bottom row, reclining just behind the man with the officer's peaked cap. The eyebrows, the large ears, and the down-turned mouth were the giveaways, as was his unnervingly direct expression. I was staring at the assured, rather cocky figure of my grandfather, just turned twenty a couple of weeks before the picture was taken, and I marveled at how supremely comfortable he looked surrounded by his fellow nationalist warriors. I wonder what pride of place that photograph must have occupied, and what satisfaction it must have aroused in him to discover that *this* picture now graced the opening pages of such an important Nazi publication. He was in the history books. No wonder he declared that the Frontbann had "fulfilled his expectations." You can see it clearly in his face: this is a twenty-year-old entirely happy for you to be utterly in awe of him, and all that his membership in the Frontbann signifies.

Röhm had huge ambitions for his new organization, which were spelled out to all its new recruits, Bruno included. The Frontbann was there to act as a spearhead with which to assail the Weimar Republic and one day help bring about a new Germany. Bruno was part of this growing counterrevolutionary movement. Even more significantly for Röhm, this was a mission for which the Frontbann had the field to itself. With Hitler in prison, his Nazi Party in disarray, and the SA banned, there was a vacuum waiting to be filled. All Röhm needed to do now was ensure that the Frontbann didn't break the law (by repeatedly reassuring the government he was there to uphold their authority, not subvert it), and the leading role in the nationalist cause was his for the taking. Unfortunately for Röhm (and, by extension, for Bruno, too), Hitler had a very different idea about the role the Frontbann should be allowed to play in the struggle for power. Crossing Hitler was not something lightly undertaken.

Hitler was a man of violence, but he was a political animal first and foremost. His ambition was to become a national leader, a second Bismarck, not just the man who cleared the way for another's benefit. The Party was his main weapon, which meant that any armed militia took its orders from the politicians, not the other way round. In a nation of 67 million people, with an army still loyal to the state, power was not achievable by force alone. The 1923 Beer Hall Putsch had failed because under those circumstances all putsches would fail. The road to power lay within the framework of Weimar politics, however loathsome. It required a complete overhaul to make the Party capable of achieving politically what a military coup had failed to do with force. The Party was a shambles, too disorganized, too chaotic, and too full of dissent to take on its opponents. It couldn't even agree that Munich Party HQ should be the only place allowed to issue membership cards.

All that was going to change, and radically. Authority had to be centralized and made non-negotiable. Leadership was to be vested in one individual—Hitler himself. Then, and only then, could the Party build an election-winning juggernaut capable of smashing any obstacle in the way to power. There was a terrible irony here: driven entirely by contempt for democracy, the Nazis nevertheless became one of the most formidable practitioners in the dark arts of triumphing at the polls. Bruno didn't know it yet, but his Nazi future lay not with the Frontbann but with a ruthless, Führer-dominated Nazi Party that Hitler was in the process of constructing. Between 1924 and 1926, as Bruno was working his way toward the Führer, so the Führer was working his way toward him.

In February 1925, two months after being released from prison, Hitler could at last begin ruthlessly clearing the way to absolute power—and his first target was Röhm's shiny new Frontbann. Hitler had no desire to be supplanted by rivals, as Röhm was fast becoming, but there was a structural issue, too. What in the end was the relationship of party to paramilitary? Who led, and who followed? For Hitler, there was only one answer: The paramilitary was indispensable as a tool for intimidation and propaganda. But it followed policy, it didn't dictate it. It was time to disabuse Röhm of his overinflated sense of the Frontbann's importance and his obstinate refusal to renounce his strategy for winning power by a coup. Röhm, brilliant organizer and fearless army officer though he was, proved no match for a full head-to-head confrontation with Hitler, who comprehensively crushed him. He had little choice but to resign his leadership of the Frontbann, after which he stormed off to Bolivia in a fit of pique. Bruno the paramilitary was now leaderless.

Hitler's other serious rival for the affections of the right wing was Ludendorff, but he was even easier to deal with than Röhm. Hitler persuaded him to stand in the forthcoming election for president in 1925. The result was a disaster for Ludendorff, who won barely 1.1 percent of votes cast.[20] Hitler expressed his shock and sympathy but made little effort to conceal his true feelings: "That's all right," he told a party colleague, "now we've finally finished him."[21] Ludendorff vanished from the political limelight dazed and paranoid, his reputation in tatters. This was a powerful double blow for a young would-be nationalist such as Bruno, so keen to identify a figurehead for his political longings. In the space of just weeks, his two earliest leading lights had been taken out at the knees by a Bavarian agitator whom at that point Bruno, like most northern Germans, knew very little about.

Both these battles, however, were merely an overture to the main event, the removal of Hitler's *real* obstacle to undisputed domination of the embryonic Nazi movement. He now had in his sights the jealously guarded independence of north Germany's nationalist right, who owed the Bavarians nothing—Bruno's natural constituency. These were men with different traditions and aspirations from Hitler's—whose semirural Austrian and Catholic background stood in deep contrast to theirs. Like Bruno, they were urban, Prussian, and Protestant. They were led by a pharmacist named Gregor Strasser, alongside his young ally from the Ruhr Valley, an ex-journalist and failed novelist, Joseph Goebbels.[22] The emotional Strasser, who wore the pains of the working man on his sleeve, and the icy, ferocious Goebbels posed a powerful double act that required all of Hitler's cunning to bring to heel.

The showdown came on February 14, 1926. Summoned to the town of Bamberg, they were treated to a two-hour tirade, as Hitler raged and ranted, to Goebbels's dismay.[23] Against the weight of Hitler's onslaught, not even Strasser and his otherwise unyielding Prussian allies could put up any real resistance, and like Röhm before them, they, too, capitulated. The Bavarians had won. Hitler was the movement's undisputed leader. He had neutralized every rival, securing from all who remained acknowledgment that he was their Führer, a title that combined the roles of figurehead, chief ideologue, and sole strategist, against whom there was no court of appeal. He had become National Socialism's Marx, Lenin, and Stalin combined.

Hitler was a ruthless and formidable opponent. He confronted his rivals head-on, crushing their dissent with his irresistible tirades of rage and sarcasm. But, unlike Stalin, he also knew how to seduce his vanquished opponents back into the fold; before long, even the hesitant Goebbels was besotted with him. Gregor Strasser too, though incapable of Goebbels's total idolatry, was maneuvered back into the party, with a big job as propaganda leader. It was a victory that cleared the way for Hitler's unchallenged mastery of the Party and its ideology. The "idea" and the "leader" were indissolubly linked; no more argument over nuances of doctrine; no room to deviate from essential principles.

This was the point where I believe Bruno, too, fell under Hitler's spell. Until now he had had a series of only provisional role models—his father, Ludendorff, Röhm—but in 1926 they had all been replaced by the transcendent figure of Adolf Hitler, who appeared to have been delivered to Germany by Providence itself. Bruno was transfixed by the charisma of a newly triumphant Führer, and by the disciplined organization of the Party apparatus answerable to his will alone. What before had been shapeless political longing had been transformed into the beginnings of a leadership cult, first fawning, later obsessive.[24]

But what really excited Bruno was the sheer scale of National Socialist ambitions. Hitler promised them even greater future triumphs, far beyond mere electoral success in the Reichstag. He told his followers that National Socialism was destined to become the world's dominant belief system. It was going to be bigger than capitalism, democracy, communism, even Catholicism, because, he argued, it derived its irresistible power not just from money, or class, or God, but from the ethnic lifeblood of the world's master race.[25]

The year 1926 therefore marked the most important crossroads in young Bruno's life. In one direction, Weimar beckoned, normal, safe, and showing the first signs of achieving stability, perhaps even international respectability. As memories of the world war, Versailles, and hyperinflation started to recede, many in Bruno's generation began to exchange the hothead excesses of their politicized youth for the sober pleasures of adulthood, marriage, and family life. Bruno had every opportunity to do the same. But in the other direction stood a very different prospect: a long and difficult political road, full of uncertainty and violence, reviled and feared by the great majority of his fellow citizens. It was a decision he made free from any material constraints (being neither unemployed nor financially desperate), directed by conscience and desire alone.

On May 17, 1926, still only nineteen years old, Bruno took the U-Bahn from his Charlottenburg home to Potsdamer Platz. Here he entered the dingy basement that was Nazi Party headquarters, so full of choking cigarette smoke and pale artificial light it was dubbed sardonically "the opium den," and signed on the dotted line. From that day on, he was a fully fledged Nazi. As he said later: "I remained with the Frontbann, Charlottenburg until I joined the NSDAP (Nazi Party) on 17.05.1926." Bruno was not alone. Plenty of others of his age and background found their way into the Party via a number of earlier, pre-Nazi organizations.[26]

Party, movement, and a restless young man in search of fulfillment had all come together. Just as Bruno had moved from uncertainty and indecision to determined conviction, so the Party had moved from a myriad of competing factions into a coordinated and unified body. Bruno had found the NSDAP at the same moment the NSDAP had found itself. This was his political niche, and he remained within it until its dying day.

A few days later, his membership card arrived from Munich Party Central, informing him, in a florid copperplate hand, that he bore membership number 36,931, and owed them the first of his monthly Party dues. Though only a few marks, it was nevertheless a not inconsiderable sum, especially for a man about to start four years of dental training. The number of members was still small—the extent of the Nazi Party in 1926 barely represented a football crowd. But with that came a furtive glow for the new Party member, part of a small band of true believers, savoring the solidarity of the ideological elect. This was the great trophy of the early joiner—the aura of prescience, courage, and moral conviction that later entitled him to many Third Reich privileges.

But Bruno's new Nazi membership wasn't enough. That same day he went even further and joined the Party's other organization, the one that had taken over the military responsibilities briefly held by the Frontbann—the recently reformed SA, or Sturm-abteilung. He disdained political anonymity. Unlike the Party, the SA provided him with a uniform (which he paid for himself). Wearing the khaki shirt and jackboots of a Nazi storm trooper was a declaration of war against the status quo. He could flaunt his status as a political warrior. It also allowed him to keep company with several members of his disbanded Frontbann unit, all looking for a new paramilitary home. Between them these men formed the nucleus of a new SA battalion (or *Sturm*), which later played a key role in Bruno's Nazi story: "15 ex–Frontbann personnel later set up the Charlottenburg SA, later Sturm 33. . . . In March 1928, [Fritz] Hahn took over the 20-man-strong Charlottenburg SA." It grew into one of the most infamous of all SA regiments, with a reputation for brutality and marauding aggression that belied Charlottenburg's air of bourgeois respectability.

Bruno could not have entered his political adulthood more emphatically. Joining the Party first and then the SA was a dou-bly dramatic gesture, signaling that he was ready to become a total Nazi. What motivated Bruno was the prospect of ideology fused with violence, party doctrine, and brass knuckle; each was insufficient without the other. The hard core, the elite of the movement, embraced those few men capable of delivering both. Bruno was determined to be among them.

However, whatever the internal logic behind Bruno's deci-sion, the whole process seemed absurd. For all their bravado and tough talk, the Party that Bruno had joined was an irrelevance, even in the bear-pit politics of the Weimar Republic. They were negligible in number, minuscule in influence, and without any realistic prospect for achieving any form of real power. Still, Bruno appeared entirely immune to the meagerness of the Nazis' political standing. His Party card and SA uniform were the outer shell of a terrifying and powerful inner certainty. This went far beyond the pernicious web of ideology, hatred, politics, science, and culture that constituted the Nazi worldview, its *Weltanschauung*. This was Hitler's secret weapon, a hubris so powerful that nothing could curtail it. For all those who chose to believe in it, Hitler's willpower was strong enough to overcome any obstacle, no matter how daunting. For the Party faithful like Bruno, victory was inevitable; the only question was when and how it could be achieved.

Later that same year, the whole world got a chance to inspect Hitler's vision of a Nazi future and the source of that confidence. The year 1926 wasn't just when Bruno joined both Party and SA, it also witnessed the publication of National Socialism's gospel, *Mein Kampf*. Second only to Hitler's charisma, this was the pillar on which the early movement rested: "I had the opportunity to study Adolf Hitler's *Mein Kampf*. I was confirmed in the opinion that the book must be the Bible of all National Socialists. The more I became absorbed in it, the more I was gripped by the greatness of the thoughts expounded therein. I felt I was eternally bound to this man."[27] Bruno, a voracious consumer of political propaganda, was one of its earliest and most avid disciples.

Mein Kampf is justly reviled for both its message and the crudity of its style, derided as one long crescendo of shapeless vindictive rage. And yet it played a key role in motivating my grandfather's long-term infatuation with Hitler's politics and worldview. Reading *Mein Kampf* had clearly proved a pivotal experience for young Nazis like Bruno, who fell over themselves to join the Party in the months after its publication. So one weekend I decided to read *Mein Kampf* and sample its pernicious persuasive power for myself, to see if those who dismiss its influence were right.

I sat down, cracked the spine of an English-language translation, and began to read. No amount of forewarning quite prepared me for the experience. For a few uncomfortable hours, I had the unpleasant sensation that I was riding the Berlin U-Bahn, alongside Bruno, on his way to Party HQ, fountain pen and membership dues at the ready.

From behind its rough and shapeless prose there rose the dark, ugly outline of Bruno's Nazi dream. It was like having Hitler inside your head. For one thing, much of it sounded very familiar: this was how Bruno himself used to talk. The book reeks of the same overweening conviction with which my grandfather used to arm all his pronouncements, contradicting, declaiming, and shamelessly seizing the last word.

Bruno would have emerged from his reading of *Mein Kampf* with several key things. First, a slavish admiration for the overwhelming force embodied by the prose. Its subject matter may ramble, but its deafening volume never ceases. From its first paragraphs, this is war camouflaged in book form, one long sneer that reduces anyone with an opinion different from Hitler's to the status of whiny political cretin. This crude ferocity proved that Hitler was no *mere* author, but a scourge of human folly and rottenness, with the courage to strip the world bare of apparent sanctimonious hypocrisy. Reading *Mein Kampf* gave Bruno the opportunity to wield the sledgehammer of Hitler's dogmatic omniscience for himself, as well as exult in the grossness of its language, its ubiquitous images of putrefaction and decay. Its dominant effect is one of bloated enormity, intended to provide converts with a towering sense of their own importance.

Mein Kampf gave Bruno more than just a taste for Nazi rapture. As I read more of the book, I could see only too clearly how it attempted to define what a real Nazi was—somebody enthralled by ideas that went far deeper than just admiration for its outspoken author. It sought to convince its readers that they were participants in a cosmic battle, in the service of a prophet seeking to deliver the world from *delusion*.

Once Bruno locked on to this idea, he was no longer just reading a book that described the key moments from Hitler's early life; he was bearing witness to the rise of a political giant. For a Nazi convert, of all the evidence for Hitler's political clairvoyance, none was more sublime than his self-proclaimed ability to winnow Truth from Lies. *Mein Kampf* painted a world that had been separated into two unequal camps: one was inhabited by the deceivers, the other by their dupes. Deeply sanctified but slow-blinking Germans had to be protected from their fast-talking tormentors. For Hitler, Germany was in the grip of falsehood as large as history itself, a conspiracy of global proportions. The book's triumphant conclusion, which a Nazi like Bruno grasped as its central point, was that this corruption and decay had only one perpetrator—the "hydra of World Jewry."[28]

The battle that Bruno thought he was joining contained only two adversaries: the Führer, with his monopoly on revealed truth, and the entire phenomenon of Jewishness. The Jews were no ordinary enemy. Luckily for the Nazis, as many like Bruno could now start to see, Hitler was no ordinary anti-Semite; he and the Jews were equal and opposite forces, locked in permanent conflict, with the entire world at stake, the climactic chapter in a race war dating back 2,000 years.

Bruno must have swallowed it all. Anti-Semitism had its roots in antiquity, but Hitler was remodeling it for the modern world. Underpinning Hitler's worldview was a clutch of key concepts that became Nazi shibboleths: "the eternal Jew," "geopolitics," "the survival of the fittest," "life not worth living," *"Lebensraum"*—all of which were first coined in the late nineteenth or early twentieth century, and all of which crop up repeatedly in *Mein Kampf*.

But there was one concept that towered over the others—and that was the idea of struggle, or *Kampf*. That was why Hitler used the word in the title of his book; it obsessed him. It held true for all living things, from viruses to nation-states. *Mein Kampf*'s final gift to Bruno was a philosophy, an amalgam of the three most influential luminaries of the day—Darwin, Nietzsche, and Wagner. For Darwin, all living physical things were locked in life-or-death struggle, from which there was no escape. The strong always win, and winning makes them stronger still. For Nietzsche, struggle separated the human from the superhuman, or *Übermensch*. And for Wagner, struggle defined the whole of cosmic creation itself, with one figure, the Teutonic Aryan, triumphing over all the others. Hitler added elements of each into a toxic mixture of eugenics, philosophical posturing, and ethnic self-regard, producing what Hugh Trevor-Roper later called "bestial Nordic nonsense."[29]

This was what made *Mein Kampf* more than just an outline of Nazi *ideas*; the book and its contents constituted their most powerful weapon. The Nazis may have been impatient with academic intellectuals, but they were in awe of the power of a transcendent truth. Certainty didn't just drive Nazi fanaticism; it was its most important concept, the driving force of history. That was why Christianity had defeated the might of the Roman Empire, for all their legions. Being willing to die for their beliefs had made early Christians irresistible. The right *idea* can conquer everything, Hitler proclaimed; it can transform the raw power of the masses into the irresistible force of a *Volk*, just as it had turned a mere figurehead into the Führer. And in *Mein Kampf*, particularly its anti-Semitism, Bruno had seen that idea cohere and crystallize.

It was evident that 1926 was a highly critical milestone in Bruno's National Socialist journey. This was the moment when he committed himself heart and soul to the movement's leader and the ideological aims of the Party. But the year didn't end until it had set one final test.

For Berlin's Nazis, the year of Party consolidation had taken a very distinct form with the arrival of a new figure in Bruno's political apprenticeship, its newly appointed *Gauleiter*, Joseph Goebbels. He had completed his transformation from left-leaning skeptic into rapturous worshipper: "[Hitler] is a genius. . . . I stand shaken before him. This is how he is: Like a child—dear, good, compassionate. Like a cat—cunning, clever, and agile. Like a lion—magnificently roaring and huge."[30] Berlin was Goebbels's reward for having aligned himself with his new master, but he had few illusions about the scale of the challenge of unfurling the swastika in a city that boasted so many thousands of hard-line Communists in its population: "They all want me to go to Berlin as a savior. Thanks for the desert of stone."[31] It was only made worse by the revulsion the city's underbelly provoked in him: "Berlin by night. A sink of iniquity! And I'm supposed to plunge into this?"[32]

Shortly after Goebbels's arrival in November 1926, Bruno, along with Berlin's few hundred other Nazis, found himself summoned to Party headquarters, to be harangued by their new city boss. First, they were reminded of the critical importance Berlin held for the movement: "Whoever has Prussia has the Reich. And the road to power in Prussia is via the conquest of Berlin."[33] He then delivered his ultimatum: Only those who could commit themselves fully and without reservation, whatever the sacrifice, could take their place in the great crusade. There was no room for vacillation or shirkers. The Party had to be purged of its fellow travelers, its passengers and parasites. Of the thousand or so Party members that Berlin had, four hundred took the hint and resigned. Bruno was *not* one of them. Goebbels appeared far from dismayed at having lost so many from an already negligible party, and was quick to rally those who had stood firm: "Today we are six hundred. In six years we must be six hundred thousand!"[34] He was to be proved right.

By the end of 1926, the Berlin twenty-year-old, about to embark on his training to be a dentist, could now count himself part of a tiny, utterly ruthless inner circle of Nazis, barely six hundred, in a city of nearly 4 million inhabitants.[35] They had their marching orders. In 1930s Nazi Germany, women were defined by the three K's: *Kinder, Küche, und Kirche*—children, kitchen, and church. But at the dawn of what became the Nazi era, men, too, had their triple K's: *Krieg, Kraft, und Kampf*—war, strength, and struggle. The next decade was later nicknamed the "*Kampfzeit*," the time of struggle, and Bruno would take his place right on its front line.

Five

STREET-FIGHTING MAN

1926–1933

Like every Nazi after 1926, Bruno was driven by one overwhelming desire: to get on with the task of winning real power. With arguments over worldviews, Jewish conspiracies, and Nazi ideology settled, it was time to take to the streets and show Germans what National Socialism really stood for. It fell to one particular Nazi organization more than any other to do it—not the Party, but the armed militia of the SA. For the time being, Bruno's brown shirt proved even more decisive than his membership card.

The SA became Bruno's home away from home. A childhood in the shadow of a military barracks, and a stint with both Jungbund and Frontbann, had accustomed him to the experience of aggressive and cloistered male solidarity. He needed it. The SA was full of men who reveled in their status as social outsiders. Vandals and thugs they may have been, but in their own eyes they were the epitome of dynamic and virile activism, committed to a great and important cause.[1] Bruno's "blooding" in the SA during the years of *Kampfzeit*, the time of struggle, marked him for the rest of his career as a full-blown *alter Kämpfer*, or "old fighter," one of the Third Reich's most coveted accolades. Only just twenty-one, he had never felt so important.

I wasn't surprised to discover that Bruno spent his career as a brownshirt with two of the most infamous battalions anywhere in the SA: Sturm 33 and, later, its sister battalion, Sturm 31. Based in north Charlottenburg, they were notorious, even by the standards of the SA, for their acts of street violence and drunken murder. Bruno remained in SA uniform for eleven full years, taking it off only in 1937, when it became clear that there were better places for him to serve the cause. His SA career placed him not just in the front line of the decade's worst urban violence, but also, though he didn't know it at the time, right on top of the most significant fault line running through the Nazi movement. The tensions between the Party and SA grew worse with every passing year, culminating in the "Night of the Long Knives" in June 1934.

Back in 1926, however, the SA had only one priority: to win the battle for Germany, and in particular the battle for Berlin, home to everything they most despised.[2] Nor did they allow their low membership numbers to dilute their capacity for violence. What they lacked in size, they made up for with ideological fire: "In 1927 I turned my back on the idle and joined the active fighters of the SA. After that time I participated courageously in the demonstrations, carrying the flag of the group. During the years of the struggle I tasted many a meeting hall and street fight with the menace of the red street mobs and their screeching women," bragged one SA man.[3]

Goebbels promised to take "red Berlin" by the throat. The

SA's mission was simple: "warfare against all anti-nationalists and internationalists; warfare against Jewry, social democracy and left radicalism; fomenting of internal unrest in order to attain the overthrow of the un-German Weimar Constitution." This required the SA to boost both its numbers and its fighting spirit.[4] Bruno now knew what was expected of him, which was to help take over the streets, dominate the city, and overwhelm all opposition.

It was easier said than done. Berlin was a stubborn place. As the seat of government, it had a vested interest in keeping the Weimar Republic safe from both left- and right-wing extremists. Berlin was home to Nazism's bitterest Communist enemies, drawn from the one million–plus working families who labored in the city's vast industrial hinterland. Their catchment areas in north and east Berlin proved the hardest for the Nazis to penetrate.

Outside politics, too, Berlin was a Nazi abomination. Its reputation as the red-light capital of Europe[5] and its world-class community of avant-garde artists stuck in their throats as an affront to *völkisch* morality. The city was notorious the world over for its Expressionist art, cabarets, gay bars, Bauhaus design, and nude revues, but most of all for the availability of sex, exulting in a reputation for being "a city of no virgins. Not even the kittens and puppies [were] virgins."[6]

Bruno had no problem despising Berlin's distinctive modernist high culture, which, like most Nazis, he regarded as willfully obscure, Jewish, and seditious. Berlin's depravity was more problematic. On the one hand Bruno was never more at home than in the raucous pubs of backstreet Berlin. He took his pleasures very seriously, and there was little that was refined about them. But that didn't stop him and fellow SA men from distinguishing their own hedonism from that of other Berliners, especially when tangled up in issues of apparent sexual deviancy, as so much of it was. Either way, the SA got to indulge both their ferocious appetites for drink *and* the self-righteous pleasure of promising to clean up the city's moral sewers.

Goebbels had at his disposal barely a couple thousand men, Bruno included, but this was *not* going to be a covert war. Nobody knew better than Goebbels how to fight the kind of running battle where notoriety and headlines were as important as casualty figures. He taught his tiny SA how to think big, turning his storm troopers into an intimidating force: "The sight of a large number of . . . uniformed and disciplined men marching in step . . . will impress every German deeply. . . . If whole groups of people in planned fashion risk body, soul, and livelihood for a cause, it simply *must* be good and true."[7] Bruno and his brown-shirted storm trooper colleagues were soon a threatening and ubiquitous feature of city life. Harry Kessler first noticed them in 1925, standing on street corners looking menacing: "On the Potsdamer Platz just a few swastika-carrying youths, with heavy cudgels, blond and stupid as young bulls."[8]

Winning Berlin required breaking heads. The SA had perfected the art of marching through the heart of working-class Berlin taunting Communist residents, and Bruno didn't have long to wait to put it all into practice. On November 14, 1926, he joined a formation of 280 SA heavies as they marched through the streets of Neukölln, a Communist district of working-class Berlin. The march, culminating at Hallesches Tor, triggered a series of ugly brawls that saw thirteen storm troopers badly wounded. It was hailed a propaganda triumph.

Battalions of SA hard men regularly patrolled Communist

areas, where they were soon engulfed in violent mêlées: "An enormous roar greeted us; a hail of rocks, bottles, junk, full chamber pots came flying through the air. Women, in particular, were acting like crazy, jumping around and shrieking, spitting on us, showing their bare behinds."[9] This mayhem became routine: "There was not one of us who did not get it with a chair or a beer stein. . . . Our slogan was always 'Germany, Awake!'" gloated one punch-drunk Berlin storm trooper.

Beating up Communists was gratifying, but ineffective if nobody knew about it. The Nazis needed the limelight of national headlines, and in January 1927 Goebbels and the SA adopted new tactics intended to deliver them. Bruno found himself attending raucous political meetings, staged in halls and auditoriums in the middle of Communist areas. It worked like clockwork. First, the Nazis invited sympathetic speakers to come and whip up an audience packed with Nazi brawlers. Then they sat back and waited for enraged locals to burst in and start heckling, when all hell broke loose. The first of many such meetings took place in Spandau, to the far west of the city, a hotbed of Berlin Communists.[10]

Goebbels wasn't content with just news reports. He soon built these sordid confrontations into the stuff of legend. By now, Bruno and his SA comrades were no longer playing a part in mere violent scuffles; once Goebbels had finished talking them up, they had been transformed into heroic set pieces. The most celebrated took place in February 1927, in Pharus Hall, a large auditorium to the north of the city, in the suburb of Wedding.

Deliberately choosing a location right in the middle of a Communist area, the meeting in Pharus Hall was advertised with posters that borrowed the rhetoric of proletarian jargon: "The bourgeois state is approaching its end. A new Germany must be forged! Workers of the brain and the fist, in your hands lies the destiny of the people!" Local Communists duly retaliated with posters of their own: "Red Wedding for the red proletariat! Whoever dares to put his foot into the Pharus Hall will be beaten to a pulp!"[11] Bruno was part of a drunken, seething crowd that had been worked up to a frenzy before Goebbels even took to the stage. The merest provocation from the back was all it took to trigger an eruption of bottle and chair-leg throwing.

Instead of running for cover, Goebbels stood his ground, shouting above the fray, surrounded by the most seriously wounded SA men. He later glorified his men as the "aristocrats of the movement," political giants who were guaranteed to whet the interests of the city's newspaper editors, who duly devoted whole pages to them. It was a sequence of events repeated regularly over the next six years. Politics had become equated with violence, both rhetorical and physical.[12] Bruno had become part of a sensation, both on the streets of Berlin and on the pages of its press.[13]

All-consuming as this was, Bruno still had to find time to complete his dental training. Though less academically demanding than the full-scale university degree required of a *Zahnarzt*, the German *Dentist* still had to master the fundamentals: extractions, fillings, the fitting of false teeth, though they stopped short at root canal work or tooth reconstruction. Only then could he report for duty. Every minute of his day (as well as most nights and every weekend) found him with either a drill or a Nazi banner in his hand.

Bruno's chosen career lifted him into an elite minority within his SA regiment, otherwise dominated by manual laborers and the unemployed. Most storm troopers had to lay aside their politics when not in uniform, but as a trainee medic, Bruno found plenty of scope to gratify his *völkisch* cravings even when out of his brown shirt. Almost by accident he had chosen a world gripped by intellectual revolution every bit as far-reaching as the wider sphere of politics: that of medicine.

Until now, Bruno's *völkisch* nationalism had drawn its impetus from the pens of Pan-German League folklorists, the cranks of the Thule Society, and other racial theorists. But doctors also had a role to play. With their calipers, stethoscopes, and germ theory, a new generation of physicians set out to redefine where humanity ended and medicine began. As a result, Bruno was a soldier in yet another *Kampf*, what the Nazis called their "race struggle," or *Rassenkampf*, the ultimate goal of which was so-called racial health, or *Rassenkunde*. As important as a nurse's spotless uniform or a scrubbed-down hospital ward was a sepsis-free body politic. Spurred on by a torrent of books and propaganda, many German doctors embraced their new responsibilities with a vengeance.[14] Even as a trainee dentist, Bruno was taught that he was no longer a mere doctor. His responsibilities as a medic covered not only the well-being of his individual patients but also the health of the entire nation.

But for all the SA's furious activity, the Nazis had virtually nothing to show for all those broken bones. Their election results in 1927, both national and local, remained pitifully low. Their noise and notoriety were simply not yielding any political dividend. The rallies continued, as did the beatings and the intimidation, but the movement itself seemed to have stalled, stuck at a threshold of a few tens of thousand *überzeugt* fanatics.

And they were in trouble with the law again. The SA had kept as close to the line of legality as it could, but had still overstepped it. In 1927 the Nazis were slapped with yet another in their long run of political bans. The SA uniform was outlawed, and Goebbels was prohibited from speaking in public. According to Sturm 33's battalion chronicle, they were forced to abandon their marching and flag waving and replace them with evening discussions held in cellars, "friendly" flats, or premises outside the city limits.

But the SA refused to be demoralized. Germans might not yet be voting for the Nazis, but the country was still deeply and aggressively nationalist. The fiercely authoritarian von Hindenburg had been elected chancellor in the 1925 elections, and Germans in the hundreds of thousands enthusiastically turned out to commemorate national celebrations and *Stahlhelm* processions.[15] The great majority of Germans mistrusted the left-wing Weimar government of the 1920s and loathed the specter of Communism. Nor did the Nazis alone feel the pain of old national wounds. It had been more than ten years since the end of the First World War and the reviled Treaty of Versailles, but there were few Germans for whom these weren't still powerfully emotive subjects.

To the Nazis' great frustration, these burning resentments were failing to influence most Germans' voting plans, which remained dictated by firm class and religious loyalties. A great number of the population were emphatically nationalistic in everything *except* how they behaved at the ballot box. National Socialism's message of national grievance resonated more deeply with many in Weimar Germany than its opponents wanted to believe. To prove that they were more than just another party, the Nazis needed something huge and cataclysmic to happen, a crisis so all-encompassing that the country itself would appear in jeopardy. In

Top left: My Scottish grandfather, Sergeant Donald Davidson, serving in France, 1917. He wears the uniform of the Seaforth Highlanders.

Top right: A temporary commemorative cross erected near Arras in France, where my Scottish grand-uncle Algy Davidson was killed. He was later interred at Roclincourt.

Bottom: Second Lieutenant Algy Davidson (at center, in the kilt), like his brother Don in the Seaforth Highlanders.

Max and Hedwig Langbehn, Bruno's parents, with family and friends, in the mid 1920s. Max is the bald man in the middle, and Hedwig wears the white ribbon.

Max and Hedwig, on the right, relaxing at a holiday cottage.

Left: My German great-grandmother Ida with her second husband, army officer Friedrich Pahnke, in the early 1920s. *Right:* Thusnelda and Bruno, shortly after their wedding in 1931.

Hedwig and Max seated in a meadow outside Potsdam, August 1929, two months before the Wall Street crash.

Perleberg barracks, in a state of elegant decay. This was the site of all of Bruno's earliest experiences of the military, and where his father was stationed during the First World War.

A Freikorps confrontation with Spartacists in Berlin, 1919. A large regiment o these hastily mobilized right-wing troops was stationed in Perleberg, bringin; counterrevolution and extreme nationalism to Bruno's hometown. BILDARCHI
PREUSSISCHER KULTURBESITZ

Bruno's SA *Sturmlokal* (storm trooper pub), the Zur Altstadt, located on Hebbel-strasse in the Charlottenburg area of Berlin. The pub owner was a zealous Nazi sympathizer, Robert Reisig. BILDARCHIV PREUSSISCHER KULTURBESITZ

A typical SA march through the streets of Berlin, 1932, flying the flag, and throwing down the gauntlet. Bruno participated in such marches on a weekly basis for more than eight years. BILDARCHIV PREUSSISCHER KULTURBESITZ

Bruno's SA battalion commander, Hans Maikowski, was shot down by communists on the very night Hitler became chancellor, January 30, 1933. Joseph Goebbels turned Maikowski's funeral a week later into a Nazi extravaganza. Bildarchiv
Preussischer Kulturbesitz

Members of the Wilmersdorf, Schöneberg, and Charlottenburg Frontbann (a
areas in Berlin), August 1925. Bruno is circled, reclining in the second row.

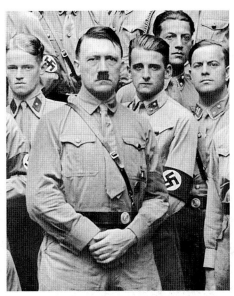

left: Bruno's Berlin Nazi boss, Joseph Goebbels, whipping up a crowd of storm troopers. Bruno was one of only six hundred Nazi Party members in Berlin in 1926, when Goebbels took over. Bildarchiv Preussischer Kulturbesitz

right: Hitler's hold over the minds of his young fanatical followers was total. Bruno was as committed to Nazi ideas as he was to the promise of power. Mary Evans Picture Library

A terror goes underground; in countless cellars, warehouses, and improvised holding cells, democrats, socialists, and communists were detained; most were beaten up, many were killed. Bildarchiv Preussischer Kulturbesitz

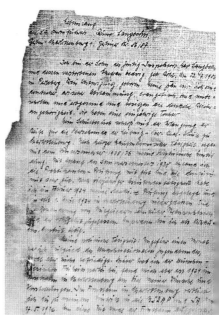

Left: The folksy brutalism of the Nuremberg Rally, 1934. Bruno is somewhere among the numberless ranks of SA and SS marching along the medieval streets of Nuremberg on their way to the vast parade grounds designed by Albert Speer, to be filmed by Leni Riefenstahl. ULLSTEIN BILDARCHIV

Right: The first page of Bruno's *Lebenslauf,* or CV, with its frayed edges and jittery handwriting, the centerpiece of his application to join the SS.

The Nazification of German dentistry: the opening of a regional office of the Reich Guild of German Dentists. Bruno was in charge of its most important office, in Berlin. BILDARCHIV PREUSSISCHER KULTURBESITZ

The SD school for new recruits in Berlin-Charlottenburg. Note the SD lozenge on the officer's sleeve, the official insignia of Reinhard Heydrich's security service.

Lfbe. Nr.	Name	Degen	Ring	SS.Sp.Al.	Feichtb.K.	Ehrenstern	Dienststellung
10036	Saalfeld Otto, ✠ I 🎖 ⊕			⬦	⬦	Υ	SD-Hauptamt
10037	Langbehn Bruno, ⊛		O				SD-Hauptamt
10038	Bauer Mathias			⬦	⬦		SD-Hauptamt
10039	Schilling Franz, 🎖					Υ	SS-»Na
10040	Schachl Josef					Υ	Stammabt. 11
10041	Wöhrnschimel Rudolf					Υ	38. Sta.
10042	Klein Walter						Stammabt. 11
10043	Mandl Josef						Stammabt. 11
10044	Ullrich Josef						11. Sta.

Bruno's entry in the SS Admissions Roll, or *Dienstalterliste*, confirming that he is a holder of the Gold Honor Party Badge and the *Totenkopfring*, and that he has been attached to the Security Service Head Office, the SD Hauptamt.

Bruno's new bosses were the most ruthless men in the Third Reich: the head of the SS, Heinrich Himmler; the head of the SD, Reinhard Heydrich; and the head of the Gestapo, Heinrich Müller, in 1939. BILDARCHIV PREUSSISCHER KULTURBESITZ

Bruno's father-in-law, Friedrich Pahnke, at work in his office in Paris, April 1942. He wears the uniform of a staff-officer captain, attached to weapons procurement

Friedrich on leave with Ida, summer 1943.

Ewald, Bruno's brother-in-law, a private who served as a motorbike dispatch rider.

The Langbehn family, July 1941. Bruno wears the uniform of an SS first lieutenant, or *Obersturmführer*.

Thusnelda and her mother, Ida take the girls and their cousin to the Berlin Zoo, spring 1943.

My mother, Frauke (left), and her two sisters, Prague, Christmas 1945.

Thusnelda, spring 1944, on the eve of moving from Berlin to Prague.

German troops surrendering in Prague, 1945.
ULLSTEIN BILDARCHIV

iumphant Soviet tanks complete the liberation of Prague, May 1945. ULLSTEIN
LDARCHIV

Bruno and Thusnelda (in the black dress) relaxing at the Berlin Dentists' Ball i
1956. The war seems very distant.

Thusnelda and Ida (standing), Christmas 1956. The large television set, we
laden Christmas tree, and Bakelite telephone provide indication of Germ:
postwar prosperity.

Bruno, looking suitably stern, with a few *Kameraden*, sometime in the early 1960s.

Bruno with Thusnelda, in Berlin in 1966, beer, schnapps, and cigarettes to hand.

Bruno and Gisela, his new common-law wife, in 1974, after his divorce from Thusnelda. Gisela's adoring look has clearly mellowed him.

The last photo we have of Bruno, Edinburgh, 1984.

late 1929, they got their wish: on Tuesday, October 29, the New York Stock Exchange collapsed.

The Wall Street crash, and the Great Depression that followed, hit Germany hard. All the Weimar glitter, the musicals, the movies, the restaurants, the neon, and the nightclubs had been paid for by American short-term loans. Its love affair with the ballsy chutzpah of America had earned Berlin the reputation as an outlying satellite of Hollywood and Broadway, to the horror of cultural conservatives, such as ultra-nationalist composer Hans Pfitzner, for whom the "jazz-foxtrot flood" represented "the American spiritual assault on European culture."[16] But thousands of ordinary Berliners were bewitched by sensational performers like the African-American dancer Josephine Baker.[17] Bruno's preferences were for the light classics, operettas, and marches, mostly, as well as the kinds of songs he could sing along to with a tankard of beer in his hand, but he was no stranger to the siren call of Berlin's nightlife.

The withdrawal of American money plunged Germany into economic havoc. Unlike what had happened in the crisis of 1923, the result wasn't runaway prices in hyperinflation, but catastrophic deflation, which caused mass unemployment. This turned out to be the biggest boon to Hitler's "politics of catastrophe." The numbers are chilling.

In 1929, 31,800 Berliners had been out of work. By the end of September 1931, the figure was 323,000. By April the following year, 603,300 were registered unemployed, while the actual figure was estimated at over 700,000. Berlin now contained more than ten percent of the total unemployed population of Germany. The persistent poverty wore people down. It was the second time in a decade that the Weimar system had failed them, and their anger was palpable.[18]

No wonder Stephen Spender was sure he could detect an "all-pervading smell of hopeless decay . . . [that] came out of the interiors of these grandiose houses now converted into pretentious slums."[19]

Germans, with their pronounced work ethic, had always found unemployment particularly hard to bear. Joblessness pulled the nation apart, driving a wedge into families and neighborhoods and, worst of all, male pride. The novelist Christopher Isherwood, who was living in Berlin at the time, described the despair that resulted:

> Morning after morning, all over the immense, damp, dreary town and the packing-case colonies of huts in the suburb allotments, young men were waking up to another workless empty day to be spent as best they could contrive; selling bootlaces, begging, playing drafts in the hall of the Labour Exchange, hanging around urinals, opening the doors of cars, helping with crates in the markets, gossiping, lounging, stealing, overhearing racing tips, sharing stumps of cigarette-ends picked up in the gutter, singing folk-songs for a penny, or *Groschen*, in court yards and between stations in the carriages of the Underground Railway.[20]

But the real impact of unemployment was how it made its victims feel. The Depression brought back to the surface traumatic memories of the post–First World War nightmare from which National Socialism had sprung in the first place, when the nation had never felt so broken or reviled. As a contemporary article put it:

> With the loss of work the needed earnings are not all that is taken from the man; his sense of life is also taken. The unemployed man sees the ground beneath his feet disappear, and with it his position and rank are gone. Through the workplace, the worker had his place within the community of human society. By losing work, he loses his justification to be, and not only in the community of the Volk, but also in his small family circle.[21]

It played perfectly into the hands of Nazi propaganda, which saw the global financial meltdown as a perfect allegory for the Darwinian struggle in which all nations were locked—a struggle that Germany was losing.

The Depression also reinforced the scaremongering of Nazi anti-Semitism, central to which was the myth that the world's money was controlled by the Jews. To millions of angry young Germans, blaming Jews for Germany's economic calamity felt more and more gratifying. Resistance to Nazi polemic was starting to weaken. Christopher Isherwood saw opinions that before had been the preserve of the Nazi fanatic set to enter the mainstream: "Here was the seething brew of history in the making . . . which would test the truth of all political theories, just as actual cooking tests the cookery books. . . . The Berlin brew seethed with unemployment, malnutrition, stock market panic, hatred of the Versailles Treaty, and other potent ingredients."[22]

For Bruno, the Great Depression was the miracle the Nazis

had been looking for. Goebbels had told them back in 1926 that they could achieve their breakthrough only if they mobilized hunger, despair, and sacrifice. One immediate consequence was that the SA was flooded with new recruits looking for a refuge from the ravages of unemployment. *Stürme* that had typically numbered around sixty or so had doubled and even tripled in size by 1930–1931. The SA's influence quickly spread even more widely and deeply across the city, especially in working-class areas, where unemployment had its most devastating effect. The SPD newspaper *Vorwärts* reported an interview with a new recruit to Bruno's SA Sturm 33: "When the nineteen-year-old high school graduate Konrad Domning . . . was asked why he had taken up with the SA, he gave the classic answer: 'My dad was broke, it was already winter, and I had no chance of an apprenticeship!'" Walter Stennes, commander of the SA Eastern Division, reported to Ernst Röhm, head of the SA, that sixty-seven percent of his *Stürme* were unemployed men.

Even more attractive for the unemployed German man was that SA battalions were based not in barracks, but in local pubs, called *Sturmlokale* (battalion locals). The combination of drink, cigarettes, and the camaraderie of shared resentment acted as a magnet for the disaffected, especially those otherwise condemned to spend their days in tiny flats, surrounded by anguished wives and crying children.

Bruno's Sturm 33 was no exception. It took them a while to find suitable premises, as bar owners were wary of attracting trouble, but they finally lighted on a bar whose landlord was amenable to the Nazi cause. As the battalion records later put it: "Back then it wasn't easy finding a suitable *Sturmlokal*. . . . It used to mean the pub owner's having to take a big risk. But soon after, we found the pub, Zur Altstadt, Hebbelstrasse 20, which was ideal, its publican one Robert Reisig."[23] It remained Bruno's favorite watering hole, and base for his SA activities for the next several years, being only a few minutes' walk from his North Charlottenburg home.

The Nazis weren't the only political extremists to benefit from the chaos of unemployment. So, too, did the Communist Party, whose numbers rose dramatically. Berlin's two opposing forces now included thousands of men, both hard-line veterans like Bruno and bewildered, furious newcomers. As their numbers climbed, so did their capacity for violence. Goebbels's publicity campaigns helped the SA to build a ruthless cult out of the resulting bloodshed. The more blood that was spilled, the more he rhapsodized SA heroism and sacrifice. The Communists couldn't match it.

The SA was moving into a new era. Meeting-room bundles and rowdy demonstrations weren't bloody enough. They gave up using chair legs and bottles and turned to guns and knives instead. As the scale of the violence intensified, one Berlin *Sturm* acquired the fiercest reputation of the lot: Bruno's Charlottenburg Sturm 33. They became a newspaper sensation, a synonym for Nazi violence at its most unapologetic and brutal. Formed from the remnants of Bruno's old Frontbann battalion, Sturm 33 was based in the north of Charlottenburg, right next to a Communist stronghold in an area called Kleine Wedding (Little Wedding). The surrounding streets were a flashpoint for violence.[24]

Though clearly built on extremist right-wing attitudes, SA Sturm 33 considered itself the true representative of working-class angst, describing its outlook as defiantly plebeian in its regimental propaganda. They operated in the "proletarian districts of Old Charlottenburg, not the Kurfürstendamm" (a fashionable shopping area).[25] For Bruno, their local neighborhood was simply a microcosm of the wider national struggle. Their proudest achievement was to have "hounded off all the Jews" and made the area fit once more for "their German brethren, [by] winning it over for the message of the Third Reich."[26] Bruno was fighting a racial, not just a class, war against alleged ethnic betrayal as much as alien ideology. Their declared enemies included not only the reds of the far left but even members of the respectable bourgeoisie, namely *any* middle-class Berliner "guilty of turning a blind eye to the needs of his *Volksgenossen* [race comrades], with an 'I'm all right, Jack' attitude; or whose cowardice let Marxism gain a foothold in the street; or whose shameful lack of race instinct failed to recognize the danger posed by the Jew."[27]

Sturm 33 was commanded by one of the SA's most charismatic young officers, Friedrich Eugen Hahn (Fritz to his colleagues), an old friend of Bruno's and an early mentor. In 1936, Bruno described his relationship to Hahn in an SA affidavit: "I have known Standartenführer [Colonel] Hahn since 1924, from our time together in the Charlottenburg Frontbann. I have been a member of the Charlottenburg SA till today, with one short break." He had been asked to speak up for him, after a "clique of SA men had started a whispering campaign against Battalion Leader Hahn." Bruno leaped to his defense: "Standartenführer Hahn has always been an upstanding comrade for the twelve years I have known him and carried himself with superb military bearing, with everything about his conduct unimpeachable."

Hahn's upbringing was virtually identical to Bruno's: the son of an army major, he had belonged to a number of quasi-military nationalist organizations before crossing paths with Bruno in the Charlottenburg Frontbann. At the age of twenty-one, while working as a bank clerk, he was made the commander of the new SA Sturm 33. Nicknamed "Roter Hahn" (literally, "red Hahn," but more jokingly—and obscenely—"red cock," as the word *Hahn* means "rooster") because of his bright ginger hair, he was infatuated by all things military. Kurt Daluege, head of the Berlin SA, and later head of the Berlin SS, described him as his "longest-serving and best officer." At the end of 1931, however, Hahn was forced to leave Sturm 33. He had murdered a Communist, and he fled to the Netherlands.[28]

Hahn was replaced as commander of Sturm 33 by another contemporary of Bruno's from Frontbann days, Sturmführer Hans Maikowski, who picked up where his predecessor had left off by expanding and intensifying their campaign of terror, earning Bruno's battalion even greater notoriety. On Tuesday, February 3, 1931, the left-wing paper *Die Welt am Abend* (Evening World) screamed: *"Mörder-Eldorado in Charlottenburg!"* ["Charlottenburg, the Eldorado of Murder!"] . . . The tally for a few weeks of fascist bloodshed: two dead, a dozen wounded, thanks to Hahn's column of death!" The battalion proudly reprinted the headline in their recruitment literature.[29] Their atrocities became so routine that one journalist, Gabriele Tergit, writing in *Die Weltbühne* (The World Stage), was forced to throw his hands up and declare, "We know it, this is Sturm 33 . . . this is terror. But no newspaper bothers to report it anymore; not even the police think it's news. We have just grown so accustomed to this city war; we don't notice it anymore."

Sturm 33's roll call of bloodshed offered a frightening picture of how grim Berlin's back streets had become. In November 1930, twenty of its men were in a Charlottenburg dance hall, the

Eden-Palast, when they spotted members of a rival Communist group, the Falke (the Falcon); a fight broke out, shots were fired, and three Communists lay badly wounded.

The Eden-Palast attacks triggered one of the most extraordinary episodes in Berlin's pre-Nazi history, as I discovered. I had been discussing Bruno's career in Sturm 33 with one of my German cousins, a lawyer. His ears pricked up on hearing the battalion name, and he asked me if I had heard of a man named Hans Litten; I hadn't. He explained who Litten was: a Weimar-era lawyer, whose name is commemorated in a humanitarian law prize awarded by the German bar to this day. His story was astonishing. At the risk of his life, Litten had tried to prosecute not just the SA men from Bruno's Sturm 33 accused of the Eden-Palast shootings but, even more incredibly, Adolf Hitler himself, whom he accused of having ordered the SA attack.[30]

Hans Litten, a Jewish left-wing lawyer, not yet thirty, was convinced that the Eden-Palast atrocity proved Hitler was a man of violence planning to overturn the state by force. Litten astonished Germany by subpoenaing Hitler to appear in the trial and defend himself from the accusation of being responsible for a campaign of murder and intimidation. In May 1931, Litten finally got his day in court, when members of SA Sturm 33, charged with attempted murder, appeared in the dock. The real sensation, however, was the cross-examination of Hitler himself, conducted by Litten. Crowds of SA and Party supporters flocked to the court to heckle the stooped figure of the young Jewish lawyer and ogle their beloved leader. So, I asked my cousin, do you think Bruno had been one of those who barracked the courtroom? He just laughed; the idea that Bruno had missed the biggest Nazi scandal of the entire year was risible. How could the storm trooper son of a justice inspector have resisted it, with his own SA comrades in the dock?

Litten opened by attacking Hitler's claim that his fellow Nazis had renounced violence in their plans to win power. Hitler resorted to party cliché: "his SA" was merely a "bodyguard," there to protect "a purely spiritual movement." The cross-examination went on for some hours.[31] Though Litten drew blood with his rhetorical swipes, backed up by evidence from Sturm 33 infiltrators, he failed to convict Hitler of perjury. But the trial had been enough. As far as Litten was concerned, Hitler the would-be statesman had been unmasked in the full glare of national publicity as a conniving liar and violent thug. Bruno's Sturm 33 was also held up to the world as the true face of Nazi doctrine. It was the last time Hitler was ever made accountable in such a way. A few months later he was in power, and no such attack was ever again possible.

Litten's name may be all but forgotten now, but his actions over that week in 1931 represent the most devastating and prescient critique of Nazi methods and the lies that sustained them ever mounted in Weimar Germany. Litten's courage in the courtroom, and the audacity of his cut-and-thrust interrogation, visibly rattled Hitler, as well as revealing to the world what Bruno's SA was really like. The price for being the Führer's public accuser, however, was to prove high for Litten. As soon as Hitler came to power he had him arrested and sent to Dachau. Litten endured five years of agony in the concentration camp, targeted from the moment he arrived for special levels of abuse, before committing suicide in 1938.

The trial, sensational though it had been, proved only a temporary distraction and did little to stop the crescendo of Sturm 33 violence. On New Year's Day 1931, a month after the Eden-Palast assault, three members of the Reichsbanner, the SPD paramilitary organization, were ambushed by storm troopers from Sturm 33, who stabbed them repeatedly with kitchen knives. Two of them, brothers, were so badly injured they took months to recover; the third man was maimed for the rest of his life.

The end of January 1931 saw Sturm 33's first killing. Four Communists were drinking at the bar of the Zur Altstadt, Bruno's SA *Sturmlokal*; an SA man recognized them and raised the alarm. Minutes later, one of them, who had tried to flee out the back, lay on the floor bleeding to death. Another, Max Schirmer, was hurt so badly he never walked properly again. On February 1, 1931, a twenty-three-year-old Communist, Otto Grüneberg, was shot through the heart and died in yet another late-night pub brawl.

Sturm 33 led the tally of SA bloodshed and was denounced by the Social Democrat paper *Vorwärts* (*Forward*) for its "fearsome, bloody tit-for-tat" (*"fürchterliche Blutbilanz"*) on the streets of Berlin. Maikowski's SA battalion relished its murderous reputation and basked in the Nazi acclaim it earned them. They incorporated their tabloid nickname, *Mördersturm*, into their regular marching song: *"Wir sind die Nazi Leute vom Mördersturm Charlottenburg!"* ("We're the Nazi boys from Murder Squad Charlottenburg!"). The Berlin Communist papers boomed in outrage: "By all accounts, it's clear, a fully mobilized Nazi death squad is active, all around Hebbelstrasse."

Goebbels was ecstatic: this vindicated his tactics of ceaseless provocation and intimidation. He published a jubilant justification: "*Tempo! Tempo!* That's the slogan for our work! In this blinding frenzy of struggle between good and evil, there can be no quarter." Sturm 33's kudos as the most effective storm trooper unit turned it into a shorthand for the entire SA. The newspapers quoted a letter leaked to them, written by an SA man to his commander: "Hey, you've seen the popularity Sturm 33 has got itself. . . . I know your every effort is about 'doing a *Maikowski*,' or, better still, going one further, that's the way to impress people!"

The Communists responded in kind. The violence went both ways, as Bruno found out for himself, on March 6, 1932. Luckily for him, his assailants weren't armed with either knives or a revolver, just heavy sticks. Flaunting his SA brown shirt and blue-lined cap proved a perilous thing to do. In an affidavit ("Eidesstattliche Erklärung"), which all Nazis who had been on the receiving end of physical violence proudly filled in, Bruno recorded what had happened to him:

> I came from the cemetery in Seestrasse, having visited my mother's grave [she had died the previous year], and I wanted to visit my relatives in the Antonstrasse, flat 2. When I came out about an hour later, I was set upon in the hallway. Eyewitnesses reported that three men armed with cudgels entered the building just after I had gone in, and after they had failed to find anything looking through the courtyard windows, they had then waited by the doorway. The culprits do not seem to have been from the area. That is why I suspect I had been followed for some time. I was wearing a blue cap, with a Sturm belt.

To the question *"Wer hat den Unfall verschuldet?"* (Who was responsible for the injury?), there was only one answer he was likely to give: "My assailants were Communists."

Bruno was fortunate: he escaped with some serious knocks, lacerations, and a burst eardrum and was ordered to take ten days' bed rest, but he was still alive. Berlin's hallways, courtyards, stairwells, and alleys had been turned into potential death traps. Needless to say, Bruno and his SA comrades were not required to fill in documents to account for all the violence they meted out.

The SA had a new weapon to help them with their struggle, Goebbels's *Der Angriff* (The Attack), first a weekly and later a daily Berlin paper. It acted as a megaphone for the atrocities and the standoffs dominating life in the capital. Every SA scrap became epic news, while every headline spurred on ever more violence. Goebbels's articles all followed the same pattern: upstanding SA men going about their business, ambushed by despicable and cowardly Communists, with nothing but their fists and their faith in the Führer to sustain them, battling their way to victory after victory, upholding German law and order and saving the country from the left-wing plague. The SA was repeatedly depicted as the front line of civilized decency, holding back the red tide. It was all part of the big lie that repeatedly dramatized the SA as the victims of violence and outrage, and never as the instigators. Many Germans standing on the sidelines were prepared to believe it.

Goebbels reinforced this with a series of SA martyrs, in a pointed echo of the First World War cult of the "fallen," deliberately evoking the sanctity of trench camaraderie. The spirit of Jünger was alive again, not in the trenches of Flanders, but on the streets and in the pubs of frontline Berlin.[32] Goebbels was shameless in the way he did it; he considered no hyperbole too mawkish.[33] He garlanded his descriptions of SA thuggery with Wagnerian symbolism. Fusing both Christian sentiment and First World War nostalgia, he transformed Nazi storm troopers into Aryan heroes battling "Jewish-Bolshevik sub-humanity." Anyone falling victim to a Communist bullet was ripe for Nazi canonization.

Goebbels finally found the perfect candidate, a young, popular commander of Berlin's Sturm 5, shot in the back by alleged Communist assassins. His name was Horst Wessel, and his life story was eerily similar to Bruno's. He was born in 1907 and joined the SA in the same year as Bruno, 1926. Like Bruno, after a few years of "adventure, stirring up putsches, playing soldiers," fulfillment had come in the form of his "NSDAP . . . political awakening."[34]

It was in death, however, that Horst Wessel served the Nazis best. The fact that he had been killed, not in some heroic tussle on the streets of his beloved Berlin but in an argument over a prostitute with her pimp, offered Goebbels no obstacle to creating the ultimate Nazi icon.[35] Goebbels used every medium available to him: poetry, biography, film, music, and ceremony, including the creation of a national day of remembrance, complete with statues, monuments, indeed an entire cult to which even Hitler paid repeated tribute. Capping it all, however, was a marching song, a rousing piece of kitsch whose lyrics the dead SA man had written and that Goebbels elevated into the Nazi version of "La Marseillaise." Henceforth known as the "Horst Wessel Song," it became the movement's most potent anthem.

Wessel's funeral and its aftermath consummated the legend. Bruno took part in a huge SA turnout at the cemetery, drawn from every *Sturm* in Berlin. Goebbels couldn't have scripted it better. On the way to the grave, there was a fight with jeering Communists, while the cemetery was daubed with obscene graffiti, courtesy of some "murder-crazed, degenerate Communist bandits," as Goebbels labeled them. Lying on top of his coffin was Wessel's *blaue Mütze* (blue cap)—the same sort that subsequently got Bruno attacked.

A few months later, Goebbels even released a Horst Wessel movie, featuring Aryan courage, Communist villains, and religious symbolism, depicting Berlin as a Jewish "asphalt" den of decadence and corruption. The dead pimp was shown marching alongside SA columns from beyond the grave. "With his song, sung today by millions, Horst Wessel has won a place in history. . . . Even after millennia have passed, when there isn't a stone left standing in the city of Berlin, the greatest of the German freedom fighters and its poet will be remembered." That left one piece of unfinished business. The accomplices of the man who had shot Wessel, as well as the assailant himself, were quietly dispatched: the first two were guillotined; the shooter (who was already serving a six-year sentence) was driven out of prison to a wasteland on the outskirts of Berlin and brutally gunned down.

Throughout 1930 and 1931, the SA continued to grow. New battalions were formed and old ones split. Soon, Sturm 33 had to bow to the inevitable and create a subsidiary to soak up the excess. This became Sturm 31, also based in north Charlottenburg. Bruno, along with sixty other SA men, made the transfer around the turn of the year.

Sturm 31 never matched the exploits of Sturm 33, but Bruno found life in his new battalion full of drama of a different sort.

Within weeks of his arrival, he was embroiled in an even more significant battle, not against the Communists, but against his own Nazi leadership. It had been simmering since the previous year, but in spring 1931 it erupted in the single biggest rebellion Hitler ever faced, and Bruno was caught up in the middle. It was a battle that had enormous consequences for the future of the SA and played a key role in Bruno's journey toward the SS.

Sturm 31 was run by another powerful SA personality, Sturm-führer Heinrich Kuhr. He had a prickly, aggressive streak that made him deeply unpopular with his men, Bruno included. But that was only the half of it. The real issue was Kuhr's allegiance: Was it to the Party or to the SA? This was simply another way of asking: To whom did the SA answer, to Hitler or just to itself? This had been a constant issue since the days of Röhm and his troublesome Frontbann. Hitler regarded their subordination to his political leadership as settled, but deep within the SA, there lurked deep disquiet. The fracture that opened in the middle of Sturm 31 came to threaten the whole Nazi movement.

Kuhr's prime loyalty lay with the man who ran the Eastern SA (including Berlin), his commander, Walter Stennes. Stennes was old-school SA in the Ernst Röhm mold, with very clear ideas about its role—ideas that didn't coincide with Hitler's. For Stennes, the SA was a new model army, built on the solidarity of the German working man, freed from social hierarchy and economic exploitation. More worryingly for the Nazi leadership was the fact that the man who ran the entire SA, Franz Pfeffer von Salomon, shared Stennes's puritanical Prussian values and publicly supported him. Pfeffer, Stennes, and Kuhr clung to the idea that the SA was there to seize power by force of arms, not via the ballot box. It was also their opinion that the Party owed the

SA its allegiance, not the other way around. Röhm may no longer have been in the country, but his founding vision for the SA endured, even if it had been driven underground.

Things had come to a head a few months earlier in the summer of 1930, while Bruno was still in Sturm 33, about to make his transfer to Sturm 31. Pfeffer's tireless lobbying for Hitler to grant the SA full independence had worn the Führer's patience so thin that he sacked him. Stennes and his supporters, among them Kuhr's Sturm 31, reacted instantly, by calling a strike. All SA activities in Berlin and surrounding cities ground to a halt. No Nazi speech makers were protected from hecklers; there were no marches, no leaflets, and no assaults. In August 1930 Stennes and Kuhr proceeded to do the unthinkable.

Far from apologizing for his startling impertinence, Stennes ordered Kuhr's SA Sturm 31 to "seize the Berlin party headquarters and the offices of *Der Angriff*."[36] What was later to become Bruno's new *Sturm* then rampaged through the city's two most important Nazi buildings, beat up their SS guards, and barricaded themselves inside. Goebbels was ignominiously locked out of his own offices by drunken storm troopers, men he was supposed to be in charge of. Sturm 31 had perpetrated an act of open mutiny. Fortunately, order was quickly restored, tempers calmed, and the status quo reestablished. Stennes and Kuhr were reprimanded but kept their commands.[37]

In 1931, Bruno made his move, exchanging the brutal Sturm 33 for the rebellious Sturm 31. It made me wonder if Bruno had been transferred there deliberately, to leaven their troublemaking dissent with some of 33's murderous loyalty. Whatever the motive, within weeks of his arrival, he was in trouble. Bruno's commitment to Hitler far outweighed any sentimental attachment to SA solidarity. The records show not only that he failed to sympathize with Kuhr's campaign, but that he openly dissented. Bruno and four other pro-Hitler opponents of the Stennes rebellion found themselves threatened with expulsion from the regiment by an outraged Kuhr.

On November 27, 1930, a committee member of the Berlin USCHLA[38] sent a report to the Reichs-USCHLA in Munich, informing them that there were a number of SA men in Sturm 31 who "had worked their way up the *Sturm*, and hence merited respect, among them Bruno Langbehn, aged about 25 years, 'tooth artist'" (aka trainee dentist), whom their *Sturmführer* (Heinrich Kuhr) was trying to kick out. Bruno appealed against the decision—and won. He was reinstated in Sturm 31 by the order of SA HQ in Munich. But it wasn't over yet. Stennes and his ally Kuhr refused to back down. Once again muttering and grumbling grew in Sturm 31.

In the spring of 1931 Stennes ordered a second rebellion. It was even bigger than the first. "Unlike September, the revolt spread throughout eastern Germany. Of the 25,000 men on Stennes's Group East, 8,000 to 10,000 joined the rebellion. The Berlin police estimated the breakdown as 1,500 in Berlin, 2,000 in Brandenburg, 3,000 in Silesia . . . and 2,000 in Pomerania."[39] Another SA strike was called in Berlin, and all electioneering, leafleting, and marching stopped. Once again, Kuhr dispatched Sturm 31 to assault Party HQ, take possession of the building, and beat up any SS guards who refused to join the protest. It was an even bigger crisis for Hitler than the first rebellion in the summer of 1930 had been.

The repercussions spread rapidly across the rest of the SA. Obergruppenführer Kurt Kremser called on every storm trooper to stand up in Stennes's defense. He savaged "the political leaders who even today are of the opinion that the SA is here only in order to die." In the time-honored fashion of all reluctant revolutionaries, he justified his support for Stennes as an expression of solidarity with the downtrodden, sharing their contempt not for the Führer, but for the parasites who surrounded him. They claimed it was they, not the Party, who best embodied the principles and the hopes of National Socialism. To the rest of the SA, Stennes's supporters made the following defiant declaration: "In the person of Captain Stennes, the whole SA is under attack. Now the SA have done their duty, they can go. They are now a cumbersome conscience, reminding people of the betrayed Party program and demanding the fight for the old ideals of National Socialism. . . . With our flag held high and our ranks tightly closed." The SA marched. Stennes took over command.[40]

The gloves were off. This wasn't just gangster rivalry, one power-hungry operator out to topple another, but the galling spectacle of a senior SA commander denouncing Hitler as a capitalist sell-out surrounded by sycophants with their noses in the trough. The SA rebel demanded an end to cronyism and insisted that Hitler declare his opposition to both Catholicism and capitalism. Above all, he argued for an end to the charade that power could be won "legally." This was a revolutionary charter and it tore the Berlin SA down the middle. Hitler was in real danger of letting the northern SA slip through his fingers.

Goebbels, locked out of his own offices for the second time in as many months, fled Berlin and pleaded with Hitler to help quell the uprising. Hitler leaped into action, first with a series of loud and aggressive articles in the *Völkischer Beobachter* (People's Observer, the Party newspaper), vowing to "stamp out root and branch this conspiracy against National Socialism." The SA would have to choose either "Police Sgt. (retired) Stennes or the founder of the National Socialist movement and the Supreme Leader of the SA, Adolf Hitler."[41] Then he set off for Berlin, to mount a tour of north Berlin SA *Sturmlokale*, including Bruno's Zur Altstadt, whipping up ecstatic support from the disgruntled storm troopers in a face-to-face charm offensive.

The tactic worked, and Stennes's breakaway movement quickly fizzled out. For all their indignation about workers' rights, and their call for internal moral zeal, what really defined the Nazi phenomenon was Hitler himself. Nothing could rival him. Bruno had recognized this; Stennes (and Kuhr) had not. One rebellion was just about tolerable, but two was open insurrection. Hitler expelled Stennes and Kuhr from the SA.

The episode had subjected Hitler to yet another SA insurrection. His authority was absolute, and it was time the rebellious SA knew it. He issued an order requiring every SA officer to take an "unconditional oath of loyalty"; soon every member of the SA had to do the same. Hitler was to be formally addressed as "Führer," his leadership beyond question: "I hope the world will bow to that as quickly as it has bowed to the Holy Father's claim." But, in one final irony, he welcomed back to the Nazi fold the thorniest SA commander of all, Ernst Röhm, who had returned from Bolivia, anxious to be reinstated by his Führer's side. His reward was to be given, for a second time, the command of the entire SA—just so long as he remembered the SA's place in the Nazi scheme and didn't get above himself.

Bruno watched all this unfurl right in front of him. He had been forced to choose sides and had backed Hitler against the majority of Berlin's pro-Stennes storm troopers. It had been a disaster for the SA, who had once again shown themselves to be thoroughly unreliable. Even worse, Bruno could hardly fail to notice that the episode had produced some enviable winners—not the SA of course, but the SS.[42] Their loyalty to Hitler had proved unbreakable. Although the SS was tiny in number, its members were fanatical and unswerving; their actions during the Stennes mutiny earned them Hitler's heartfelt applause, as well as a new motto and watchword; from that moment on: *"Meine Ehre heißt Treue"* ("My honor is my loyalty") was engraved on all SS daggers and belt buckles. This was more than just a formula, but the core of their future Nazi role, later reaping them power and favor that the bolshier SA could only dream of. Bruno took note.

For the time being, however, the SS (with barely three hundred members) was no substitute for the SA in terms of the job at hand—namely, clearing a path to power—and Hitler was careful to let Bruno and his brownshirt compatriots know how greatly he still claimed to value them: "Don't forget that it is a sacrifice when today many hundreds of thousands of men of the National Socialist movement protect meetings, put on marches, sacrifice night after night and return only at daybreak. . . . Believe me, that is already a sign of the power of an ideal, a great ideal!"[43] At the end of 1931, both Sturm 31 and Sturm 33 were amalgamated into a new larger regiment, 1/1 (Standart 1, Sturmbann 1; Battalion 1, Regiment 1); these were types of formations introduced by Röhm to help absorb the vast influx of men to the SA—now numbering hundreds of thousands. Bruno was again back in the company of his comrades from Mördersturm 33.

But none of this addressed Hitler's most pressing priority: How *was* the Party going to win power? A new controversy was looming. Hitler's decision to renounce overt violence (while happily endorsing it as a carefully rationed short-term method) was becoming more and more resented, as political success continued to elude them. The decision to avoid breaking the law stuck in the throats of the SA: "A portion—probably the greater portion of the rank and file—say to hell with legality," wrote one SA commander. "No one [in the ranks] believes in the path of legality." Fighting spirit was in danger of sinking into apathy: "The most active and best elements came to the movement and joined the SA to bring about a decisive change," but in the current situation, "even old, trusty, and completely reliable SA leaders, who have always maintained a high degree of optimism, are slowly becoming silent men."[44]

Hitler could hear the rumblings and retorted: "I am accused of being too cowardly to fight illegally. I am certainly not too cowardly for that. I am only too cowardly to lead the SA to face machine-gun fire. We need the SA for more important things, namely for the construction of the Third Reich. We'll keep to the constitution and will still come to our goal."[45] For the moment, the Nazis carried on as they had started, bending the law whenever possible, but avoiding breaking it altogether. And that meant winning elections, which suddenly came thick and fast— five in 1932 alone.

Bruno the political Nazi was as busy as Bruno the storm trooper, elaborating strategy, attending meetings, distributing leaflets, and tirelessly hectoring potential voters.[46] It was all part of Hitler's determination that this "legal" way to power could never be accused of lacking energy or resolve. Not a single element of modern campaigning was overlooked: posters, recordings, films, leaflets, a nationwide campaign tour by air, and speeches—dozens and dozens of speeches. And behind the propaganda, there was political calculation, too: endlessly taking the temperature of different constituencies, switching from one group to another as soon as it appeared advantageous. When they discovered they were failing to make any inroads into the urban working class, they redirected their efforts toward a different section of the electorate, farmers, peasants, and most fruitfully of all, the dairymen of Schleswig-Holstein. Having been Nazi skeptics, they were won over and notoriously gave the Nazis their biggest single majority in the key national elections that eventually saw them win power.

However, none of this interfered with the storm troopers' more traditional pleasures—smashing Jewish shop windows and prowling the Kurfürstendamm, looking for anyone of Jewish appearance to beat up (particularly popular on Sundays and Jewish holidays), and singing their favorite song while doing it, to the tune of music from Bizet's *Carmen*:

> *If it's raining or it's hailing,*
> *If there's lightning, if it's wet,*
> *If it's dark or if there's thunder, if you freeze or if you sweat,*
> *If it's warm or if it's cloudy,*
> *If it thaws, if there's a breeze, if it drizzles, if it sizzles,*
> *If you cough or if you sneeze, it's all the fault of all those Jews!*
> *The Jews are all at fault for that!*[47]

It was all in a day's work. As one storm trooper noted in his SA diary:

Reichstag opening. The whole afternoon and evening mass demonstration by the Nazis. During the afternoon they smashed the windows of Wertheim, Gruenfeld, and other department stores in the Leipzigstrasse. In the evening they assembled in the Potsdamer Platz, shouting "Germany, Awake!" "Death to Judah!" "Heil Hitler!" Their ranks were continually dispersed by the police, in trucks and on horseback. . . . For the most part, the Nazis consisted of adolescent riffraff who made off yelling as soon as the police began to use rubber truncheons. . . . These disorders reminded me of the days just before the revolution, with the same mass meetings and the same Catilinian figures lounging about and demonstrating.[48]

The English poet Stephen Spender was a witness to a "sensation of doom" that he felt characterized this *"Weimardämmerung"*:

The feeling of unrest in Berlin went deeper than any crisis. . . . In this Berlin . . . was the tension, the poverty, the anger, the prostitution, the hope, and the despair thrown out on the streets. It was the . . . grim, submerged-looking Communists in processions, and the violent youths who suddenly emerged from nowhere in the Wittembergplatz and shouted: *"Deutschland Erwache!"*[49]

The SA vindicated the hopes Hitler and Goebbels placed in it. No other Nazi organization came close to equaling the formidable part it played stamping Hitler's mark all over the face of the Weimar Republic. By 1933, Bruno's street army was the most visible symbol for the replacement of German democracy by barbarism. Sebastian Haffner later wrote:

Hitler's NSDAP possessed an uncanny dynamism from the start. It obeyed only *one* dominating will . . . and it was, down to the smallest units, full of fighting spirit, a hissing and pounding steam engine of an electoral machine. . . . The SA far outstripped all other political fighting units in fighting spirit and aggressiveness, and of course, in murderous brutality. Among the political private armies of the day the SA alone was genuinely feared.[50]

And of them all, few SA battalions came close to matching the ferocity of Bruno's Sturm 33. For all their size and muscle, however, it wasn't the SA who delivered the final breakthrough that resulted in the Nazi "seizure of power" in 1933; it was Hitler himself, whose profile was rising even more rapidly than the numbers voting for the Party. The threatening nature of his paramilitaries made him impossible to ignore, but it didn't account solely for the extraordinary transformation in his fortunes. Hitler came to the fore by turning his personality as Party leader into a political force in its own right. Voting Nazi no longer appeared to mean voting for a "party" at all. Hitler offered *himself* as Germany's route to salvation. The Communists could only point to subservience to Moscow. The other parties were hostages to democracy and capitalism.

Hitler exploited all the political dividends thrown up by the Great Depression. He vilified the traditional parties as slaves to vested interests. Ordinary voters leaped over the special pleading of rival parties and found themselves face-to-face with Germany itself, in the fleshed-out figure of the Great Dictator. This was where the dynamism of the SA became an asset, too. Even if ordinary Germans didn't like what they got up to in the streets, many of them grudgingly admired what they stood for, namely, a guarantee against the one thing they most despised in their politicians—that they were all words and no action.

In the end, the Nazis seized power after a string of elections and a sequence of four separate chancellors, all under the watch of an increasingly senile president, Hindenburg. Hitler had positioned himself as the man who could deliver the support of the mass German population to the conservative right wing, which had made the terrible mistake of thinking they would be able to exploit that support, while controlling Hitler as their mouthpiece and puppet. They were very wrong. Thanks to a nightmarish sequence of miscalculations and continuing self-delusion, a succession of political mediocrities proceeded to walk Germany to the brink.

On January 30, 1933, it was all over. Having refused the previous year to settle for the position of vice-chancellor, Hitler stood appointed as chancellor. Berlin's right wing erupted in mass euphoria. Absolute power now lay within their grasp; the keenly anticipated dictatorship was close to becoming a reality. Their Communist rivals were in tatters and quickly shrank back into the shadows, surely aware of what was coming next. Hitler was there to stay and wasn't going to let anything stop him from turning his Third Reich into the antithesis of all that he had so despised about the Weimar Republic.

The wilderness years that Bruno and his fellow Nazis had endured through the 1920s and early 1930s had finally ended. For nearly a decade, Bruno had been a street-fighting political outsider; at a stroke, 1933 transformed the twenty-seven-year-old dentist into one of the regime's new breed of Party insiders. It was an opportunity he exploited ruthlessly.

Six

TRIUMPH OF THE WILL

1933–1937

The night of January 30, 1933, saw the most triumphant piece of marching that Bruno ever took part in. The entire Berlin SA, alongside the SS and civilian and veteran *Stahlhelm* formations, had embarked on a six-hour torchlit procession through the heart of imperial Berlin. Adolf Hitler, their leader for more than fourteen years, had finally breached the inner citadel of German power, having only hours earlier secured President Hindenburg's approval to become chancellor. In the words of one storm trooper present that day,

> an incredible burst of joy awaited us as we marched through the Brandenburg Gate. Thousands of bareheaded spectators sang "Deutschland über Alles" and the "Horst Wessel Song." . . . Standing at the window of the Chancellery was Hitler, between Göring and the leader of the SS, Himmler. . . . Later that night, we returned to our *Sturm-*

lokal, where we fittingly celebrated the event that had recompensed us for all our struggles and sacrifices.[1]

Twenty-four hours earlier, Bruno had been just another hothead, spitting with nationalist fury and venting his contempt for democracy. Today, January 30, as he and his fellow brownshirts streamed up the Wilhelmstrasse toward the presidential palace, he could draw huge personal satisfaction from the long and important part he had played in the fight that had just reached its climax. He didn't care that electoral success still fell far short of absolute power (that would come a year or so later), or that his beloved Nazi Party was still a minority in the Reichstag (with only three Nazis with seats on the cabinet). It was enough to know that as the storm troopers goose-stepped their way through the Brandenburg Gate, they were marching from one era into another. Weimar was dead. Hitler's Germany had been born.

It was an awesome sight, as the French ambassador, André François-Poncet, who witnessed it, testified: "From these brown-shirted, booted men, as they marched in perfect discipline and alignment, their well-pitched voices bawling warlike songs, there rose an enthusiasm and dynamism that were extraordinary. The onlookers, drawn up on either side of the marching columns, burst into a vast clamour."[2]

For Melita Maschmann, another spectator of the great procession, the cheering and the marching didn't feel like political jubilation at all:

The crashing tread of the feet . . . the flickering light from the torches on the faces . . . were at once inflaming and

141

sentimental. For hours the columns marched by. . . . At one point somebody suddenly leaped from the ranks of the marchers and struck a man who had been standing only a few paces away from us. . . . I saw him fall to the ground, with blood streaming down his face, and I heard him cry out. . . . The image of him haunted me for days.[3]

But there was something else stirring in this particular onlooker, who was honest enough to admit the potent, almost euphoric quality experienced when surrendering to violence:

The horror it inspired in me was almost imperceptibly spiced with an intoxicating joy. "We want to die for the flag," the torchbearers had sung. . . . I was overcome with a burning desire to belong to these people for which it was a matter of life and death. . . . I wanted to escape from my childish, narrow life and to attach myself to something that was great and fundamental.[4]

Lining the route of the march, Bruno and his fellow marchers were thrilled to see the figures of Berlin policemen, so often in the past their adversaries, but now proudly showing their true colors by brandishing swastika armbands. It meant only one thing. Nothing now existed that was strong enough to hold the Nazis back.

As soon as the procession was over, Bruno and his SA cronies wasted little time turning their attention to the immediate business at hand. The pent-up "brown tide" of SA righteous violence could now engulf the face of German life with unfettered, licensed brutality, wiping out opposition and laying down the foundations for the new Germany. Bruno could hardly wait. They were free not just to take the law into their own hands, but also to define what was legal in the first place.

Bruno would have no trouble summoning up the aggression and resolve to play his part in this new era. The timing simply couldn't have been better for the SA dentist—all of this had been achieved before his thirtieth birthday. His professional, political, and personal lives were all coming to the boil at the same time. Bruno was now married. As a recently graduated dentist, he had met the extraordinary figure of his future mother-in-law, my great-grandmother Ida, a fellow dentist. She had taken a shine to this thrusting young man. Her views, scarcely less forthright than his own, had enthralled him. Ida always had a soft spot for clever, assertive young men and soon introduced him to her daughter—Thusnelda, a year Bruno's junior.

Like Bruno, Thusnelda was a Prussian, born in 1907 in Osterode, deep in the east of the province. Her family were true Nazi believers, if of a rather unusual kind. The power in Thusnelda's family revolved around the formidable character of her mother, Ida. After Ida's first husband had been killed on the western front, she had put herself through dental school in Danzig and supported her family by practicing as a dentist in her own right, a most unusual achievement for a woman of her generation and background. When she married for a second time, she refused to drop her own name, Lietzner, in favor of that of her army officer husband, Pahnke, agreeing only to double-barrel it with his, as Frau Pahnke-Lietzner. But her unorthodox female assertiveness did not stop her from embracing the Nazi ideology, which, had she followed its tenets in her own life, would have consigned her very quickly back to more traditional female preserves. What brought Thusnelda and Bruno together went further than just political sympathies. She was smitten by him from the start; he, for his part, was bowled over by her sweet-natured, wide-eyed infatuation for him. Under Ida's stern and conniving gaze they were engaged, and they married in the spring of 1932, in a wedding officiated by his fellow SA storm troopers. Buoyed up perhaps by the example of his mother-in-law, Bruno, who had worked for four years as a dental assistant, now opened his first practice.

Not only was Bruno coming of age, he was doing so in the best possible location for a career at the heart of the National Socialist dream—Berlin, soon to become one of the great power capitals of the world. For all Hitler's dislike of the place (it could never compete for his affections the way his Bavarian mountain retreat in the Obersalzberg could), there was never any question that it would serve as the hub of the new Nazi regime, the source of all its power, the home of all its institutions, and, in time, the springboard for the colossus that Nazi Germany strove to become.

But first, there was unfinished business with all those who *still* refused to bow to history and acknowledge the triumph of Hitler's National Socialism. This would be their day of reckoning too. For many in the SA, there was no time to lose moving from celebration to revenge. Top of the list were, of course, Berlin's Communists and Socialists. For the man who commanded Bruno's old Mördersturm 33, Sturmführer Hans Maikowski, the night of Hitler's triumph, January 30, was still young. Six hours of marching and singing himself hoarse had only inflamed his aggression. He itched to mark the significance of the day. He led a gang of carousing SA men out of the Zur Altstadt, Bruno's favorite Charlottenburg storm trooper pub, looking for trouble. They tore up and down the familiar Communist streets of neighboring Kleine Wedding, looking for someone to beat up, this time as the victorious representatives of Hitler's new regime. They made it as far as Wallstrasse before encountering a large and dejected band of Red Front Communists, still reeling with disbelief at the events of the day. In seconds, a fight ensued—but this time, when the inevitable shot rang out, it was SA Sturm-führer Maikowski who fell dead to the street.

Hans Maikowski, the man who had lent his name to "doing a Maikowski" (any act that surpassed the SA's usual level of violence and thuggery), had reaped what he had sown, even if, for the Communists who shot him, it was a Pyrrhic victory, a gesture of futile rage by enemies of the new regime, who must have had few doubts about what now lay in store for them. News of the shooting electrified a city still in the convulsions of the Nazi triumph. "Maikowski will be buried like a king," retorted Goebbels, whose "state funerals" were by now a well-oiled ritualistic machine. Maikowski, who had spent the day singing the "Horst Wessel Song," was set to join the song's eponymous composer on the pantheon of Nazi martyrs.[5] His funeral was a Nazi extravaganza.

But Maikowski's legacy would take a much more violent form than just an elaborate obituary. Whatever satisfaction the beleaguered Communists had taken from gunning down their Nazi nemesis, it was to be very short-lived.[6]

Bruno hardly needed to have it spelled out. From now on his SA would enjoy carte blanche to flatten the remnants of their old Weimar foe, the Communists, and their Socialist stooges. It was a Nazi article of faith that nothing worth achieving came without violence. Actions had only one test, and that was the level of will and ruthlessness they required to succeed. If it was an "iron fist" they wanted, he would be happy to help provide it. SA Standart 1 was just one regiment among many, demanding the chance to round up and persecute non-Nazi deviants.

While Maikowski's death had shocked Berlin's SA, a few weeks later the whole country was plunged into an even greater state of emergency. At around nine o'clock on the night of February 26, reports started reverberating around Berlin that smoke was belching out of the Reichstag building. By the time firemen and police converged on the parliament building, it had become an inferno. For the Nazis this was the most fortuitous disaster imaginable, an act of sabotage that justified a full-scale emergency clampdown. In the words of one SA man unable to contain his glee:

> God grant that this is the work of the Communists. . . . You are witnessing the beginning of a great new epoch in German history. The fire is the beginning. . . . You see this building? You see how it is aflame? If the Communists got hold of Europe and had control of it for but two months the whole continent would be aflame like this building.[7]

Like every other hard-core SA man, Bruno wasn't overly concerned with the niceties of what actually happened in the smoldering ruins of the old parliament building. All he needed to know was that it was (surely!) a prelude to an all-out Communist uprising. As another SA witness asserted, the Reichstag's destruction provided them with the inspiration for the action they had been dreaming of:

The burning beacon of the Reichstag building . . . lighted our way. . . . I had put together a small *Rollkommando* [mobile squad] of my *Sturm* from the most daring of the daring. . . . Who was going to strike the first blow? And then it came. [There were] signs of fire all over the country. Finally the relief of the order: *"Packt zu!"* ["Go to it!"] And we did get to it . . . wiping the lecherous grin off the hideous, murderous faces of the Bolsheviks for all time.[8]

The burning of the Reichstag was indeed no accident, but the result of arson, carried out by a disaffected simpleton by the name of Marinus van der Lubbe. He claimed to have had vaguely Communist motives for his attack, which suited the Nazis perfectly, even though it was clear he had been working alone.[9] Goebbels went to work, ratcheting up the sense of national atrocity, and demanded total "retribution." President Hindenburg granted broad emergency powers to enable the government to protect "people and state," and these were further reinforced after the elections held in early March.

For the sixty or so men who made up Bruno's section of SA Regiment 1/1, Charlottenburg was transformed at a stroke. Its few square miles of streets, tenements, pubs, and squares became their corner of the Nazi state, answerable to no one. Their "manor" was now a battlefield. They knew what was expected of them. They marched whenever and wherever they wanted. Bruno was in his element. Years later, even when mellowed by age and a glass or two of his favorite cognac, there were traces of the old intransigence: a face that would move in a flash from a leery grin to a steely-eyed "Do not cross me," the expression of a man who grew up believing that a readiness to mete out violence represented the highest of manly virtues.

And this time it would be different: no longer just a series of scuffles on the streets, or back-alley knifings, but an orchestrated campaign of institutional repression. Bruno and his SA comrades may have struggled in their efforts to appear a "real" army, but they found no difficulty whatever in adapting to their roles as the jailers and torturers, crushing the opposition. It was the job of veterans like Bruno and the other "old fighters" to convert the SA from abrasive street menace into a fully fledged paramilitary force. They proved frighteningly good at it.

As the Prussian police chief Rudolf Diels later explained:

The SA storm-squads, however, had firm plans for operations in the Communist quarters of the city. In those March days every SA man was "on the heels of the enemy," each knew what he had to do. The storm-squads cleaned up the districts. They knew not only where the enemies lived, they had also long ago discovered their hideouts and meeting places. . . . Not only the Communists, but anybody who had ever spoken out against Hitler's movement was in danger.[10]

The SA set about converting their *Dienststellen* (the pubs, rented apartments, and bits of office space they had been using as command posts) into improvised holding cells and torture rooms; most pubs had cellars, which could house internees as well as barrels of beer. There were more than two hundred such buildings in Berlin that different units of the SA soon transformed into hubs of terror. These *Sturmlokale* became outposts from which groups of SA men patrolled the streets, as well as centers for the collection of information about the activities of political opponents. And it was back to these adapted pubs, apartments, and other commercial premises that countless people were brought at gunpoint. After being "arrested" they were "questioned," "processed," and then sent on to larger, hastily erected SA detention facilities (General-Pape-Strasse in Tempelhof, for example). Even Berlin's "ordinary" police got in on the act, turning their HQ on the Alexanderplatz into an impromptu political prison, providing the veneer of bureaucratic due process to what was simply arrest without charge.

Few of those detained in SA premises escaped without being beaten up. Some didn't escape at all; they were murdered, or left to die from their injuries. SA premises were filled to bursting and had to be supplemented by so-called wild camps, which were thrown up virtually overnight, to provide yet more space for the SA. But even these proved insufficient, and soon SA men were constructing the first of Germany's formal concentration camps (*Konzentrationslager*, or KZs), first in Dachau, near Munich, and then in an old brewery in the Oranienburg district of Berlin. The former remained in use for the duration of the Third Reich, as did many of the techniques of arrest, imprisonment, cruelty, and degradation first practiced in these makeshift hellholes. Nobody will ever know for sure how many people passed through them, but it is unlikely that it was fewer than 100,000.

Bruno's SA pub, the Zur Altstadt, was too small for the new role required of it. Far more suitable as a base for terror and repression was his Regimental HQ located at Rosinenstrasse 4. Only a few months previously, this had been an important Social Democrat building. Not anymore. Seized by the SA, it was renamed Hans Maikowski Haus and converted into a holding facility with room for up to forty prisoners in its cellars. It wasn't long before it witnessed its first murder. The victim was Fritz Kollosche, a prominent member of a Communist antifascist militia. He died in a local hospital as a result of the savage beatings he suffered at the hands of senior SA officers.

In November 1933, Maikowski Haus played a central role in the suppression of the Charlottenburg Socialist Workers' Party (SAP), a KPD (Communist Party) spinoff. A few months later, in March 1934, two local Communists, Walter Harnecker and Walter Walz, were clubbed to death inside Maikowski Haus. Bruno's HQ had lived up to the brutality of the man whose name it had taken. It was merely one of thousands where the same things were going on, throughout the whole of Germany. There are no records to tell us what role Bruno specifically played in all of this. Before I started my research into his Nazi career, I would have found it impossible to conceive that my grandfather could ever have been one of the men depicted in the few surviving photos of the time, enforcing SA torture and imprisonment. I had anticipated that Bruno's later years would prove the most alarming. But what I was reading about the SA, and about the Charlottenburg activities of its most aggressive *Sturm*, changed all that. As horrible as it was for me to picture Bruno in one of those cellars, holding somebody down or wielding a truncheon, it was entirely consistent with what I now knew about SA activities in Berlin in the weeks after Hitler's victory.

The facts were that he was one of the longest-serving men in a *Sturm* that had a core membership of around sixty. The violence that exploded after Hitler had won power represented the chance for Nazis to settle old scores with their bitterly opposed political enemies. The SA reveled in its opportunities for brutality. Its members were proud to be defined by it. They never forgot that more than fifty percent of the electorate had, in fact, not voted Nazi at all, but for alternative parties, including thirty percent who had voted for Socialists or Communists. Their priority was to rout this considerable source of political opposition, and to do so immediately. There was no greater trophy for an SA man than to be seen playing a key and personal role in this, their most heroic chapter. Bruno had been a vociferous and energetic participant in the Nazi struggle for eight long years. His every effort had been directed toward this outcome, and he had never flinched from the aggression and sacrifices it had demanded. Why would he have stopped now that his party had the whole of Germany—including their hated political enemies of the left—at their feet?

After all, there was little fear of arrest or even reprimand; on the contrary, the barbarity enjoyed the sanction of the SA's top leadership. High-ranking SA commanders—Prince August-Wilhelm of Prussia, son of the last Kaiser, and Karl Ernst, commander of the Berlin-Brandenburg SA—visited several of these "interrogations" and even had the mutilated prisoners paraded before them. In December 1933, Bruno's SA superiors, Standartenführer Hell (of Standart 1) and Sturmführer Kuhr (probably the very man who later killed Harnecker and Walz) were honored by Gruppenführer Ernst for their "outstanding work in fighting elements hostile to the state." If German royalty found all this so edifying, I don't imagine it bothered Bruno too much.

But beating political dissenters into submission was only one small part of Bruno's contribution to Hitler's new state. As a dentist in a world of soldiers and thugs, he was never going to strike the same kind of figure as Hans Maikowski had done, but he had what most in the SA did not, namely a surefooted ease with the key ideologies of National Socialism. Bruno would prove his mettle preaching Nazi doctrine, as well as by hunting down dissenters.

Nothing was more volatile than German politics, and the Nazis were only too aware how easily their new regime could find itself rejected, alongside the dozens of other political parties that had come and gone during the turmoil of the Weimar years. Bruno and his fellow Nazis had emerged from oblivion and had no desire to return to it. All those millions of citizens who hadn't voted for Hitler now had to be seduced into joining the millions who had. Terrorizing them wasn't enough. The next battle was the political one, convincing Germany that National Socialism represented their deepest hopes, and that all the other forms of politics were dead in the water. They had to be shown the light, and surrender to it.

Nazi rhetoric hammered home the point. Democracy didn't work because it subordinated the *Volk* to the mediocrity of mass opinion, where the best were always drowned out by the worst. Old-style German monarchy didn't work, either; it was effete, divisive, and the product of privilege, not historical destiny. Communism was the worst of all—handing over power not just to the proletariat, but to their paymasters in Moscow.

Hitler knew that he had to give ordinary Germans a glimpse of Utopia, in which politics itself appeared redeemed, a single anthem of national purpose. There was one promise that above all constituted the source of Hitler's popular appeal—that of racial unity. All the violence and upheaval were the price that had to be paid for their greatest creation, what the Nazis called a *Volksgemeinschaft*, a "people's community," which claimed to be both classless and selfless. It was a powerful dream, and Hitler turned himself into its symbol. "I recognize neither bourgeois nor proletarians, I recognize only Germans," he had proclaimed back in 1927.[11] Many Germans, including those ill disposed to the Nazis, grasped the prospect with open arms.

Within a few weeks, even the agnostics found themselves mesmerized by the spectacle of Hitler's brand of charisma politics. Millions of conservative Germans were as impressed by the ruthlessness with which he had crushed the left as they were enraptured by the way he embodied their deepest dreams and hopes. For many of Bruno's age, it felt like nothing less than a sacramental awakening.[12]

Even more seductive, Hitler's politics appeared to be underwritten by a doctrine of national *justice*. He ceaselessly berated the iniquities under which he claimed Germany continued to suffer, both the injustices of the past (the "stab in the back" of 1918, the Treaty of Versailles, inflation, and unemployment), and those of the future (Germany forever denied its rightful place in the sun). These crimes against the German *Volk* had been perpetrated by the same traitors who had ushered in Weimar and sold out Germany's destiny. With justice came *justification*. It was *justice* that Bruno and his fellow SA thugs were meting out in the basements and improvised holding cells: not random brutality, but retribution.

Nazi justice had no room for compromise. Opponents were to pay for their political treason with pain, humiliation, and even death. The Nazis felt entitled to their self-righteous vindictiveness because those who stood against them had forfeited the right to pity. Their ruthlessness represented the Nazis' most formidable political weapon. Victory against the forces of Bolshevism didn't mark just the triumph of the Party, but the moment that Germans could leave politics behind and assume their rightful role as Europe's dominant people, its master race. There was a price to pay for this, of course, which was total obedience to the will of their Führer, whose leadership represented in exaggerated and sublime form all that was best in the *Volk*. The reward? Hitler's magical infallibility paving the way to a unique and exclusive future.

There *were* limits—not to criminality, but to motivation. Not every aspect of the new Nazi regime was free from Hitler's censure. The men of the SA who had helped to deliver victory were also the ones who most threatened it. With power achieved, there were many in the political mainstream who were uneasy at the licensed brutality of the SA. They distrusted the swaggering brownshirts and recoiled from the pleasure they so visibly derived from torture and terror, all of which reflected on Hitler himself, who had to appear respectable as well as resolute. No matter how disillusioned people had been with the privations and frustrations of Weimar, not everyone thought handing over the country to an army of unemployed and dispossessed renegades was a good idea.

And among the SA there were mutterings, too. Where was their reward? Rounding up their old opponents and being given a free hand to terrorize and intimidate was not enough. It was time for the Party to settle its debts. For some in the SA this simply meant the booty of victory, helping themselves to money and jobs as befitted those who had "won." For others, it meant harboring the dream that it would be they, not the Party, who would dominate the new Germany, running it with a junta of senior storm troopers. Instead, they were aghast to see the new regime appear to renege on all they had promised the SA and start making overtures to those very elites the SA had considered their political enemies. Hitler courted the civil service, the officer corps, the captains of industry, the lawyers, the intellectuals, and the career politicians, all of whom (in SA eyes) represented the worst of bourgeois complacency.

For many in the Nazi hierarchy, the storm troopers of the SA were both an embarrassment and a rival power bloc. They had helped lead the way to power; now it was time for them to shrink and vanish. A whispering campaign began. Röhm, the head of the SA, was not to be trusted, they said, claiming he had always nursed an ambition to trump Hitler and turn the Führer into the SA's political mouthpiece. He was plotting a new putsch. He was conspiring with foreign powers. The relentless bad-mouthing was making its impact felt. Hitler, unlike Stalin, felt profoundly bound to the world of his old fighters, but not at any price. It wasn't hard to convince him that this kind of sedition was only too typical of Röhm and the SA in general. The SA's history had been littered with it. It had seen Röhm forced to exile himself to Bolivia in 1925, his successor, Franz Pfeffer von Salomon, sacked in 1930, his supporters' attempted mutiny (under Stennes), crushed in 1931. Once again, the rift between Party and SA deepened.

The army, so crucial to Hitler's future plans, had also made it clear that they would never tolerate being subordinated to Röhm, or even being made to compete with the SA for arms and resources. For Hitler, harboring greater ambitions than even the army's generals could hope to understand, this was a genuine dilemma. The army, despite its negligible size, had genuine offensive and strategic value. The street vigilantes in brown had none, now that they had discharged their main role—namely, helping pave the way to power. Hitler had no intention of forever looking over his shoulder in fear of an SA knife in the back or, even worse, having to limit his ambitions because of ceaseless internecine bickering.

Hitler may have revered Röhm's organizational skills, but he distrusted his motives. Now, so Hitler was being told, the SA was not only fomenting a "second revolution," but also actively conspiring with foreign powers (notably France) to bring him down. By late spring 1934, his paranoia was turning into open panic. Even Bruno, who was as well connected as any party apparatchik, could have had no idea of the forces that were being ranged against Röhm and the SA leadership. Indeed, the entire SA was caught out, the price for not having an effective intelligence system, and for being so roundly outmaneuvered by their many rivals.

Röhm, oblivious of the trouble he was in, blithely ordered the entire SA to take extended summer leave, starting on July 1. For Himmler, Göring, and the others actively conspiring to bring about Röhm's downfall, there was now an urgent timetable for action. After July, it would be impossible to sustain the claim that the SA was planning an imminent coup, not if they were all out of uniform and on holiday. Trumped-up evidence of SA "death lists" was waved in front of Hitler. With only a day or two to spare before the SA went on their summer break, Hitler pounced.

Röhm had begun his own vacation in the spa town of Bad Wiessee in Bavaria, nursing a number of ailments. He had a heart condition and was suffering the ill effects of wounds he had received during the First World War. He and his entourage (including his harem of male consorts) were now staying in a hotel, unaware of the trap that was about to spring. Hitler and a small group of senior SS officers arrived by car early on the morning of Sunday, June 30. They crashed their way through bedroom doors, arresting a startled, uncomprehending group of SA men, Röhm among them. Berated, jostled, and loudly accused of treason, they were taken to Stadelheim Prison in Munich. Röhm, now prisoner 4034, was locked up in cell number 474, supposedly the same cell he had occupied after being arrested in 1923 after the Beer Hall Putsch. Similar arrests took place in Berlin and Breslau.

The end was swift and merciless. Eighty-five or so met their ends during the so-called Night of the Long Knives, either where they stood when arrested—in their homes, behind their desks—or in front of firing squads deployed in Munich, Berlin, Breslau, and Dachau. The SS used the chaos to settle a number of scores with prominent critics of the movement, including the man who had recently written a hostile speech given by Deputy Chancellor von Papen.

Finally it was Röhm's turn. The man who had been Hitler's mentor and closest ally was given a loaded revolver with which to kill himself, but he refused to collude in the charade of his own guilt, baring his chest instead and facing down the two SS officers who entered his cell and promptly shot him at point-blank range. "All revolutions eat their own children," he was reported to have said. The killing was ordered to stop before July 2, and those who fell after that date had their death certificates backdated accordingly.

The SA was finished as a force in its own right, and for the rest of its history, it never slipped the leash of party control.[13] It continued to exist, but in greatly reduced form. Most of its weapons were confiscated and handed over to the army. Its numbers plummeted from nearly 4 million to just over 2.5 million by September 1934. By April 1938, that number fell by a further 1.5 million. Its senior political offices were abolished, and it was no longer represented at the highest levels within the Party. After the war, this loss of decision-making power saved it from being declared a criminal organization by the Allied authorities.[14] Bruno was not the only storm trooper who had to come to terms with the fact that the SA leadership had gambled so badly and lost.[15]

The German population accepted the official explanation given to them over the following days: the rowdy, rebellious SA was not popular, and nobody seemed in the mood to pick apart Hitler's self-serving version of events. Hitler, though he had been reluctant to kill his oldest comrade, was soon rewarded for his ruthless actions. He had barely a month to wait to see if the gamble had paid off. On August 2, the aged President Hindenburg finally passed away. Hitler immediately appropriated his office, which at last gave him power over the whole country, not just the Reichstag. Two weeks later, he sought a retrospective ratification for his move in a plebiscite, held on August 19. Eighty-nine percent of those allowed to vote endorsed the move; four and a half million Germans, even at this late stage, were brave enough to say no, but to no avail. It was a landslide.

Hitler's price for neutralizing the SA leadership was to insist on a personal oath of loyalty from every single serving soldier in the Reichswehr—and he got it. "I swear by God this holy oath that I will render unconditional obedience to the Führer of the German Reich and people, Adolf Hitler, the supreme commander of the armed forces, and as a brave soldier am willingly prepared to risk my life for this oath at any time." Killing Röhm had delivered a huge political bounty. The army formally renounced its independence; the truculent brownshirts had been curbed; even right-wing opposition had been outmaneuvered. Killing Papen's speechwriter told the conservative opposition (many of whom still harbored the idea that Hitler could be "tamed") that their days of political troublemaking were over. The nationalists and the monarchists and all those clinging to the old Prussian hierarchy were banished.

It is ironic that only in its demise had the SA succeeded in offering Hitler the ultimate service, clearing the way for the assumption of absolute power. Röhm ended up being far more valuable dead than he had been alive. The murdered storm trooper had been transformed into a powerful emblem of Hitler's resolve and his willingness to make whatever sacrifices law and order demanded. Nothing accommodated the waverers in Hitler's Germany more to the new regime than the spectacle of Hitler brutally curbing his own henchmen. The SA was appalled, but mainstream middle-class Germany applauded.

For those *inside* the movement, like Bruno, there was a very different lesson to be learned. Röhm's naiveté had proved even more dangerous than outright treason. The future of Germany lay with Hitler and his party, not with armed storm troopers. This was a racial dictatorship, not just a military one. The prizes went to those who could operate with ideology, not simply with weapons. This was lucky for Bruno, who, alongside his SA uniform, possessed an even more powerful token boasting his value to the Nazis—his political acumen. Bruno had sided with the Party, rather than the SA, because, unlike the great majority of his storm trooper comrades, he could see the larger picture and understood that National Socialism was too important to be reduced to short-term personal advantage. It was a loyalty that had won him one of the new regime's most potent trophies—which he wore proudly on his tunic.

The Nazis were good at rewarding their party faithful. Hitler understood the power of symbols. At the end of the previous year, 1933, the Party had instituted a system of prizes and medals, a glorified loyalty program that allowed the old fighters to stand out from the late joiners. The most important of them took the form of a Gold Honor award, a round, gold-fringed badge, given as proof of the wearer's elite status within the movement. The criteria were strict—long and unbroken Party membership, and a Party number below 100,000—and Bruno found himself one of barely 22,000 Berliners who qualified. Wearing it earned the veteran Nazi both prestige and an envied nickname: he was a "golden pheasant" (a nod to the golden wreath that ran round the badge's circumference, and the red braid that Party officials liked to drape over their epaulettes, but also one that mocked the strutting display indulged in by those who possessed one). It would remain a powerful signifier of his VIP status within the new Germany for the duration of the Third Reich.

Of course, many who received the award did so simply because they had been in the Party for many years. Bruno's affiliation to the movement went even deeper than that. For having sided with the Party over the SA, Bruno received a second, and more explicit, accolade, a nomination into the SA Honor Court (Ehrengericht). This was acknowledgment not just that Bruno had avoided siding with the troublemakers, but that he had earned the recognition of his superiors as being a highly useful asset in the SA's struggle to regain Hitler's confidence in the aftermath of the bloodshed and had played a key role in the SA's attempt to rehabilitate itself.

The court that Bruno is referring to, the so-called Ehrengericht, or Honor Court, was a direct response by the Nazis to the turmoil of the "Long Knives" summer. On August 1, 1934, the Supreme SA Command (OSAF) decreed that a special court, the Sondergericht der OSAF, be established to inquire into and pass judgment on cases that "have and will become acute due to the purge." The courts were supposed to look into cases directly related to the putsch of June 30, 1934, but also to rid the SA of all unwanted members, in particular those guilty of an unsuitable way of life, which included immorality, careerism, materialism, fraud, drinking excesses, bragging, and wastefulness.

The court was, in effect, the Party's way of further tightening its grip on its mutinous storm troopers and justifying the killings in June. As the official version was keen to stress, Hitler's actions had been reluctantly forced on him and were motivated only by selfless concern for the national well-being. The Honor Courts helped ensure that this version of events stuck. For Bruno, it was further proof of how greatly his political superiors valued his reliability. Only those with long-established track records of pro-Hitler activism, who had not been, to use the Nazi phrase, "subject to the symptoms of SA disease," were qualified to sit on them.

The Berlin-Brandenburg Honor Court was set up on August 8 by Bruno's new Berlin SA boss, Obergruppenführer Dietrich von Jagow. It had an important new home, in the SA's big central premises, Tiergartenstrasse 4—the building that later accommodated the Nazi euthanasia program, and from which it took its name "T4." Bruno was appointed to sit on one of its key panels, surrounded by officers many ranks higher than his. His staunch loyalty to Hitler, his ideological convictions, and his immunity to contamination by SA disobedience had received their official blessing from the Nazi hierarchy. And this went much further than just receiving a badge. This Honor Court role required him to act as a kind of proxy for the Party, policing and punishing transgression. What greater vindication could there be for Bruno as a Party activist than to sit in judgment on all those the Party found wanting.

Of course, for all the trappings of due process and "honor," Bruno was participating in little more than a charade. The SA's attempt to distinguish the lawful from the illegal was farcical. Bruno had no problem legislating against breaches that included pilfering, drunkenness, or just being "unreliable," while at the same time condoning torture, false imprisonment, intimidation, and murder, none of which seemed to compromise the SA's sense of "honor." The Nazis' moral compass was never more haywire than when it codified and legitimized their own actions.

This brutal suppression of the Party's revolutionary wing marked a watershed moment in how the regime operated. Until now, the Party's priorities had been revolutionary and quasi-military, crushing old opponents and enforcing conformity within its own limits. But that was just an overture to the job of building the Third Reich itself.

After nearly two years of ceaseless turmoil and agitation, it was the perfect moment for Hitler to demonstrate the extent of his absolute leadership. There had been marches and processions, but this would be on a completely unprecedented scale, an assault on history itself, demonstrating to the *Volk* that the Nazis now operated at a level beyond conventional politics, neither accountable to it nor bounded by its usual rules. Of course, behind the gestures and the spectacle, there was always a covert agenda in everything Hitler did, and this was no exception. Having eliminated the SA's leadership, it was vital for the Nazis to draw the more than 3 million storm troopers back into the fold. Hitler called on his most powerful stage managers—Goebbels, the master of persuasion, and Albert Speer, his young court architect—to deliver the intended spectacle. The Nazi regime was defined by propaganda, mass activism, and ritualized physical participation, and there was one place, even more than Berlin, where these all came together—the Nuremberg Rallies. I know from his SS records that Bruno attended four of these annual rallies, in 1929, 1933, 1934, and 1935. They were the high points of his Nazi calendar. Their scale, their hubris, their idolatry, and, once darkness had fallen, the drinking, bingeing, and roughhousing that characterized any gathering of SA men, were all designed to strike awe into rally participants.

The rally of 1934 was to be the masterpiece. The Brandenburg Gate victory march of January 30, 1933, had marked the Nazis' political arrival; Nuremberg was incomparably bigger and communicated a quite different message—the announcement of the Nazis' thousand-year Reich. The 1934 rally has since gone down in history as the high-water mark of prewar Nazi triumphalism—no wonder that Hitler later christened it the "triumph of the will." It could not have been more fortunate in its scheduling, taking place barely weeks after the death of President Hindenburg removed Hitler's last obstacle to being declared Führer. With its combination of imperial durbar, Roman triumph, trooping the color, and ticker-tape parade, the 1934 rally marked the moment all effective opposition to Hitler ceased.

Bruno was one of more than 5,000 Berlin-based Party members and SA storm troopers who piled onto their specially chartered trains between September 1 and September 3, their destination the northern Bavarian city of Nuremberg. It was an escape from Berlin, a chance for him to immerse himself in the movement's spiritual home—bucolic, ancient Bavaria—rather than gray, up-tight Prussia.[16]

The setting was deeply symbolic: first, there was the medieval splendor of the city of Nuremberg itself, close to the geographical center of the country, deeply associated in German history with the Holy Roman Empire. Its wooden houses and narrow, twisting streets provided a congenial and pleasingly *völkisch* alternative to the "asphalt" modernity of Berlin. But Nazi power brokers wanted to do more than just evoke national heritage. Hitler therefore commissioned his talented young architect, Albert Speer, to design and construct a sparkling new mega-stadium in which to organize vast chessboard formations of marching storm troopers. It was completed just in time for the 1934 rally. Together, Nuremberg's half-timbered fairy-tale medievalism and Speer's shining, clenched-fist concrete gave Hitler's rallies their distinctly double-faced appearance: a collision of the old and the new, individual and mass, folksy and brutal.

What drew Bruno year after year was more than just habit; he was entranced by the scale of the proceedings. The Nazis wanted to bask in myth. Hitler always saw himself not as Germany's god, but as its greatest artist, and Nuremberg was his canvas. The rallies allowed to him to dramatize Nazi politics as a vast expression of the national popular will, even as it despised the democratic process. But behind the pomp and the symbolism of 1934 lay a very particular political purpose: to address the men in Bruno's brown uniforms and, if possible, heal the breach between Party and SA paramilitaries, for whom memories of the events of June 30 and the Night of the Long Knives were still raw and uncertain. The rally was to be the SA's biggest test of loyalty after the bloodshed, their chance to accommodate themselves to Hitler or face even further purges.

In the end, the Party had nothing to fear. For men like Bruno, there was no sacrifice in demonstrating to the Führer that the SA was once again integrated into the Third Reich, its days of troublemaking over. Hitler got his victory parade, and it marked the final separation between the turmoil and bloodshed of the *Kampfzeit* and the golden age of his new Reich.

The rally itself, though bigger than any before, exploited the same well-established pattern of march-bys, consecrations, roll calls, and torchlight processions. This time, though, it was able to take possession of the vast new concourse of Speer's converted zeppelin field, with its gargantuan plinth and even vaster parade ground, the perfect forum in which to locate mass gatherings, where Führer and *Volk* could physically be set off against each other. Bruno and his SA comrades were accommodated in great tent cities, erected in fields on the outskirts of the city, alongside those housing the huge contingents from other organizations.

It opened on Tuesday, September 4, with receptions for members of the international press, culminating in Hitler's own arrival. The rest of the week was given over to a series of themed "days," starting with the Day of the Opening of Congress, where proclamations were read out in the Luitpoldhalle by Rudolf Hess and other paladins. Thursday, September 6, was the Day of Labor, which involved a vast congregation of the Labor Service, the men recruited for the major road-building projects with which Hitler planned to tackle national unemployment. The political organizations took center stage next, followed by the Hitler Youth on Saturday. The final two days were given over to the SA and SS, and in a fitting climax to the behind-closed-door dealings of the spring and summer, the rally concluded with the army proclaiming its new oath of mass personal loyalty to Hitler himself.

Each of these special "days" involved a familiar set of ingredients. There were speeches—some indoors, some outside, in daylight, but also at night, illuminated by smoking torches and raking lights. Just laying eyes on the vastly swollen numbers of the Nazi faithful was awesome enough. The movement had always been counted in thousands and, just occasionally, in tens of thousands. But membership levels were off the scale now. Just compare the image of a 1934 rally with the photograph taken in 1925, a mere nine years earlier, of Bruno reclining surrounded by his Frontbann colleagues, all easily contained within the frame of one photographic negative, with every individual face clearly discernible. Now, as architect Speer had intended, Bruno's presence at Nuremberg was rendered virtually invisible. There is no magnifying glass powerful enough to find him in these enormous formations. He's there somewhere, of course, but is completely lost among the great gathering of representatives of the new *Volksgemeinschaft*: not just the familiar SA, and their SS counterparts, but legions of Hitler Youth, Party members, and various other armies of Nazi functionaries.[17]

Over the course of that week, Bruno listened to speeches given in the Luitpoldhalle by senior Nazis (including Hitler himself), in the middle of an audience that exploded in ecstatic applause, arms stretched to breaking point in endless Nazi salutes. Once darkness fell, old SA habits resurfaced, and Bruno joined his Charlottenburg comrades in nocturnal drinking sessions, brawling their way around both town and camp, sparking numerous fistfights and landing dozens of SA rivals in hospital.

> A report by one SA leader of events in the brown shirts' camp during a single night at the Nuremberg Rally in 1934 indicated [that] everyone was drunk, and a large fight between two regional groups at one in the morning left several men with knife wounds. On their way back to the camp, storm troopers attacked cars, threw bottles and stones at the windows, and beat up their occupants. The entire Nuremberg police force was mobilized to try and stop the mayhem. A brown shirt was hauled out of the camp latrine, into which he had fallen in a drunken stupor, but he died of chlorine poisoning shortly afterward. The camp was not quiet until four in the morning, by which time six men had been killed and thirty wounded, as well as another twenty who had been injured by jumping on or off cars or trucks.[18]

Most memorable, however, was the dressing up in full uniform and taking part in the great set pieces that have become synonymous with Nazi spectacle: the choreography of vast marching columns, tens and tens of thousands of helmeted men in perfect formation, like a tidal wave of indistinguishable faces. For someone who had spent his life intoxicated by the trappings of military power, this was exhausting, but blissful. Boots, helmets, gleaming leather, a powerful symbol for the mobilized might of the legendary storm trooper. Here at last was the spirit of

Bruno's beloved Ernst Jünger, transported from the carnage of the western front and brought back to life in formidable and immaculate form.

But this year there was even greater incentive for Bruno to march his heart out, to stand as tall as possible on the parade ground, and to help play his part turning the assembled tens of thousands into a vast, living tableau. This year it was being filmed. Even at its most monumental, the rally alone was not enough to satiate Hitler's craving for immortality, especially in its new "thousand-year" guise. Among the most important of its monuments would be those built out of celluloid. Germany was in love with the big screen and its extraordinary technological novelty; the recent introduction of recorded sound was just the latest in a long line of innovations. There were cinemas all over Germany by the early 1930s. Film conveyed national emotions even better than the written word—a fact that Goebbels completely understood. Hitler decided to commit the rally to film.

Bruno, no stranger to the world of Berlin nightlife, a lover of movies and with a lifelong eye for women, was very well acquainted with the name of the ex-dancer turned actress and director who had been given the job of turning all that speechifying and goose stepping into an epic image of a nation on the march: Leni Riefenstahl. This Berlin sensation, with her glamorous looks and ruthless ambition, was commissioned to create a cinematic masterpiece to celebrate the regime, the same way triumphal columns and victory arches had earlier ones. She rose to the challenge with her imperious arrogance, an unlimited budget, and more than a dozen of Germany's finest cinematographers operating her cameras, in what became the world's largest outdoors broadcast. Scale was her specialty; she knew that there was nothing smaller on screen than the world's largest set; she would capture the *dynamism* of Nazism's mass arousal, not just its size.

Leni Riefenstahl had made her name starring in, and directing, a string of so-called mountain films, overblown melodramas set thousands of meters above sea level, combining vertiginous photography with kitsch story lines.[19] It was her genius to transfer this vocabulary to the rallies. Instead of the Zugspitze, Germany's highest mountain, the summit to which her cameras now achingly aspired was Hitler himself. In place of the crevasses, canyons, peaks, and granite slopes of the Alps, she substituted the vistas of men in uniform, her high crane shots turning the visual expanse of Nuremberg's parade ground into an unlikely combination of *Ben-Hur*'s Circus Maximus and a Caspar David Friedrich landscape. Speer's Nuremberg architecture, with its gleaming marble and shining granite, represented for her a living vision of Sparta, the perfect meeting place for bodies, weapons, flames, and assemblies. No other film director could call upon so large and disciplined an army of extras—the hundreds of thousands of men like Bruno, determined to make this an event to remember—nor a central star of such transcendent charisma as Germany's new Führer. Earlier rallies had paid tribute to the spectacle of mass adulation, but the 1934 rally moved the spotlight toward the beacon of the great Führer himself. She used close-ups of Hitler's stern and furrowed visage to depict a Leader elevated beyond the realm of mere politics.

It was months, though, before anyone got to see the results of her astonishing efforts: the film had its gala premiere on March 29, 1935. As Bruno was a senior Party member and had actually attended the rally, it is safe to assume there was little chance he missed seeing the film. As the lights dimmed, he knew he was about to savor the greatest cinema experience of his Nazi life. At two hours and twenty minutes long, it was, and remains, one of the defining landmarks of movie megalomania.

It was a film that I came to know very well when, in 1993, I persuaded the BBC to broadcast it, as a way of responding to the recent, much-publicized release of Riefenstahl's autobiography, *The Sieve of Time*. I made a forty-minute documentary introduction to it, interspersing clips of the film with interviews with historians, moviemakers, and commentators. For weeks and weeks, in a miniature version of Riefenstahl's own efforts, I sat at an editing desk in London's West End, spooling back and forth through *Triumph of the Will*, shaping an account of what kind of film it was, while looking to get some kind of handle on where in the history of film it deserved to sit. I realized how unusual it had become to watch the film in its entirety, having gotten so used to seeing it stripped for images and sequences. Riefenstahl clearly intended that the film should deliver pure cinematic rapture. So it came as a genuine surprise to discover that for every shot that astonishes with its "very nasty magic,"[20] there were so many moments of genuinely bizarre incompetence.[21] It also feels very shapeless—nobody watching it now would be able to remember remotely what order the sequences come in, or even how it ends. Of course, this could hardly have mattered less for its intended first-night audience, who were looking for radiance, not insight.

At the time, I had no idea that my grandfather had played any part in it. It had never occurred to me that he might be one of those grim-faced SS hoplites marching in the film's endless formations. When I watch it now, the experience feels very different. Now I try to see it through Bruno's eyes, as he must have that late March night. As I do so, it becomes clearer just what Riefenstahl managed to achieve, in what she later used to describe as her "film of peace."

Like the Führer himself, it is a work that appears to have no specific "program."[22] What it offers instead, and what its partisan early audiences found so arousing, is its overwhelming image of the fascist state working like a well-oiled machine: unity fused with hierarchy, the great Leader embodying, and at the same time shaping, the national will, the assembled masses feeling the power of their own collective strength at the very moment they surrendered all their authority. Above all, the film defied its viewers to resist its great, irresistible invitation: Come, march with us! I can only imagine with what kind of exultant swagger Bruno left the cinema.

Of course, as exhilarating as he found the film, it merely symbolized all he already knew. Even its ulterior purpose—healing the rupture between the traumatized SA and the victorious Party—was something he had long been committed to.

For a storm trooper as ambitious as Bruno, by late 1935 the Röhm business was ancient history. Unfortunately, so too was the SA. Their power was waning by the month. Simply coming in out of the cold and being reconciled to the Party leadership might have been a big enough aspiration for the SA rank and file, but not for Bruno. He surely hated how low the SA's fortunes had fallen. Going through various SA papers attached to his personal records, I discovered an extraordinary document, an affidavit that painted a shocking picture of the desperation he felt to stand out from the SA crowd and the ruthlessness with which he was prepared to do it. Like his SS CV, it was written in his own hand and consequently offered a vivid snapshot of what kind of Nazi he had become.

This new episode in Bruno's Nazi career wasn't a reprise of the mutinies and rifts of the Stennes/Röhm years, when those on the left of the Nazi movement had sought greater levels of socialism in Hitler's politics. In fact, it was the opposite. Throughout the Third Reich, corruption, cronyism, and chronic profiteering had become endemic. This was the dark side of the bonanza of new political power, in a regime that believed might was right and that the point of power was to seize all the prizes available to it. Of course there were Nazis who took it too far. A zealot like Bruno, however, was dismayed. He appears to have drawn a distinction between the legitimate reward for years of loyalty and sacrifice and simply sticking a snout in the trough. He took it as the badge of a true fanatic to refuse to ignore immorality, *even* within the ranks of his own SA battalion—an attitude that was the legacy of his months serving on the SA Honor Court. The SA surely had to do whatever it took to become the incorruptibles of Hitler's empire once again. If it couldn't, then it was all over for the storm troopers. In 1936, Bruno got his chance to match words with actions, by becoming an SA whistle-blower.

The victim of Bruno's raptorlike vigilance was one Heinrich Rohmeyer, a fellow officer in SA Sturm 31, a man he had known for years. He was an exuberant loudmouth, but was considered a "useful" character in the battalion. It was his raucous behavior in their SA pub Zur Altstadt, also referred to as the Robert Reisig (after the name of the bar owner), that caught Bruno's attention. Here was a man who claimed to be unemployed, but who threw large amounts of money around, buying endless rounds of drinks and cigarettes. Bruno was convinced that there was something highly dubious about the man, so he decided to put him under surveillance: "I didn't trust his abundant generosity one little bit, or believe his activities abroad. So I began to monitor him."[23] He shared these suspicions with his boss, Sturmbannführer Feldmann, the new head of Sturm 31, who encouraged Bruno to take the matter further.

Bruno's one-man operation quickly spread beyond the SA, as, warming to his task, he got in contact with old "party comrades" who were now working in the Gestapo and the Security Service. The file on Rohmeyer slowly grew thicker as allegations against him were gathered and investigated. Eventually Bruno had no choice but to broach the matter with Rohmeyer's immediate superior, SA Standartenführer Hahn, whom he had known since his Frontbann days. But here, Bruno hit a brick wall. Hahn didn't even try to deny that Rohmeyer was an unsavory character. But "lay off," he told Bruno. "Rohmeyer is too useful to us, I don't want him touched." His particular talent, it turned out, was his ability to "acquire useful materials"—and Hahn didn't want too many questions asked, certainly not by an overzealous fellow SA man with a point to prove. For Bruno the inference was obvious: Rohmeyer was some kind of embezzler, and his old friend Hahn was either turning a blind eye to it or, more likely, actively colluding.

Other files from the archives tell the full story. Rohmeyer had been responsible for the refurbishment of the regiment's new HQ on Kastanienallee 1, a lavish but dilapidated villa in a smart district in central Berlin. The building costs had overrun their original estimate. Rohmeyer meanwhile, though officially jobless, was regularly chauffeured to work in his own limousine and was never short of cash. What had started off as merely "acquiring" building materials had quickly escalated into the appropriation of fully fledged financial "donations," and before long he was raking in thousands of Reichsmarks. It was part of a much larger scam involving an accomplice in the Reich Air Ministry, precisely the sort of behavior that so many in the SA now considered the prerogative of power, and which Bruno was determined to expose. Of course it didn't bother Bruno that the Kastanianallee building had been the location for any number of SA atrocities during the months of terror in 1933. That was just business as usual. The real sin, the one that required more than a year of active investigation, months of SA tribunals and courts-martial, and finally a criminal trial, concerned the misappropriation of 15,000 Reichsmarks and some building materials.

Unfortunately for Rohmeyer and his boss, Standartenführer Hahn, the SA hierarchy, anxious to protect their reputation in the eyes of the Party, shared Bruno's view of his activities, and when the case finally made its way to the SA Honor Court, they found him guilty. The SA concluded that Rohmeyer had indeed "acted against SA discipline," and they expelled him from their ranks. It was a triumphant result for Bruno's tenacity. His rectitude had proved even stronger than the SA solidarity created in the *Sturmlokal*, cemented by the drinking, the boasting, and the atmosphere of being a law to themselves. Nazi fanaticism came first. Bruno was doubly vindicated, not only because his suspicions had been borne out, but also because he had stood up against corruption, placed Nazi propriety above the behavior of his battalion comrades, and proved to the security services what a cool operator he was, not just in words, but with deeds. For Rohmeyer there was worse to come. After the SA had finished with him, his case was handed over to the criminal courts, where he was promptly convicted for embezzlement and sentenced to over two years in prison.

Yet there is a hint of regret in Bruno's documents. He must have been conscious that his actions would cast the SA in yet further bad light; there was awareness, too, that he had helped bring about the downfall of Fritz Hahn, his old colleague and mentor. He therefore tried to limit the impact by adding a coda to his affidavit, outlining his long-term admiration for the soldierly and irreproachable conduct of his old comrade. Bruno had always regarded Hahn as "straight and sincere," as "striking the best impression as a man," as he put it in the affidavit's rather mealymouthed concluding paragraph. But it was to no avail. Hahn too was expelled from the SA and closely avoided going to jail. Fortunately for him, the court gave him the benefit of the doubt; they concluded that as an "old fighter" he had not actively participated in Rohmeyer's felony, he had merely been duped by it. Bruno was sorry to see his comrade's reputation bespattered, but it couldn't be helped. Bruno had been compelled to act. He had done the right thing and he had served the Nazi cause by doing so.

Of course, what is so striking reading the documents today is how inverted—perverted, even—Nazi judicial values had become. Hahn was expelled from the SA over the matter of some stolen building materials. In reality Hahn was a violent and murderous thug. Even Bruno's new commanding officer, Sturmbannführer Feldmann, knew this, acknowledging (not without reservation) his "aggression and capacity to strike fear." In 1931, Hahn had shot a Communist, in cold blood, and fled to the Netherlands to avoid prosecution by the Weimar police; he was able to return to Germany once the dust had settled. For Bruno these were the kinds of decisive actions that earned men like Hahn more respect, not less—if only he hadn't succumbed to grubby temptation.

There was no doubt that the Rohmeyer episode had enhanced Bruno's standing—though maybe not with his immediate storm trooper colleagues. There was no doubt, either, that Bruno's appetite for this sort of investigative work had clearly been whetted. Perhaps for all these reasons, this turned out to be the last chapter in Bruno's long SA career, one that had spanned the violence of Hans Maikowski's Sturm 33 and the treacherous rifts of Heinrich Kuhr's Sturm 31. Bruno was too astute an observer of the Nazi power grid to have failed to notice the SA's steep decline in prestige and influence. For the first time in twelve years, the SA could no longer deliver him the "political fulfillment" he so valued. He would have to invest his ambitions elsewhere. As 1936 drew to its close, Bruno had made his most momentous decision. It was time to abandon the SA and make his bid to join the real winners of the Nazi revolution: Himmler's men in black—the SS.

Seven

MEN IN BLACK

1937–1939

I t took Bruno from January to August 1937 to manage it, but after seven months of displaying the right combination of loyalty and ideological reliability, he finally received the most consequential letter of his Nazi career: "With effect from September 12, 1937, I am taking you as an SS man and promoting you to the rank of SS *Untersturmführer* [second lieutenant]." He had wooed the toughest of Nazi selection boards: "SA Sturmführer Bruno Langbehn, Party number 36,931, dated May 17, 1926, belonged between 1924 and 1926 to the Frontbann, before joining the SA on May 17, 1926, where he served with SA Regiment 1/1 as regiment dentist. On March 20, 1937, Langbehn joined the SS, where he was able to use his network of excellent contacts to very great effect. He sees to completion all his tasks with great circumspection and energy. He is mentally agile and intellectually above average. It is recommended that he be commissioned into the SS as an *Untersturmführer*."

The rest was a formality. With confirmations from senior

officers in the Berlin SS, and formal endorsement by Obersturmbannführer (Lieutenant Colonel) Falkenberg, Bruno was in: "There is no objection against SA Sturmführer Langbehn being accepted as an . . . officer in the SS. The SS Regional Office agrees that SA Sturmführer Langbehn should be given the rank of an SS *Untersturmführer* and be formally admitted to the SS, and requests approval of this recommendation." It might have seemed to those unfamiliar with the complex hierarchies of the National Socialist establishment that he was simply transferring from one branch of the Nazi state to another, but Bruno knew this was not the case. He understood that his admission to the SS marked a new and greatly accelerated phase in his journey toward the heart of the Nazi elite. This was the moment when he became the Nazi equivalent of a made man, when it must have seemed that his long and violent apprenticeship had at last delivered the recognition and approbation he had so ardently wished for.

But if 1937 represented a personal apotheosis for Bruno, it was a year of similar significance for the nation as a whole. It marked the culmination of an internal battle for Germany's soul, a struggle to redefine the whole country in the Führer's image.

It had been waged since Hitler's accession to power in 1933, and Bruno had played his part in it to the full. But no successful Nazi apparatchik ever stood still. As the Third Reich evolved, so too did Bruno. It was hardly surprising, given the role played by violence, that he had earned his first Nazi spurs in the brown shirt of an SA storm trooper. What few might have predicted, however, was that in his capacity as a dentist and bureaucrat he found his true Nazi vocation. The first four years of Nazi rule would see Bruno the street-brawling "old fighter" develop into a very different kind of perfect Nazi and, in so doing, mirror far more ominous changes taking place deep within the regime.

Before 1933, Bruno's formative period had been characterized, as he knew only too well, predominantly by the experience of being an outsider. After 1933, all that changed. From then on, the war was fought from within, with Bruno and his like-minded allies setting the agenda. They held the levers of power now and were determined to use every means their new insider status delivered into their hands to achieve their ends. It was a campaign designed to win over the hearts and minds of susceptible Germans, and to browbeat and intimidate those less sympathetic to their new style of government. It was, in effect, a process whereby the whole of society was Nazified, permeated by the ideas, processes, and terminology of the Party.

No aspect of life was either too important or too trivial to be colonized by Nazi patterns of behavior. For a highly motivated *Volksgenosse*, or race comrade, like Bruno, every day offered fresh opportunities to parade his Party credentials. There was a whole new specialist language to embrace, starting with the now virtually compulsory "Hitler greeting" (straight-arm salute, combined with a loud *"Heil Hitler"*), and extending to include the many new Nazi organizations, ranks, and concepts that flooded the Third Reich. This was a world awash with abbreviations,[1] abstractions,[2] and Party ranks,[3] and how good they must have sounded to Bruno, conclusive proof that nation and Party had become one and the same.

He had always been a compulsive joiner, a man at his happiest inside institutions, a natural committee member. Later in his life, long after the war, when German society had lost much of its earlier formality, Bruno still loved participating in associations, attending formal functions, collecting insignia. He was a stickler for official protocol his whole life, even in an age that later largely discarded it. In a system that measured loyalty to the Reich through mass membership of societies embedded in every aspect of daily existence, he must have been in his element. Of course, passive membership was not enough to satisfy the suspicions of the new government. On a regular basis, Germans were forced to advertise their adherence to the Nazi state and their loyalty to its values in more actively demonstrative ways. There were innumerable, large-scale ceremonies, national days, processions, charity drives, all requiring enthusiastic participation, sometimes with donations of money, always with flags and cheering. A pillar of the regime like Bruno made the most of every one of them.

Every apartment complex—every street, every neighborhood—had its "block warden"; together, they constituted an army of sharp-eyed lookouts waiting to pounce on any minor transgression or perceived act of disrespect. For many ordinary Germans, the consequences of overheard jokes, or even just careless eye rolling, were horrifying. But not for Bruno; he had no need to resort to "internal exile," the private withdrawal into mental retreat undertaken by Germans unhappy with Nazi authority. He had flaunted his political affiliations since he was a teenager, even during periods when they had been made illegal by the Weimar government. Engaging in them now wasn't just a duty; it was a source of profound satisfaction, turning every day into a miniature Nuremberg Rally.

Bruno got to dress the part, too. This was a society in which everybody aspired to wear a uniform, no matter how modest their job: mailmen, railway officials, civil servants. Even prior to the SS, in his brown SA tunic, complete with Gold Honor Party Badge, Bruno had a ten-year lead on them all. The use of uniforms was a deliberate ploy by the Nazis so that, according to Hitler, "Germans can walk together arm in arm without regard to their station in life."[4] Uniforms replaced the unregulated distinctions of informal dress with a carefully calibrated hierarchy of status controlled by the Party leadership.

In the Nazi state, even leisure time was to be directed toward properly approved goals. This was no problem for Bruno, who had always loved the pleasures of the collective life and expected to spend what spare time he had from work and Party duties enjoying himself with like-minded companions. His Nazi CV alluded to his work for the Kraft durch Freude (Strength Through Joy) tourist organization. This was intended to organize holidays for loyal German workers and ensure that they would be able to take them in suitably uplifting settings. The KdF combed the German landscape looking for places both associated with the rise of National Socialism (sites of monuments, important battles, any location that had formed the backdrop to their rise to power) and of natural beauty outstanding enough to inspire the visitor with a vision of Germany's native wonder. Even on holiday, there was no time off for the perfect Nazi.

The process by which every last aspect of German life was rebuilt to reflect Nazi values had, of course, its own name—*Gleichschaltung*, or national "coordination." Leni Riefenstahl's *Triumph of the Will* had offered ordinary Germans a cinematic vision of this process. But it was never supposed to be limited to movies and myth making. National Socialism would not rest until it had seeped into every pore and penetrated every corner of the German *Volk*. This applied especially to the world of work, including the middle-class professions, and Bruno's was no exception.

Few white-collar institutions threw themselves at Hitler's feet as enthusiastically as those of law and medicine. Doctors, apothecaries—and dentists—were rivaled only by judges, lawyers, and magistrates for the speed and the totality with which they put themselves at the disposal of the new regime. Bruno was as fervent a Nazi in his dental surgery as on the SA parade ground. Both his civilian and his paramilitary efforts served prime national concerns. In fact, it was as a dentist, not as a storm trooper, that Bruno got to claim the most significant reward for all his years in frontline service to the movement.

One of the most powerful new Nazi institutions was the DAF—the German Labor Front, which had replaced, at a stroke, all Germany's trade unions and ensured Nazi control of the national economy. Both blue- and white-collar workers were among the first of Germany's population to feel the force of Hitler's social experiment. For Bruno, this was a golden opportunity. Still barely in his thirties, he was appointed to a senior position within this umbrella Workers' Front—as a *Gaufachswalter*, or senior supervisor/administrator. This was just the first of two important roles; he soon landed an even bigger one.

The largest and most significant professional body representing dentists was the Reichsverband Deutscher Dentisten (RDD—Reich Guild of German Dentists), which could boast 18,000 members in 1934 (ninety percent of all the *Dentisten* in Germany). This was one of a number of such institutions dating back to Weimar days that were quickly reorganized along staunchly Nazi lines in 1934 and 1935. Its regional offices were renamed *Landesdienststellen* (regional departments), to reflect their new political affiliation, and their old bosses were replaced by reliable Nazis. Playing every card in his hand, Bruno landed the biggest professional jackpot of his life, when at some point in the late 1930s (I couldn't track down the exact date) he was appointed *Landesdienststellenleiter* for the whole of Berlin—by some margin the most senior of all the regional offices. He was now responsible for the careers of the capital city's 2,000 practicing *Dentisten*. This would have been impossible under the Weimar Republic, which would never have entrusted such a major role to someone so young. His unwavering dedication during all the Party's wilderness years had now paid off in the clearest and most tangible way.

For Bruno, it didn't end there. His Party membership not only landed him his job, but dictated how he would exercise it as well. As a senior DAF dental functionary, Bruno had responsibilities that went far beyond the mundane issues of dental "pay and rations"; his medical expertise ensured his involvement with the social policy that defined Nazi strategy and thinking: public health and the value of human life.

As soon as they came to power, the Nazis sought to purge and reshape Germany's medical professions to reflect their ideological convictions. If there was no absolute equality of value when applied to human life—if, as they believed, some lives were inherently more worthwhile than others—then it was necessary that existing structures of health care be restructured to reflect that belief. This would lead eventually to acts of unimaginable evil conducted in the name of perverted medical science, but it had its beginnings in a simpler question. If protecting the health of a racially pure *Volk* was the first duty of the state, who was to be charged with achieving this all-important task? Before it arrived at the issue of who was worthy of receiving treatment, the Nazi state sought to define who was fit to deliver it. Who should be allowed to practice medicine at all? For Nazis like Bruno, the answer was a simple one. There was no profession that carried a greater responsibility within the "race community" than that of doctors and dentists. As a result, it was one from which Jews must be strictly excluded.

Hundreds of Jewish physicians were dismissed from their posts. In Berlin, Bruno's *Reichsverband* was responsible for doing the same thing to Jewish dentists. Those who couldn't be persuaded to give up their profession were subjected to outright defamation: "Non-Jewish doctors had no inhibitions about destroying professional competitors. . . . Measures against doctors soon applied to dentists, who were subjected to *Stürmer* smear tactics, involving photographs of dirty equipment and squalid surgeries. One of them, Professor Heinz Moral of Rostock, author of Germany's most outstanding dental diagnostic textbook, committed suicide after being dismissed from his university post."[5]

Alongside smear tactics and outright dismissal, Jewish medical practitioners also found themselves the targets of bureaucratic persecution, the hallmark of the Nazi state. By excluding Jewish dentists from the complex system of private and state funding that effectively paid their wages, the Nazis steadily and surely drove them out of the profession. As a practicing dentist himself, Bruno had relied on a wide range of different kinds of payments: from the state, from charities, from private health insurance schemes. Now, as head of the Berlin Dentists' Guild, he made sure that access to these essential sources of income was denied to Jewish professionals. Victor Klemperer wrote in his diary of this ominous portent for the future: "The sudden exclusion of non-Aryan doctors from the private insurance schemes" filled him with alarm; he interpreted it as yet more evidence of "the screws being tightened on Germany's Jews."[6]

Klemperer was right to be concerned. The restructuring of Germany's health care system had implications that went straight to the malign heart of Nazi policy. In vicious bureaucratic backwaters throughout the Hitler state, men like Bruno were grappling with questions that would lead to the darkest possible outcomes. Whose health was most valuable to the *Volk*? Who was to be protected and nurtured as racially and socially useful? Who, on the other hand, had nothing to contribute? Who, on grounds of race, behavior, or capacity, were effectively disqualified from full participation in the future of the Reich? Few debates were more central, or more routine, in the Third Reich than this. They were different ways of asking, What is the value of one *life* over another?

Reflecting on these questions—and finding ways to turn their implications into enforceable directives—was what men like Bruno did all day. They were the administrative vanguard of a policy that effectively rewrote the tenets on which the whole of Western morality had been based; they became the bureaucratic outriders of evil. The Nazis had begun their regime by *politicizing medicine*—by excluding the racially unqualified from being allowed to practice, by making it all but compulsory for doctors, dentists, and pharmacists to become active Nazis if they wanted to keep their jobs, far less win promotion. As head of the Berlin Dentists' Guild, Bruno not only benefited personally from this, but also played a significant and active role in extending it across the capital. But in doing so, he and others like him were responsible for an even more profound shift in thinking. The Nazis had *medicalized politics itself*. From now on, the two were indivisible. Every question of state—not just relating to hospitals and surgeries—was posited on this central biological principle, and accountable to it. The right to health and well-being—indeed the right to life itself—was no longer to be considered an absolute human value. Instead, it was one to be assessed, analyzed, and decided upon by those qualified, by expertise and ethical soundness, to pronounce on fitness. Bruno, as both a bureaucrat and a medical man, was the perfect exemplar of this role.

At home, too, Bruno's personal life was moving forward at a considerable pace. He and Thusnelda, married for more than three years, had their first child in spring of that year, a daughter to whom they enthusiastically gave the resoundingly *völkisch* name Gudrun (as had Himmler to his first child). The increase in his salary (now over 450 Reichsmarks a month—not a fortune, but comfortable) allowed him to move his new family into a larger apartment, on the Berliner Strasse (Otto Suhr Allee today), in the heart of his favorite district of Charlottenburg. Thusnelda, for her part, was now a member of the Nazi Association of German Women. Her brother Ewald had followed Bruno's path into the SA and was proudly wearing his own brown shirt. Ida, her mother, still very much the family matriarch, retained her own dental practice, which was highly unorthodox for a respectably married woman. She liked to host high-powered social soirées, at which her most influential acquaintances were given the chance to ventilate the issues of the day. She had an extensive social network and was entirely at home in the new Germany, with its harsh preoccupation with conformity and hard work. Ida's second husband, army officer Friedrich, was meanwhile working in the Reichswehr, liaising with arms manufacturers (thanks to his diploma in engineering), doing his part to help the army evade the conditions imposed on it by the Treaty of Versailles. As though to underline just what a zenith the Langbehns had reached in 1936, Thusnelda's closest friend, Gisela, won a place, against stiff nationwide competition, to perform in the opening ceremony for the Berlin Olympic Games as a eurhythmics dancer. This was Nazi Germany's proudest moment, as the rest of the world poured into the country to inspect for themselves a brutally sanitized version of what Hitler had achieved. Bruno and his immediate family were its proudest advocates.

What more could Bruno have wanted? There was no part of his life—personal, family, professional, or political—that had not absorbed, and profited from, the first four years of the Third Reich, except for one—and it must have cut him to the quick. Bruno fitted in perfectly in the new Germany—and that was the problem. So too did tens of millions of others. For more than a decade, he had enjoyed belonging to an elite Nazi minority, the early joiners. Now *everyone* was trying to get into the Party—so many, in fact, that Party membership had to be temporarily suspended to avoid being swamped. The Führer cult was in full, frenzied swing, drawing into its clutches vast numbers of the German population. What had been exclusive was now mainstream. This threatened to rob Bruno of his most distinctive and jealously guarded prize—the kudos of the old fighter. The last thing he would ever have wanted to be was an ordinary Nazi— but that was precisely what he was becoming, unless he acted quickly and decisively.

By this point, too, not even Bruno's SA uniform could guarantee elevated status in the eyes of his countrymen. No matter how hard he, and other, like-minded SA men, had worked to help rehabilitate their status after the Röhm affair, it had all been for nothing. The SA was a spent force, reduced to menial Party tasks, providing bouncers for meetings and handing out leaflets.[7] By itself, this might not have mattered. But Bruno knew differently. There were no "also rans" in Nazi Germany; you were one of the regime's fêted inner circle, to whom the most important jobs were delegated, or you were nobody, a predicament Bruno was not prepared to contemplate. He had learned the Third Reich's most important lesson too well to make that mistake.

Behind the illusory social unity of the *Volksgemeinschaft*, Bruno could see clearly this was a system that rewarded only one thing— predatory instinct. Advancement came to those willing to prey on others, no matter the cost. Goebbels's gushing and incessant propaganda paid lip service to the virtues of classlessness and merit, but it was its rapacious ability to set human beings against one another that really drove the Third Reich. The only bonds that mattered were those of proximity to power and mastery over others; all the rest—compassion, reciprocity, cooperation— were redundant. The SA was of no more use to Bruno, and it would have to be jettisoned.

But there was more than just self-interest dictating Bruno's ambitions; there was powerful idealism at work, too. The administrative chaos, even anarchy, that characterized Nazi power politics[8] belied a singular truth: for all its rivalries and internecine fighting, the Third Reich was moving in a distinct and terrifying direction—driven by Hitler and the growing clarity of his ultimate aims—aims for which the successes of the previous four years were simply the overture.[9] As a long-term committed National Socialist, Bruno was as determined to play a part in that future crusade as he was to avoid being left behind.

Hitler was possessed by three as yet unfulfilled ambitions, which emanated from deep within his "core body of ideas," and from which not even the fruits of power could deflect him.[10] Prominent in the Nazis' list of urgent tasks that had not yet been accomplished was dealing with the First World War, which *still* lay unavenged. Twenty years had elapsed since the ignominy of defeat, but the wound had never healed. Only when France and Britain lay utterly vanquished, and the Treaty of Versailles was annulled, could Germany regain the greatness that was its due.

Second, there was the call to empire, which grew louder as Hitler's hold over Germany grew firmer. Having dominated the homeland, it was inevitable that he would start looking farther afield. Hitler never lost his fixation with the prospect of a vast *Lebensraum* in the east, which, once acquired, would make Germany masters of Europe for generations to come. Bruno's entire involvement in the politics of right-wing German nationalism had been premised on both these central experiences, and on the dreams of future success that they had given birth to. All the *Gleichschaltung* and material prosperity in the world could not compensate for a German future in which these categorical imperatives remained unresolved. That was as true for the fanatic like Bruno as it was for Hitler himself. The Third Reich would fulfill itself only when it had crushed the memory of the First World War, and Germany dominated the entire continent.

What made both of these aspirations especially terrifying was that, in Hitler, Germany had a leader uniquely capable of acting on them, no matter the size of the gamble or the consequences of failure. It was Hitler's malign genius to be able to convince his followers that securing Germany's military and imperial destiny was nothing less than a divine mission, and that only he possessed the willpower and the vision to ensure its successful achievement.

There was, however, a third directive, one that exerted an even more obsessive hold on Hitler's mind than war or empire, and that would prove the most catastrophic of all: the question of what to do with Germany's Jews. Hitler had no specific plan for how to solve the issue, but that didn't prevent him from believing that Germany would be held back from its quest for greatness as long as a single Jew still lived within its borders.

For hard-core Nazis, anti-Semitism went far deeper than race hatred; it was National Socialism's defining article of faith, one that pervaded—and perverted—every aspect of the Third Reich. In 1935, Bruno stood on parade at the annual Nuremberg Rally, as he had done so often before. Unlike the previous rally of 1934, in which he had helped to celebrate Germany's new Führer, the purpose here was very different. Pride of place went not to Leni Riefenstahl's cameras but to something far more pernicious—the proud announcement of so-called Nuremberg Laws, anti-Jewish legislation designed to isolate Germany's Jews, by stripping them not just of their citizenship but also of any remaining protection under the law. On September 17, Klemperer noted in his diary: "The Reichstag in Nuremberg [has] passed the laws on German blood and German honor: Prison for marriage and extra-marital intercourse between Jews and 'Germans.'" A few months later, he sardonically noted Hitler's justification for his demagoguery: "I am not a dictator, I have only simplified democracy."[11]

This was the core of what it meant to be a Nazi, far more than the paraphernalia of uniforms, salutes, Hitler greetings, and "coordinated" institutions. Anti-Jewish invective had been the foundation of Bruno's entire political career, confidently held up by the Nazis as more than mere prejudice. To help "justify" their racial loathing, anti-Semites looked to authoritative modern science, as well as a number of experts in the arts, culture, and politics, all of whom regarded Jews with suspicion and hostility.[12] It was a Nazi truism that Jews were at the same time both subhuman and superhuman: underevolved, degenerate *Untermenschen*, but also over-evolved, cosmopolitan sophisticates effortlessly controlling the infrastructure of the modern world.[13] Traces of baleful Jewish influence were omnipresent in the minds of Nazis like Bruno. Every time they wrote to their banks, paid their rent, shopped in the new department stores, listened—however unwillingly—to American music, encountered references to Einstein's theory of relativity, or debated the contradictions of capitalism, they were convinced they were dealing with the specter of international Jewry. They saw its mark all around them, claimed they could locate the fingerprint of Jewishness when examining the behavior of bacteria down a microscope, or when confronted by the jagged primitivism of modern art; Jewishness underwrote the militancy of left-wing political posters, as well as dangerous follies such as pacifism or feminism.

If this was the diagnosis, the "cure" was only too predictable. Hostility against Jews soon encompassed everything from routine acts of daily spite to harassment, physical intimidation, and relentless demonization in print and film. The "healthy sense of justice of every German" was sanctimoniously and repeatedly invoked, as Victor Klemperer, with his brilliant ear for the nuances of Nazi cant, sardonically noted in 1938, when, as a Jew, he had his right to drive legally rescinded: "Jews are unreliable, [and] are therefore not allowed to sit at the wheel, also their being permitted to drive offends the German traffic community, especially as they have presumptuously made use of the Reich motorways built by German workers' hands."[14]

The pattern was set; widespread anti-Semitism was a reality to which ordinary Germans busily accommodated themselves, some with heavy hearts, others more receptive to the alleged reasoning behind it. Even those who declared themselves free of any obvious personal grievances against their Jewish neighbors nevertheless found it impossible not to acknowledge the all-encompassing nature of the "Jewish Question." Employers were forced to decide whether or not to sack Jewish colleagues. Wibke Bruhns records the following entries in her father's diary, as he agonized over just such a question in the company he ran: "April 3, 1933: Evening, employers' association re. poss. expulsion of Jew Jacobson—sign of the times. . . . April 13: Morn. First office, then board meeting of employers' association, in which because of political developments Herr Jacobson, as a Jew, must be expelled."[15] I have encountered more than one older German, as appalled as it is humanly possible to be about what later happened in the Holocaust, who nevertheless confided to me in a hushed voice that back then their "parents and grandparents" had been dealing with an "issue" that demanded some kind of solution—just not mass murder. "You have to understand," they reasoned with me, "the Jews *owned everything*—the department stores and the newspapers. It just couldn't go on."

There were those who tried to maintain that anti-Semitism was an obsession unique to Hitler himself, an aberration in an otherwise robust social system; for Sebastian Haffner, writing in the late

1930s, this refusal to acknowledge the centrality of Jew hatred was pure self-delusion: "It shows how ridiculous the attitude is, still found in Germany, that the anti-Semitism of the Nazis is a small side issue, at worst a minor blemish on the movement, which one can regret or accept, according to one's personal feelings for the Jews, and of 'little significance compared to the great national issues.' In reality, these 'great national issues' are unimportant . . . while the Nazis' anti-Semitism is a fundamental danger and raises the specter of the downfall of humanity."[16]

For a number of Hitler's foreign admirers, it was precisely his refusal to camouflage his anti-Semitism that made him so attractive. Most notorious was the English aristocrat Unity Mitford, described by one German observer as "somewhere between archangel and model for a toilet soap ad," who courted Hitler, determined to "become Queen of Germany."[17] For Hitler, however, displaying this fervent anti-Semitism was just the start. He wanted to know how his "Jewish Question" was going to be solved. As this was the Third Reich's most emphatic racial priority, it was hardly surprising that every Nazi agency competed for the chance to play a decisive role in providing the answer. There was only one state organization, however, which combined the necessary ferocity of beliefs and cold-blooded administrative ruthlessness to be delegated the task of realizing Hitler's as yet unfulfilled dreams—most notably the "Jewish Question"—and that was the SS.

Bruno's decision to apply to join the SS therefore signified much more than opportunism or ambition; it placed him at the crux of the Third Reich's crucial transformation from authoritarian fascist dictatorship to fully fledged Nazi state, premised on racial exclusion and licensed international aggression. The Third

Reich was on the move, laying the foundations for all that was yet to follow, when everything Hitler stood for moved from rhetoric to active policy.

The SS, fully aware of the critical role it was destined to play in the transition, insisted that only the most suitable Nazis could apply for membership. Back in 1926, when Bruno had first joined the Party and the SA, the drive to maximize numbers had meant there was no selection process at all. By 1937, however, the SS were far more discerning and required only officers of the highest caliber. Unlike Bruno's SA, the SS was not forged as a response to such external pressures as war, unemployment, or economic disaster, but had emerged from deep within the Nazi worldview. Its members weren't impelled by despair, or reckless naiveté; they were mature men who had absorbed, and then embraced, the true meaning of National Socialism. Was Bruno one of them? Did he have the *inner* resolve to behave genuinely *aus Überzeugung*—out of conviction? How useful an asset could he be in helping to realize Hitler's vision of a powerful, racially purged German superstate, a crusade that required total commitment from those charged with achieving it? The SS was quite prepared to take a number of months finding out if Bruno had what they were looking for.

In January 1937, Bruno's probation period started. It comprised low-level monitoring work, done out of his apartment, and did not entitle him to wear the black SS uniform. He was required to move unobtrusively through his old right-wing circles; absorb, analyze, and report on all their activities; and note their attitudes toward the administration and its leadership. Bruno was a well-connected man and relished his clandestine role. Finally, sometime in August, he was given the good news:

he had successfully completed his assessment. A few weeks later he was formally inducted into the SS and given a new Nazi designation to go alongside the 36,931 of his Party membership: SS serial number 290,261. He had arrived.

It wasn't hard to see what had drawn Bruno to apply to join the SS. No other Nazi organization exuded such a dark, menacing aura. It was more than just the latest in a long line of paramilitary formations, but possessed an esprit de corps steeped in the kinds of mysticism and ritual that Nazis equated with secret knowledge. The SS knew how to look the part, too, with their amulets and insignia—the runic twin-lightning silver flash SS, the rings, the daggers, and the death's-head badge, all framed by their iconic black tunics and caps, white shirts, and stark red armbands—the colors of the nationalist flag.

In a state that claimed to have flattened social hierarchy, the SS represented the apogee of Nazi doctrine. All Germans belonged to a master race, but the SS proclaimed itself to be a master race above them all, bound by ties that Himmler insisted had characterized all of history's most powerful secret organizations, such as the Jesuits or the Teutonic Knights. They were the ultimate carriers of national blood, linking Germanic ancestors to the future descendants of the *Volk*. Behind their façade of terror and intimidation, they proclaimed themselves the embodiment of honor and chivalry. Bruno obviously found all of this deeply attractive.

And for that, Reichsführer Heinrich Himmler, head of the SS, was responsible. Nobody worked the levers of Nazi power as astutely as he, or had such shrewd command of Hitler's twin imperatives, his brutal will to power and his unshakable worldview, to which Himmler responded with a mix of pragmatism and blind fanaticism. The lightly spoken, weak-chinned *Reichs-führer* SS knew better than any of Hitler's other senior paladins how to wield authority in the Third Reich—in other words, how to deal with the Führer.

Hitler's rule was based on a paradox. He was a man driven by a small and finite number of unchanging dogmas that never admitted of qualification or amendment. But as a day-to-day political leader, his modus operandi was characterized by the exact opposite. Sloppy and dilatory in his daily habits, constitutionally incapable, it seemed, of ever making a decision, far less sticking to it, his overwhelming priority was to surround himself with structures that made rival power blocs impossible. He dispensed with the parliamentary rule of the Reichstag altogether, ignored his political cabinet, and routinely delegated power to more than one person, thereby ensuring that each would become a violent rival of the other, preventing alliances from being built against him. Himmler understood this and ruthlessly turned it to his own advantage.

The SS wasn't just fanatically loyal to Hitler himself, it believed it acted as a kind of proxy for Hitler's unspoken desires. The SS understood Hitler's aims, even when Hitler was unable, or unwilling, to spell them out. Neither the SA nor the army ever managed this. As Nazi atrocities grew worse over the years, this was the system by which the unspeakable could remain unsayable, while at the same time remaining unequivocally clear for those charged with making them happen. The result was what one historian so memorably described as "working toward the Führer," a system of delegation and compliance in which ambitious Nazis exceeded the letter of their remit, in deference to its spirit, even in the absence of specific instructions. With clinical effectiveness, Himmler made the SS indispensable to Hitler, pandering to his megalomania, without triggering his paranoia.

First, Himmler seized control of the penal system, supplementing the traditional network of prisons with specially constructed concentration camps, modeled on the original at Dachau. Next came the police. He fused Germany's separate regional forces, first in Bavaria, then in Prussia, into a single national entity, which he then subdivided, not by geography, but by function. The plainclothes detectives of the recently established Gestapo (literally, secret state police) were separated from the criminal police, now called Kripo (Kriminalpolizei, or criminal police). Later Kripo and Gestapo would fuse under the umbrella heading Sipo (Sicherheitspolizei, or security police), as Himmler's empire spawned ever more departments and annexes. All these different forces shared a chain of command that culminated in Himmler alone.[18] By 1936, what had begun as the tyranny of a state police run amok had become a fully fledged police state.[19]

Nazi Germany was no different from other dictatorial regimes. The Soviets, too, had their secret policemen, their camps, and their draconian and arbitrary rule of intimidation and injustice. What made the SS unique was the role played by eugenics. The Nazi state was defined racially. It was a social truism that societies were organic, which meant that they could be "healed" and made more fit for purpose. But it also meant that they were vulnerable to being "undermined" or even "contaminated" by the vagaries of the population, their "human stock." Himmler turned powerful currents of 1930s German intolerance for all those who wouldn't, or couldn't, join the *völkisch* dream into a virulent campaign of biological terror. Using a lethal combination of legal and medical criteria, the SS rooted out anyone who "offended" the "healthy instincts of the people." The SS prided itself on its capacity to instill deep-seated ideological compliance, which they delivered with far greater precision than the blundering brutes of the SA.

The Nazis were never more fulfilled than when categorizing types and degrees of social outsiders, or *Asozialen*. These ranged from the Third Reich's passive enemies, people whose offenses were usually related to either work or sex: "who through minor infractions of the law demonstrate that they will not comply with the social order that is a fundamental condition of a National Socialist state, e.g., beggars, vagrants [Gypsies], prostitutes, drunkards, those with contagious diseases, particularly sexually transmitted diseases, who evade the measures taken by the public health authorities." More biologically suspect were the physically and mentally handicapped, whom the SS diagnosed as "worthless," because they "jeopardized" future generations.[20] More dangerous still were those considered to be National Socialism's active enemies, groups accused of posing both a biological and a moral threat to the German "river of blood." These were "race aliens" (*Rassenfremden*), defined—and legislated against—as a kind of ethnic disease (Roma and Sinti "Gypsies," for example).[21]

And finally there were those branded not simply as race aliens, but "race enemies" (*Rassenfeinde*), a community that, just by virtue of living at all, could bring down the whole of the Aryan Reich: the Jews. Nobody could rival the SS's place in the Third Reich, or the priority of its mission, in policing the German state, and its biological essence, too. No wonder Bruno was so determined to join them.

Yet if passing the SS selection process wasn't gratifying

enough, there was even better news for Bruno. He had been appointed not to just any department within the SS, but arguably to its most important: the SD Hauptamt (Security Service Main Office), as well as the RFSS—the Reichsführung SS—a senior department within the SD, attached to the SS leadership. In one decisive move, he had been reinstated on the front line of the Third Reich's most critical struggle—combating not just their racial opponents but so-called enemies of the worldview, a conflict with which only the most rigorous and dependable loyalist could be entrusted.

The SD was the brainchild of one of the dark stars of the Third Reich, Reinhard Heydrich, Himmler's second in command, and for many an even more fearsome figure than his SS boss. Few men so embodied the great paradox of Nazi power: he was as at home with his fencing sword and his violin as he was orchestrating mobile death squads and teams of Holocaust bureaucrats. He grew the SD from a tiny and marginal party organ into one of the Third Reich's hardest-working policy instruments. Soon, there was scarcely a part of the Nazi system in which the SD did not in some way have an interest. Heydrich even styled himself "C," in conscious mimicry of the British Secret Service he so claimed to admire.

Heydrich was determined to infiltrate the SD into every major institution, company, body, or organization in Germany. He made no distinction between information about mass public opinion and incriminating evidence against Party members that could be stored and used later. Indeed, much of what we know about "public opinion" during the Third Reich derives from SD reports designed to take the temperature of the public mood at key junctures. But this was no Nazi "mass-observation unit." This was pure knowledge as power. He kept tabs on everything his SD agents were doing, compiling their results as on a scorecard: "Parallel with information from the highest circles of power, 'C' . . . collated Gestapo reports from all *Gaue* for the daily score on how the suppression was proceeding. The report for October 13, 1936, for example, lists arrests as: Berlin 36, Hamburg 21, Duesseldorf 17, Dortmund 12, Bielefeld 10, Frankfurt/Main 4, Frankfurt/Oder 1."[22]

From the start, the SD's purpose was different from that of the rest of the SS. It wasn't involved in the camps or in providing Hitler with a bodyguard.[23] Its main sphere was *intelligence*, in every sense of the word, building a network of spies and data collation, which, in parallel with the (state-run) Gestapo, would tap and collate everything Germans were thinking and saying.

But far more than just a national eavesdropper, Heydrich wanted the SD to become the intellectual driving force for the whole movement, drafting and then executing the Nazis' most pressing policies. In 1934, a few days after the Night of Long Knives, an order "set out the division of labor between the SD and the [Gestapo]—the police would fight the enemies of the National Socialist state, while the SD would fight the enemies of the National Socialist *idea*."[24] As Heydrich put it, his purpose was far loftier than one of *mere* street-level arrests: "As the Security Service, we are not interested in, shall we say, whether or not the KPD cell apparatus in Berlin-Wedding has been neutralized. That is a matter for the executive . . . that doesn't interest us."[25] Heydrich had built a Praetorian Guard, not just for Hitler's person, but for Hitler's entire view of the world.

The SD was more than just a Nazi seminary. It also had a job to do.[26] The battle against those who opposed National Socialism had moved on. The Nazis no longer targeted the political left, as they had done in the early days of the improvised terror cellars and the SA detentions without charge. There were no more Communists or Socialists for them to detain. That didn't mean opposition had vanished, only that it took a different—and in their eyes, more sophisticated—form.

The SD that Bruno joined was divided into three main offices, or *Ämter*. Amt I was responsible for administration and organization. Amt II covered security within the borders of the Reich, in particular targeting all those institutions and individuals enthralled to alien politics incompatible with National Socialism, the so-called enemies of the worldview. Amt III extended these covert operations abroad; Heydrich wanted to preside over an international as well as a domestic intelligence network. And for all of this he needed new recruits—men just like Bruno, with impeccable Party credentials, unwavering conviction, and the energy to help drive the Nazi project toward its future goals.

The third week of September 1937 was one of the most fulfilling in Bruno's early adulthood. A few days after he received formal confirmation of his SS appointment and his new promotion to *Untersturmführer*, Thusnelda gave birth to their second daughter, Frauke, my mother. Bruno's SS role was only part-time (he still worked as a dentist, and for the Reichsverband Deutscher Dentisten), and it was unpaid. There was nothing unusual about this. Few SD officers were paid a salary—part of Heydrich's strategy to eke out their always meager financial resources. It made no difference to their seniority or their status. Bruno never thought that the SD would make him rich, only valuable.

Bruno's first attachment was to the second of the SD's three

main offices, Amt II, dealing with Nazism's philosophical enemies. Its main mission was to spearhead the battle against all
those who stood opposed to the governing principles of the Nazi
system. This was the most esoteric department within the SD, indeed within the whole of the Nazi state, whose members loved
to flaunt their status as cerebral high achievers. Bruno's new colleagues were very different from those he had had in the SA. He
was surrounded not by the spit-and-sawdust bullies of the SA
Sturmlokal, but by the (self-appointed) cream of German uni-
versities, particularly its law departments. As such, it was a deeply
flattering appointment for a man like Bruno, who, though educated, had never gone to university. Even in the SS, the SD considered themselves an elite within an elite.

These included men such as academic lawyer Reinhard Höhn,
whose warped jurisprudence sought to justify launching wars of
aggression against countries that fell into Germany's "sphere of
influence." Among other leading lights in the new-look SD was
Otto Ohlendorf, a year younger than Bruno. He had pioneered
the Reports from the Reich, which provided Nazi leadership
with snapshots of opinion and levels of morale across Germany.[27]
The man who lent the SD its intellectual pretension was journalist and academic Franz Six, who laid the groundwork for *Gegner-
forschung*, "research into the opposition," with an infamous
index-card system of his devising, whereby color codes denoted
different classes of political heresy. For the fine-tuning of SD
administration, Heydrich had brought in another lawyer, Werner
Best, who helped to articulate the best legalistic methods for
prosecuting the war against the Jews.[28] And then there was Walter Schellenberg, who by 1938 was virtually Heydrich's deputy.
He would later play a key role in Bruno's own SS career.

What was significant was that these men were all roughly the same age, yet more products of that key generation to which Bruno himself belonged.[29] Like Bruno, they had had experiences early on that impelled them to embrace right-wing nationalism, a choice that culminated in their rise to the senior echelons of the SS's most politically engaged department.[30] Bruno never rose to the dizzying heights to which men such as Six or Schellenberg had climbed, but he was an astute enough interpreter of "enemy ideologies" to win his coveted place in the SD's most self-regarding department. It was their ambition that no thought, opinion, polemic, thesis, or social analysis could appear in Germany without the SD's knowing about it. Bruno found himself working in what was tantamount to a superior clippings service, collating and annotating every single pamphlet, newsletter, piece of journalism, almost every printed word in German, scouring them for evidence of the kind of covert oppositional thinking that for Heydrich represented Nazism's gravest threat. It was all part of the SD's job to identify and control Nazism's "internal enemies," before neutralizing—and liquidating—them.

This meant maintaining a file on every high-profile German thinker or public figure whose opinions required monitoring. One document, titled "Erfassung führender Männer der Systemzeit" (Registry of Leading Men from the System Time—the denigratory Nazi term for the Weimar years), gives a flavor of what form these took. It's a very odd sensation to run an eye over it today, exactly as Bruno must have done more than seventy years ago. Broken into their different categories of background and belief, over six hundred names are listed, the preeminent figures of the immediate pre-Nazi period, from Waldemar Abegg to Bruno Walter. In between crop up the names of future West German political giants Konrad Adenauer and Theodor Heuss, writers Max Brod and Thomas Mann, artists Emil Nolde and Käthe Kollwitz, and impresario Max Reinhardt. And that is before you even get to Albert Einstein and Sigmund Freud. After 1933, these lists expanded exponentially, groaning under the weight of thousands of new names of those who had attracted the attention of the secret police.

The grouping together of opponents of Nazism into recognizable categories was a task the SD undertook with systematic thoroughness. Each SD *Amt* was broken down into smaller units, or "desks," each of which was assigned to a separate "enemy," creating ever more Byzantine descriptions of threats allegedly creeping their way into the Nazi state. The SD's departmental structure came to represent a microcosm for the whole world. There was virtually no sect too small, or too weird, not to find itself denounced as anti-German: the Jehovah's Witnesses, the Rotary Club, even the Boy Scouts were all seen as fronts for international sedition, to be monitored closely.

At the top of these lists weren't the Marxists, but the Freemasons. Again and again in SD files, *Freimaurer* are defined as the ultimate example of National Socialism's dark antithesis, their number-one enemy. Even more than the established churches and the great political systems of the other superpowers, it's the Masons who crop up repeatedly as the most feared of all their bogeymen. Entire SD desks were dedicated to seeking out the Freemasons' secret influences. Heydrich constructed a museum in his SD headquarters, full of ghoulishly displayed Masonic artifacts, which he enjoyed showing off to VIP guests.[31]

I couldn't resist a hollow chuckle reading these numerous SD descriptions of Freemason wickedness. At the very same moment, back in 1924, when Bruno had first joined the Frontbann, my *other* grandfather, the Scottish one who had fought in the trenches of the First World War, had himself become a Mason. His motivation had been a benign combination of mutual self-help in the world of postwar economic uncertainty and a determination to keep in as close contact as possible with a large number of his "pals" from the Seaforth Highlanders. He had even converted the ex–Masonic Lodge in his hometown of Dingwall into the area's first working cinema, which he ran until his death in the mid-1950s. The idea that this could have presaged the beginnings of a plan to take over the world is utterly risible. The Nazis, however, remained convinced that they faced no enemy more diabolical.

Bruno found himself working on a different desk: Amt II/123. His specified target wasn't Jewry, or Catholic priests, or even Masons, but what the Nazis called the *Reaktion*, or "conservative reactionaries." This referred to all those on the German right wing whose loyalty was deemed suspect. They sound on first inspection to be the least intimidating of all Nazism's opponents. Unlike Communists or Social Democrats, these were people whose politics overlapped with National Socialism; they were authoritarian, jingoistic, and expansionist. Ensconced in their officers' messes, in their company boardrooms, and on their landed estates, these wealthy and important vested-interest groups owed much of their good fortune to Hitler's style of leadership. The majority of them applauded Nazi doctrine, especially its demolition of democracy.

But they had reservations. Many of their grievances were, of course, due to their blue-blooded condescension toward Hitler himself, the vulgar demagogue, with his "pimp's forelock . . . hoodlum's elegance, the Viennese suburban accent, the intermi-

nable speechifying, the epileptic behavior with its wild gesticula-
tions, foam at the mouth, and the alternately shifty and staring
eyes . . . the threats and cruelty, the bloodthirsty execution
fantasies."[32]

However, some of their objections went deeper than social
contempt. Among their ranks could be included both *völkisch*
Bolsheviks on the left and closet monarchists on the right. They
each claimed to be the *real* inheritors of the defunct Weimar
Republic, hankering after the values of the Kaiser on the one
hand or preaching a higher nationalism in whose name social
hierarchy was to be abolished on the other. Either way, they had
the potential to form a genuine caucus of opposition to the Nazi
Party. As Sebastian Haffner wrote:

> The only opponents or rivals whom Hitler had to consider
> seriously and whom at times he had to fight in the domes-
> tic political arena . . . were the conservatives. . . . With their
> well-dug-in positions in army, diplomatic service, and ad-
> ministration, [they] always remained to him a genuine
> political problem—indispensable to the day-to-day opera-
> tion, half allies but also half opponents and occasionally, at
> least some of them, total opponents.[33]

Their most dangerous heresy, however, was to believe that it
was possible to enjoy the benefits of the Third Reich without
enslaving themselves to the Führer. They were at best provisional Nazis, delighted with their newly empowered German
Reich, but unwilling to jeopardize hard-won social and economic
status in pursuit of war and racial empire building. To the Nazi

purist, they were worse than backstabbers, they were backsliders, men who sought to hold back the Third Reich not by sabotage, but by relapsing into their old, comfortable ways. Just when Hitler wanted the Third Reich to embark on its decisive next chapter, these men, bloated with complacency, threatened to rein him in. He was having none of it. Bruno's Amt II/123, far from being a backwater, was in fact located right on top of Nazi Germany's most important internal battle line, responsible for monitoring what was, by 1937, the last source of plausible opposition to Hitler. Unlike Jews and Masons, who were in reality powerless, and whose threat to the Nazis was pure delusion, the reluctant right did control a formidable proportion of German infrastructure.

Bruno had spent years inhabiting far-right *völkisch* nationalist circles. He knew these men and their organizations intimately and could spot conservative dissidence from a mile away. Bruno's father had steeped him in their ways of thinking, having been a long-term sympathizer with a number of veterans' groups.[34] He therefore had little trouble getting his feet under his new SD desk, one of a team of specialists dedicated to protecting the integrity of Hitler's authority, backed up by the awesome power of the SS. For the first time in his life, this must have offered Bruno a taste of real power. All those men on the right wing, the patricians, the senior officers, Germany's upper class, were now accountable to a small team of intelligence officers, which included Bruno the thirty-one-year-old dentist and long-term Party member. Any grandee deluded enough to entertain misgivings about Nazi policy now had to run the gauntlet of the SD, in the shape of men like Bruno (or Klaus Barbie, future head of the

Gestapo in wartime France, recruited to Amt II/123 at the same time as him, though not to the same Berlin office). Bruno had won the trust of the most powerful men in the Reich and was now acting in their name.

Joining the SD represented the high point of Bruno's Nazi activism; what had begun hot, violent, physical, and indiscriminate had turned into something very different: cool, objective, rational, and hard. These were the watchwords for the new generation of Nazi functionaries to which Bruno now belonged.[35] Like him, they had matured in their application of violence. Early Nazis had distinguished "fist" from "head"; they had always maintained (disingenuously) that violence and politics were separate things. This was no longer true. For the SS, and especially the SD, violence had been sublimated into the quiet but deadly discipline of the bureaucrat. Too important to be left with the thugs, calculated violence informed the Nazi state at its highest levels.[36]

The SD, alongside the Gestapo, represented Himmler's security apparatus in its most concentrated form, locked in a battle to the death with its opposition, real or imagined, while at the same time endlessly defining and refining its own key values. On one side, there were men like Bruno, scanning their index cards and writing up their dossiers; on the other, a judicial system that included policemen, courts, prisons, and camps, working in deadly coalition with one another.

And yet the university-educated "thinkers" who surrounded Bruno in the SD liked to project the image that they were more than just entitled henchmen. They went about their work with a particular kind of intellectual arrogance, still clearly legible in surviving SD documents, whose preferred style was less that of the departmental memo than that of the university thesis. From liberalism to Freemasonry, from capitalism to British parliamentary democracy, there was no belief system they didn't address head-on, or whose apparent inconsistencies and absurdities they didn't relish pointing up.

And if that all felt too negative, there was a third role Bruno and his SD colleagues created for themselves: that of bearers of Nazism's "good news," disseminating the idea that National Socialism wasn't just a type of politics, but a view of the world capable of illuminating the human condition, just as Catholicism or humanism purported to do. Bruno's Amt II did this with the creation and publication of copious courses, book lists, indeed, entire syllabuses, designed to enlighten the would-be Nazi intellectual about the values that underpinned the movement. Bruno's daily reading now comprised not just the outpourings of outlawed or suspect groups, but a National Socialist literature, embracing both theory and fiction. The Berlin Document Center has dozens of SD lists and invoices, whose titles give a clear flavor of the kind of intellectual environment Heydrich's security service had aspired to become. One such lists the following:

Die geistigen Grundlagen der engl. Weltmachtpolitik (The Spiritual Foundations of English World Power Politics)

Dieser Krieg ist ein Weltanschaulicher Krieg (This War Is a War of Worldviews)

Der Weg zum Reich (The Road to the Reich)

Der Dollar rollt (The Dollar Rolls)

SS-Mann u. Blutsfrage (The SS Man and the Question of Blood)

Die Sowjetunion—Raum u. Völker (The Soviet Union—
  Land and Peoples)
Der Weg der NSDAP (The Way of the NSDAP)
Rassenpolitik (Race Politics)
Bauerntum (Farmers and Farming)
Sicherung Europas (Europe's Security)

While going through a selection of these, I came across an example of the SS in full cultural arbiter mode. On October 26,
1937, a few weeks after Bruno's formal induction into the SD,
Himmler circulated a memo announcing, *"Jedes Jahr nimmt die
SS an der Woche des Deutschen Buches teil"*—"Every year the SS
takes part in National German Book Week." That year was no
exception; the SS was even going to donate all the books bought
for this august event to the BDM (Union of German Women).
This is National Socialism masquerading as the pinnacle of com-
parative European literature, with roots deep in the Western
imagination.

There was even a list of *geeigniter Bücher* (suitable books),
those Nazi-friendly works that any self-respecting SD intellectual would have to read. At the top, Adolf Hitler's *Mein Kampf*,
followed by works of Alfred Rosenberg (*The Myth of the Twentieth
Century*) and Reinhard Heydrich (*Changes in Our Struggle*)—the
two leading ideologues second only to Hitler himself. Himmler
was modest enough to bury his own offering way down at the
end of the list: *The SS as Anti-Bolshevik Fighting Organization.*
One Hans F. K. Günther contributes the next few titles: *The Race
Health of the German People; The Rider, Death, and the Devil;
Nobility and Race;* and *Urbanization.* After that, it's a canter
through the works of Walther Darré (*Peasantry as the Life*

Source of the Nordic Race and *The New Nobility from Blood and Soil*, before a run of northern twilight novels, by contemporary northern European writers, with evocative titles such as *The Werewolf, The Book of Truth, The Men, Between White and Red, Under the Oaks,* and *Eternally Sing the Woods, The Child of the Peat Cutter,* and John Retcliffe's infamously anti-Semitic tract "At the Jewish Cemetery in Prague." Their Celtic/Nordic melancholy resonated with Nazi sensibilities, turning its back on a contemporary world scarred by slums, technology, and decadence in favor of landscape, instinct, and the primeval.

But the one that jumped off the page at me was number twenty-three on the list: Gunn, Neil M., *Das verlorene Leben*, a title that translates as "The Life Lost."[37] Even more extraordinarily, here was another connection with my Scottish grandfather, Donald Davidson, who had counted Gunn as one of his closest friends and who had been a frequent visitor to the family home in Dingwall. Gunn's novel bitterly laments an episode in eighteenth-century Scottish history that saw a generation of Highland tenant farmers evicted from the land to make way for more profitable sheep farming, and forced either to emigrate or to eke out a pitiful living on the inhospitable Scottish coastline.

Many of Neil Gunn's novels do indeed have a semi-mystical glow to them, finding wistful profundity among Highland folk, especially farmers and fishermen, whose stoic insight borders on some kind of sixth sense. The *Reichsführer* SS was clearly impressed enough by the drama of instinct and race he felt was being played out at the heart of the novel to recommend it as a good, morally consoling read for his fellow SS officers. From the vantage point of seventy years later, I found myself confronted with the spectacle of my two grandfathers communing unbeknownst to each other, via the same author, but divided by the widest chasm of comprehension possible to conceive. Donald Davidson was reading a book written by his close friend as a deeply affecting parable of the hardships of highland life, a part of the world he knew well. Bruno meanwhile, was reading an allegory of the suffering and nobility of the Nordic race community, locked in a life-and-death struggle with the Judaized "asphalt" modern age.

Of course, for all its veneer of "objectivity," the SD was hardly typical of the rest of Hitler's Germany. The book lists, the lectures, the affected scholarly prose, none of it deflected from what Nazism really was—a movement predicated on violence and murderous race hate. Bruno's move from the SA to the SD may have epitomized a desire by the Third Reich to substitute intellectual analysis for bloodlust, but the visceral brutality of its early years could still be relied upon to erupt in time-honored Nazi fashion, no matter how many "desks" the SD operated or university-educated jurists it employed. Men like Bruno straddled both worlds and felt entirely at home in either. He may have had a brand-new uniform to wear, and more select company to work with, but his storm trooper instincts were still intact.

On the night of November 9, 1938, Germany's Nazi pubs were full of carousing SA men, Party members, and their civilian supporters, toasting the anniversary of the failed Beer Hall Putsch, now one of the high points of the Nazi calendar. On this particular night, they had more on their minds than just the usual desire to get roaring drunk. They were reeling from the news that a German consular official, Ernst vom Rath, had been shot by a seventeen-year-old Polish Jew in Paris. Nazis all over Germany were seething with *Judenkoller*, or anti-Jewish rage, when communiqués began pouring out of Party HQ, ordering a nationwide act of vengeance against Germany's Jews.

What followed next came to be known as *Kristallnacht*, the Night of Broken Glass, an explosion of vandalism and arson. Nowhere in Germany saw more violence than Bruno's Charlottenburg district of Berlin, where his old SA comrades were especially active. This part of the city—especially the shopping precincts of the West End around Kurfürstendamm—was home to a large number of Jewish shops and synagogues. It is hard to suppose that Bruno, now an SS officer, hadn't been drinking with his *Kameraden* in his familiar *Sturmlokal*, the Zur Altstadt, or that he later consciously boycotted the night's actions, when so many of those he had known, and had fought with for over a decade, poured out of the pubs, armed with sledgehammers and cans of gasoline. I will never know whether he chose this of all nights to stay at home and break the habit of a lifetime by refraining from participating in the largest outbreak of Nazi anti-Semitism yet to have erupted in Germany—especially one that was mandated by Hitler and Goebbels personally, and which took place right outside his own front door. But with or without Bruno, squads of Charlottenburg SA men, party officials, and civilians out for a night of looting and mayhem rampaged through the streets around the Langbehn home and the shopping heartland of Charlottenburg and neighboring Wilmersdorf, smashing windows and starting fires. Their job was made easier by the legal obligation faced by all Jewish-owned businesses that they display signs announcing the fact. Many were high-end luxury goods shops, which made them ideal targets for not just vandalism but widespread looting.

The first Charlottenburg victim of the night was a piano

shop on Joachimstaler Strasse, off the Kurfürstendamm, a raid that climaxed in having a Bechstein grand dispatched through a second-floor window. The crowd soon moved on to an adjacent perfume shop, Kopp und Joseph, which was demolished and ransacked. They then made short work of a series of larger department stores on Wilmersdorfer Strasse—Etam and Tietz and Suss—all of which had their fronts shattered and their displays and inventories stripped bare. The marauding Nazis then began to operate in a more systematic way, controlling the plunder by posting guards at the smashed-in doorways and preventing riots. A chocolate shop on Bismarckstrasse and a nearby confectioner's were the first to be methodically emptied. The crowd had swollen and included SA men, Party members, and an increasing numbers of civilians and neighbors anxious not to miss out on the bonanza of spoils. Not even residential apartments were safe: soon, Jewish apartments were being opened by building janitors and their contents raided.

It didn't take long for attention to switch to even more conspicuous Jewish establishments—the many synagogues in the area, as well as other Jewish commercial premises. The Fasanenstrasse synagogue (the main Reform synagogue in Berlin) was the first to be raided; cupboards were broken into, prayer books torn up, the organ vandalized. Finally, the synagogue was set on fire. The fire brigade was quick on the scene but did nothing except prevent flames from spreading to adjacent buildings (there was an S-Bahn station next door). The synagogue itself was left to burn. The same thing happened to a second Reform synagogue, on Pestalozzistrasse. The Kantstrasse synagogue was more fortunate: in its main courtyard were some apartments, one of which was home to a senior Party member, who, terrified that his own home would go up in smoke, remonstrated with his SA comrades and persuaded them to direct their destructive energies elsewhere. They chose instead to attack a nearby commercial area on Meinekestrasse, home to a Zionist organization headquarters, a Jewish newspaper, and a Palestine emigration office, which were soon engulfed in flames.

Charlottenburg's last synagogue, on Schulstrasse (Behaimstrasse today), was torched later that night, once again "protected" from the Berlin fire brigade by SA men in attendance. By daylight on November 10, an estimated 7,500 shops across the whole of Germany had been attacked, and 30,000 Jews had been arrested, many sent to camps. It is believed that ninety Jews perished over the two nights, with many hundreds more succumbing in the weeks that followed.

This was Bruno's last experience of street violence. *Kristallnacht* was the climax to a decade's worth of brutality and intimidation. Over the following days, Nazis like him could sit back and congratulate themselves on a good night's work, but they knew it was the last of a kind. Even within Germany itself, the price for all that violence had been anguished disapproval. Typically, this wasn't expressed on behalf of the Jewish victims, but as disgust at the methods employed—and the gift it made to Germany's foreign critics. As one respectable upper-middle-class woman put it:

> Synagogues are set alight, the shops and homes of Jews are
> completely destroyed, we are wreaking worse havoc than
> the Huns, you are ashamed to be German, and the whole

thing is being presented as a spontaneous action, spontaneous in such a rigidly organized country as Germany!! It is a disgrace, and other hostile countries rightly say they don't need to think up any propaganda against us, we ourselves have supplied them with better material than they could ever have come up with on their own.[38]

The Jewish Question demanded a "solution" able to avoid the probing eyes of international enemy powers, and more consistent with Germany's highly cultured self-esteem. From now on, the struggle would continue, but in a more systematic and less anarchic way. *Kristallnacht* had been a rude interruption to the real work now being contemplated by the SS and its subsidiary SD.

By the end of 1939, two years into his new Nazi job, Bruno could look back with considerable satisfaction. His two main areas of interest—the German health service and the activities of the right-wing opposition movements—had been decisively dealt with. This was confirmed in the "Quarterly Situation Report,"[39] compiled by the SD, which took stock of progress made against opponents of National Socialism. The report noted that most right-wing opposition had been effectively forced to look abroad for support. But more gratifying still for Bruno would have been the report's confirmation that, partly as a consequence of the *November Aktion* (aka *Kristallnacht*), legislation had finally "closed" the Jewish Question as far as the medical world was concerned: "that with effect from January 31, 1939, the entire health service was now fully purged of all Jews, including both dentists and pharmacists."

Bruno—and the SD—could turn their attention to new goals: namely, the war of revenge against the Western superpowers that had "won" the First World War only because treachery and sedition had undermined the German home front, and the ethnic struggle against the people that Hitler was convinced were Germany's most threatening racial enemies—the Jews. The German army, or Wehrmacht, would fight the first. The SS would fight the other. Bruno had a part to play in them both.

Eight

WAR!

1939–1944

On April 28, 1939, Bruno and Thusnelda, along with the rest of the German population, were treated to a radio broadcast in which their Führer announced, in full and elaborate detail, all that he had accomplished on their behalf. It was intended as nothing less than an audit of national transformation: "I overcame chaos in Germany," Hitler informed them,

> restored order, enormously raised production in all fields of our national economy. . . . I succeeded in completely resettling in useful production those 7 million unemployed who so touched our hearts. . . . I have not only politically united the German nation but also rearmed it militarily, and I have further tried to liquidate that treaty whose 448 articles contain the vilest rape that . . . human beings have ever expected to submit to. I have restored to the Reich the provinces grabbed from us in 1919; I have led millions of deeply unhappy Germans, who had been snatched from us,

back into the Fatherland; I have restored the thousand-year-old historical unity of German living space; and I have . . . attempted to accomplish all that without shedding blood and without inflicting the sufferings of war on my people or any other. I have accomplished all this . . . as one who twenty-one years ago was still an unknown worker and soldier of my people, by my own efforts.[1]

Not one of the Langbehn or the Pahnke-Lietzner family disagreed with a syllable of this. All of them happily included themselves among the millions of Germans euphorically supporting every one of those statements. Hitler, their great statesman, had outmaneuvered the rest of Europe and done so without provoking war. Unemployment appeared to be a thing of the past; covert rearmament had made a blissful mockery of the Treaty of Versailles, and Germany had begun to loom large on the international stage. Germany without Hitler was simply inconceivable, as Bruno's SD *Reports from the Reich* regularly confirmed, despite the pockets of disaffected grumbling, which not even Goebbels's propaganda could ever entirely silence.

As far as Bruno was concerned, Hitler had assuaged the two great traumas that had undone the Weimar Republic: the humiliation of the First World War and the economic catastrophe of the Great Depression. This was why so many Germans regarded the Führer as a messiah, who had delivered *völkisch* salvation to a nation that had lost its way.[2]

And Hitler had delivered not only at home. Who could have predicted his *international* triumphs, all achieved without apparent bloodshed (the victims of *Kristallnacht*, SS repression, or Nazi Germany's racial cleansing laws didn't count). The Rhineland had been remilitarized in direct contravention of the League of Nations; most gloriously of all, in March 1938, Austria had been incorporated back into the fold in the *Anschluss*, an act that was half forceful takeover, half gleeful surrender. This was followed in September by the "Germanization" of the Sudetenland, a brilliantly organized usurping of the eastern fringes of Czechoslovakia, using the grievances of its ethnic Germans (not altogether made-up) as pretext and culminating with Hitler's running rings round Neville Chamberlain in Munich.

All these events had come close to triggering war, but on each occasion Hitler had dodged open conflict, thanks to his brinksmanship, cunning, and mesmerizing ability to make others give him what he wanted—backed up by the intimidating strength of his fast-expanding army and his apparent willingness to use it. This was a campaign waged in top hats, with diplomatic standoffs, international summits, and foreign appeasement. As a result, fear of German militarism was at an all-time high. This first round of aggressive German expansion had resulted in millions of *Volksgenossen*, or race comrades, being triumphantly reunited with the larger *Volksgemeinschaft*.[3] The German nation was on the move again, seemingly without the horrors of 1914–1918, whose baleful legacy still haunted the memories of millions of older Germans unable to forget their time in the trenches.

Hitler was happy to bask in his people's exaltation of him, to pose as their "dictator of peace"—but not forever. He started to drop dark hints: peace was fine, but it was only a hiatus; there *would* be war at some point. "For years circumstances have compelled me to talk about almost nothing but peace. . . . [But] it is obvious that peace propaganda . . . can [lead to] a spirit of defeatism which in the long run would inevitably undermine the success of the present regime. . . . It is now necessary gradually to re-educate the German people that there are things which must be achieved by force if peaceful means fail."[4]

Hitler worried that the Germans might start to grow *too* comfortable with all this avoidance of war; they had even coined a phrase for their recent sequence of victories without conflict—"flower wars," in which the only missiles thrown were garlands and bouquets. For many, the idea that German greatness could be won without paying a price was deeply seductive, but Hitler was anxious not to encourage it too much. "One day," he warned them, the "German question" would require a more forthright solution:

> I have taken it upon myself to solve the German . . . problem of space. Be aware then, so long as I live, this thought will dominate my entire existence. Be convinced further that I . . . would never shrink from the most extreme measures, because I am convinced that this question must be settled one way or the other.

Despite the speech's vagueness, these "extreme measures" clearly included war. No nation ever won its *Lebensraum* without fighting for it. The world's resources were limited. Its peoples were racially stratified, and they owed one another nothing. International relations were underpinned by mutual suspicion and deadly competitiveness. The price for *not* fighting a war was the same as for losing one: degradation, humiliation, impotence. The Depression had proved to Hitler that the global economy *was* war, in all but name.

For Bruno and other committed Nazis who shared Hitler's

ambitions, war was the purest expression of Nazi ideology. A battle-ready nation was a nation at its strongest. But war also represented the pinnacle of *Weltpolitik*. Nothing could achieve the kind of power the Nazis wanted as quickly or as decisively as conquest and military domination, and it was time that the German people got used to the idea. That especially included the army. Hitler had directed almost the entire German economy toward reequipping his armed forces, run the gauntlet of international dismay on their behalf, and swept aside all their internal enemies, both within the SA and among the wider population. It was time for the Wehrmacht to repay this act of faith and fulfill the role Hitler had planned for it.

Redeeming Germany, as Hitler conceived it, was an act so enormous in its implications that, once unleashed, it would radiate far beyond Germany's borders and engulf the whole of Europe. Perhaps there were still people in Paris or London who prayed war could be avoided by negotiation and appeasement, but I doubt there were many in the SS who thought so. Hitler had invested all his hopes in the armed forces, created a security apparatus with complete dominion over the German people, and preached his unsparing and extreme racial ideology. Nobody could seriously doubt where all this was leading, least of all a man as well placed as Bruno. By 1939 he knew that the only questions were *whom* that war would be fought against, and *when*.

What had become Poland, with its corridors dividing German from German,[5] had been a geographical affront to the greater Reich ever since the days of the First World War, when Germany had overrun so much of it. The largest of Germany's Slavic neighbors offered Hitler the key to future dreams of *Lebensraum* in the east. For Bruno it had been an exhilarating and nerve-racking spectacle watching Hitler maneuver Germany to the brink of war. But even the Führer had to steel himself before stepping off the precipice.

The ground had to be laid with two diplomatic coups, not with his enemies, but with his allies. First, Germany signed a treaty with Mussolini's Italy, in order to protect the Reich's southern flank. Then, astonishingly, Hitler concluded a treaty of non-aggression to secure the eastern front with the one government that figured most prominently in Nazi demonology (which it reciprocated in full)—Stalin's Soviet Union. This was known as the Molotov-Ribbentrop Pact, named after the two foreign ministers who helped orchestrate it. I have no idea how Bruno and his comrades managed to accommodate this extraordinary about-face, whether they understood the brazen cynicism that underpinned it or were forced to conceal their bewilderment. Either way, with these obstacles removed, the path to war had been cleared.

The SD's job was to provide the ruse that would finally trigger war. This they duly did by staging a "Polish" attack on a German border radio station, the so-called Gleiwitz incident, which was used to "justify" full-scale retaliation. On the night of August 31, 1939, SD agents, dressed in Polish uniform, seized the radio station, from which they transmitted anti-German messages in Polish. The body of a well-known Polish sympathizer was left at the site, designed to create the impression that a fierce gun battle had taken place. It was a charade intended to make Germany appear the victim of unforgivable provocation. Sure enough, triggered by this "national insult," the invasion of Poland, code-named Operation White, was launched on September 1. Hitler had at last let loose his bid to create the German empire, not around a conference table, but with the world's latest and most fearsome tanks, infantry, and bombers. The Allies swore that any invasion of Poland would be tantamount to a declaration of war. This time it wasn't a bluff. Western appeasement had run dry, and within days Germany was again at war with Britain and France.

The years of standoffs, feints, and endless saber rattling were over. Bruno and thousands like him were about to get the military adventure they had so keenly anticipated. A few weeks later, Bruno enlisted in the army. With the weight of memories bearing down on him, of his own father heading off to war back in 1917, nothing was going to stop him from joining up now that he had a war of his own: not the prospect of prolonged absence from home, not having to suspend his work for the SS, or even the loss of dental income. Active service constituted a natural culmination of a life spent openly admiring all things military. It was the biggest test with which to measure himself, not just against heroic earlier generations, but against his own Nazi rhetoric.

For the next six years the war dominated Bruno's life, as it did the lives of tens of millions of others across Germany, Europe, and eventually the entire globe. Bruno's whole family would play a part in it, some as active protagonists and others as hapless bystanders. But for all his military ardor, Bruno had to confront several uncomfortable truths. He was now thirty-three years old, not yet an old man, but hardly in the first flush of youth. And, whatever his SA pretensions, he had very little in the way of formal military training.

He found himself attached to a flak unit based just outside Berlin, though whether this was specifically an antiaircraft battery or a more orthodox artillery unit, it is hard to say. Either way, it sounded like the kind of role that best suited the belligerent but older recruit: satisfyingly close to the business end of a gun, but with the real challenge of frontline warfare left to those who were younger and better qualified. I never managed to find out what his Wehrmacht rank was because it's not mentioned in any of the documents. But I would be surprised if it was as a commissioned officer, given his lack of military experience and the modest nature of his posting. It was unusual, however, for an SS officer to find himself attached not to the Waffen SS, but to the ordinary army.

I have to admit that this surprised me. The picture of my grandfather that had emerged from the documents—of a long-term, rather ruthless ideologue—seemed contradicted by this apparent willingness to serve in so humble, one might even say peripheral, capacity. I began to wonder if his keen desire to go to fight, and his willingness to do so in whatever lowly form he was offered, proved that his memories of the First World War, whose aftermath had evidently so politicized him, were just as powerful as his more recent dealings with the SS. Was Bruno indulging in the same fantasy as the First World War poet Rupert Brooke had done twenty-five years earlier, thanking God, "Who has matched us with His hour, / And caught our youth, and wakened us from sleeping"? Bruno wasn't the only German who dreamed that combat would be a redemptive mix of the galvanizing and the purifying.[6] What mattered to him was that he was on his way west, toward France, and the giddy horizons of the new German empire. At last he could *live* the Ernst Jünger fantasy, *become* a Steel Helmet, and not have to make do reading about it.

In these early days of the war, my grandfather, great-grandfather, and great-uncle epitomized very different forms of the German soldier. Bruno, a veteran of years of street fighting, now had his chance to prove he could manage the real thing. But not even he could compete with his father-in-law, Friedrich, the poised and professional engineering graduate, veteran of the First World War, and epitome of a new generation of Prussian officers. He had been promoted as a *Stabsoffizier*, a staff officer, attached to army HQ, where he was responsible for weapons procurement, at the rank of captain, and subsequently major. Like the rest of the Wehrmacht (as the Reichswehr was renamed in 1935), he had taken a personal oath of loyalty to Hitler himself. He fought his war from a desk in Paris, dispatching memos and requisitions with patrician efficiency.

What a very different figure he cut compared with my great-uncle Ewald. I never met him, but I was very familiar with the way the rest of the family so tersely belittled him. He was my grandmother's hapless brother, of whom so much had been expected, and who had, I gathered, achieved so little. Any mention of his name was always met with that particular kind of dismissive contempt that the German language is so good at expressing. Unlike his stepfather, or indeed his brother-in-law, he never made it beyond the rank of private, as anonymous and scrappy as he appears in the only picture of him to have survived, with his loose-fitting tunic, breast pockets filled with cigarettes, and an expression of resigned passivity. Nobody was looking to this man, or the millions like him, to help shape anything. His role was to get moved from one outhouse-dotted field to another. Frowning and forlorn photos like this were the only things that commemorated these men. There is no fire burning in his eyes, no distant horizon beckoning for the wretched infantry who provide the ballast to all great armies.

By the spring of 1940, however, all three of them were in Wehrmacht uniform, and on their way west. Whatever fears they might have had that this war would follow the nightmarish trajectory of the first were rapidly and decisively dispelled. German successes were extraordinary. Bruno, Friedrich, and Ewald were all, in their different ways, participating in the German army's new and devastatingly effective battle tactic, blitzkrieg, whose spectacular speed and success ensured that there would be no repetition of the trench-bound stagnation of 1914–1918.

With every major advance, Bruno's unit broke out the beer and the accordions and sang and drank themselves into a euphoric stupor. My mother vividly recalls his penchant for the marching songs that were so loud a part of German victories. He later boasted to my father that those first few months of the war he had done a *lot* of singing and drinking. Review the calendar of Germany's early triumphs, and it's easy to see why: On April 9, 1940, Denmark and Norway were attacked; the Danes surrendered the next day, the Norwegians in early June; the western offensive began on May 10; the Netherlands, Belgium, Luxembourg were first in line; the Netherlands capitulated on May 15, Belgium on May 28. I wonder what his father, Max, nursing his First World War memories of Regiment 39 in France and the Low Countries, made of it. Did he greet the news of the stunning advances with jubilation or foreboding?

To set the right mood for the imminent assault on France, Germany's oldest enemy, Hitler ordered that "from today throughout the whole of Germany the flags shall be flown for a period of eight days. This is to be a salute for our soldiers. I further order the ringing of bells for a period of three days. Their sound may unite with the prayers with which the German nation will once again accompany her sons from this day forward."[7] They were in Paris on June 14. A mere six weeks after the campaign had begun, France was forced to sign an armistice on June 22, in the very same railway carriage at Compiègne used in 1918 by the Allies.

This was the war of Nazi expansion intended to requite the disgrace of 1918, the fountainhead of all subsequent German woe. This time it would be France and Britain's turn to feel the sting of humiliation and defeat, as Germany had twenty years before. The Treaty of Versailles and endless French incursions into the Ruhr Valley had been not just avenged but trampled into the mud.

> That under Hitler's leadership Germany should reduce France, on which in the First World War she had broken her teeth for four years, in a mere six weeks confirmed once more . . . Hitler's reputation as a miracle worker and this time also as a military genius. In the eyes of his admirers, after all his domestic and foreign policy successes he became, in 1940, also the "greatest general of all time."[8]

The rapid and easy military victory over France was offered to the German people as Hitler's greatest gift to them. The resulting Führer cult went off the scale.

The ecstatic German population spent the summer of 1940 indulging in the joy of their early victories. Bruno, Friedrich, and Ewald were riding the crest of German successes: Bruno with his artillery unit, Friedrich at his desk at army HQ, and Ewald on a dispatch-rider motorbike (a role he occupied right through the war). But one day in late spring, the war bit back. Bruno had already found adapting to the stresses of military life physically challenging, having succumbed to a crippling bout of sciatica earlier in the year. This hadn't boded very well. He hadn't even made it to the front yet, and he was already struggling. Worse was to follow.

Bruno once described to me a little of what happened next. An accident, he told me, that had saved his life. He had been on a horse, which bolted during a fierce exchange with the French army, and then thrown him violently against a wall. Although the Germans comprehensively routed the French army in 1940, they still suffered more than 50,000 casualties—and Bruno had clearly come close to being one of them. He was now *hors de combat*, badly hurt, but still alive. He had sustained some serious injuries to his left arm—his wrist was smashed, rendering his hand virtually useless. His wrist was never properly fixed and would remain visibly misaligned for the rest of his life. He later boasted that this had been a small price to pay to escape being killed. He was stretchered off and transported back to Berlin. It wouldn't be his last happy accident.

What a huge anticlimax it must have been at the time. He had spent his whole life fixated on the prospect of overturning the ignominies of the First World War, but instead was undone by something as unheroic as a nervous horse, hardly the stuff of Iron Crosses, even if his injuries were bad enough to require two months' convalescence in the Lichterfelde SS Hospital back in Berlin.

At least it gave him the chance to join the vast crowds that gathered in central Berlin on July 6 to cheer their mighty, victory-laden Führer, on the latest of his great victory parades. Berliners carpeted Hitler's route from the station to the Chancellery with thousands of bouquets of flowers, and even those who had been lukewarm screamed themselves hoarse. As Bruno's own SD testified, "Admiration for the achievements of the German troops is boundless, and is now felt even by people who retained a certain distance and skepticism at the beginning of the campaign." A second SD report asserted that the entry into Paris "caused enthusiasm amongst the population in all parts of the Reich to a degree that has not so far been seen. There were loud demonstrations of joy and emotional scenes of enthusiasm in many town squares and streets."[9]

For American journalist William Shirer, a witness to the celebrations, the spectacle was altogether more horrifying:

> Looking at them, I wondered if any of them understood what was going on in Europe, if they had an inkling that their joy, that this victorious parade of the goose-steppers, was based on a great tragedy for millions of others whom these troops and the leaders of these people had enslaved. Not one in a thousand, I wager, gave the matter a thought.[10]

Goebbels certainly didn't; for him the defeat of France had wiped away the last vestiges of German paralysis and helplessness. "One feels newly born," with the shame of Versailles "amortized." A brave future beckoned: "Nationalist Europe is on the march, while the liberal world is on the verge of collapse."

This left just Britain. But after the debacle of Dunkirk, in which the British army had been forced to abandon the great majority of its most valuable equipment and scramble home on a flotilla of hastily assembled ships, all that was required, surely, was a coup de grâce to be delivered by the Luftwaffe. It was a foregone conclusion. Even though many of Britain's troops had managed to slip away, nobody could seriously think they would be back on the Continent anytime soon. The British may not have been defeated, but they were out of the war, or may as well have been. There were plans for an invasion; perhaps it would go ahead, perhaps it wouldn't. Either way, Hitler would decide in good time.

The Langbehns and Pahnke-Lietzners couldn't have been better placed to savor the pleasures of victory. Stabsoffizier Friedrich Pahnke was by now safely ensconced in Paris; Bruno was back in Berlin. London cowered under its barrage balloons, wondering what next. In a matter of months, the *Volk* had been catapulted from First World War losers to masters of all of northern Europe. It was a staggering reversal.

The wine flowed, as did the food. For Friedrich, there was also the self-satisfaction that was available to all conquering heroes. The Germans in Paris may have had to run the gauntlet of sullen French faces, but nothing could diminish the exhilaration caused by their stupendous victories. If that didn't work, there were thousands of Parisian prostitutes on hand to help them grow accustomed to their new position as rulers of France.

As promised, this war was turning out to be very good for German civilians, as well as for those in uniform. The "fruits of tyranny" now flowed into Berlin by the trainload. The rest of the Langbehn family got its chance to indulge in them too. "The illusion of prosperity and peace in Berlin was fueled by the spoils of war. . . . By the summer, Berlin was awash with beautiful clothes, food, perfumes, and luxuries of all kinds. Enormous crates arrived filled with furniture and porcelain, shoes and boots and fine woolens, silk stockings and underwear, paintings and *objets d'art*. German shops . . . now sold French champagne. . . .

The mood of the city was reminiscent of the best days of the Golden Twenties, and few stopped to think that they were still at war."[11]

Ida's formidable collection of Turkish and Persian rugs, so large that many of them had to be hung on the walls of her postwar flat, originated from those Friedrich managed to send back from Paris. They were acquired no doubt at extremely favorable prices from dealers only too anxious not to offend or alienate their new overlords. Whatever the source of the carpets, Friedrich had an eye for quality and sent back dozens. Similarly, Bruno's lifelong love for Courvoisier and Rémy Martin dated back to this auspicious moment, when "imported" French spirits started arriving in the city's bars and restaurants by the crate-load.

More important, all this largesse vindicated why Germany had gone to war in the first place. Once added to the dairy produce and meat arriving from Norway and Denmark, and the high-quality engineering arriving from the factories of Czechoslovakia, this was booty that crucially boosted the Third Reich's otherwise unsustainable economy. Incapable of enriching its own citizens, as befitted Europe's master race, *and* servicing an overheating rearmament program, Germany had no option but to exhaust its vanquished neighbors' resources. The German economy had been geared for war, but one that could pay for itself only with an empire of plunder: "If we win, the billions we have spent will weigh nothing in the scales."[12]

Bruno, however, was wrestling with a rather more uncomfortable legacy of his short stint in the war, in the form of his severely damaged left arm, whose shattered wrist was a disaster for his dental practice. There was no way he could go on working, at least for the time being. He would have to give up his practice.

For Bruno, it was a small sacrifice. There were far bigger challenges to preoccupy him than the treatment of individual patients. Temporarily assigned to the army, he had astutely put his prewar jobs on hold[13]—posts that he quickly resumed as soon as it was clear his days as a frontline artillery soldier were over. Even more significant, of course, he was again available to serve with the SS.

In spring 1940, he wrote to the SS personnel department, informing of his new circumstances and his decision to close his practice: "SS Lt. Bruno Langbehn has given up his self-employed occupation as a dentist, with effect 31.5.1940 [May 31] and from 1.6.1940 [June 1], is primarily employed as Regional Administrative Team Leader of the Reich Guild of German Dentists." Part of this was no doubt motivated by the impact of his injured wrist, but he was a man anxious to busy himself with things of greater consequence than fillings and toothaches.

Bruno's employment was good news for the SS, too, because it meant they could carry on not paying him, always a priority for the cash-starved Heydrich. Bruno had proved himself more than capable in the three years he had been an SS officer attached to the Berlin regional office, monitoring the troublesome right wing. He was transferred from the local office behind Alexanderplatz (SD Leitabschnitt), to main headquarters in the infamous Prinz-Albrecht-Strasse, the center of Himmler and Heydrich's terror network, as part of the new Berlin *Inspekteur*, responsible for intelligence operations within the capital. He was soon busy, as before, monitoring the public mood; this was considered a particularly important task during these early stages of a war that had made so many Germans deeply apprehensive. Hitler never lost sight of how the masses, screaming in adulation one moment, could be utterly fickle the next. It was the responsibility of SD officers like Bruno to ensure this never happened.

By 1940, the SD was unrecognizably bigger and more imposing than the organization that Bruno had joined back in 1937. No longer just the SD Hauptamt, it had become the altogether more substantial RSHA, or Reich Main Security Office, under whose enormous new umbrella Himmler and Heydrich had amalgamated every wing of the Nazi police state. It had grown into a sprawling intelligence superstructure, combining both the SD and the Gestapo (among others), and was divided into seven main departments, not just the old three. Wartime conditions had given the SD's role as guardians of national security ever greater imperative. Any lingering peacetime inhibitions about the SS's dictatorial powers, or its assault on civil liberties, had been long crushed by the priorities of fighting a war. Their vastly increased sphere of activity far outside Germany itself gave them the additional advantage of operating well away from the prying eyes of the domestic population.

A network of SD premises in Berlin—including Eichmann's Jewish Office on Kurfürstenstrasse, and the building that had once housed Bruno's SA Honor Court, on Tiergarten—began to organize and execute a very different kind of Nazi policy. Each used the war as a pretext for intensifying and accelerating its particular "special projects." The outbreak of war gave T4 officials the ideal opportunity to step up their program of "mercy" killing, no longer just quarantining the mentally handicapped or those (allegedly) suffering hereditary diseases, but deliberately killing thousands of them, by lethal injection or with gas, in various institutions, first in Germany, and later in occupied Poland.

The power of the SS, and the SD within it, was about to expand still further. Till now, the army had managed to curb their encroaching influence, especially in the newly conquered countries, where they ensured SS numbers remained low, and their access to key decisions was denied. But that was the war in the west. There was a new war brooding in Hitler's mind, in which the role of the SS would be altogether more significant.

After his lightning victories in the summer of 1940, the bombing of British cities during the Blitz of 1940 and 1941, and even his Balkans campaign that bailed out Mussolini after the failed invasion of Greece, Hitler was worried that he still hadn't fought *the* Nazi war of his dreams. It was time to fight a campaign that no longer relied on mere calculation or diplomatic brinksmanship, but was motivated entirely by ideology and the vision of a landmass empire on which the Nazis could graft a biologically purified German superstate. It was time to look to the east, in what for centuries the Germans had referred to as the *Drang nach Osten*.

In July 1940, barely a month after Hitler's triumph over the French, "the greatest general of all time" had commissioned plans for the third, and largest, of his military dreams, the total racial war outlined with chilling hubris in so many of his earlier speeches. Its target was everything to the east of Poland, most notably the Soviet Union. The two wars he had fought and won, the war of diplomacy and the war of revenge for 1914–1918, would segue into the war for *Lebensraum*, with its forced resettlement of entire populations and mass murder of biologically identified subhumans. This was the war that would be the making of the SS— and of Bruno's part within it.

Just a month before that picture of Bruno and the family was taken, in July 1941, the Germans had embarked on an assault that embodied the terrifying conviction of National Socialism more completely than any other; Operation Barbarossa—the invasion of the Soviet Union, whose totality and ferocity would eventually surpass even those directed against France and Britain. Bruno was right to look grim in his family photograph. This invasion dwarfed all that had preceded it and it would dictate the outcome of the war.

From the outset, this was no ordinary conflict. Three million German troops lined the border waiting to pour into the Soviet Union. It was different, too, in how it would be fought, a war not just between old rival nation-states, but between global superpowers and the ideologies that sustained them, a racial war between the two peoples that dominated the Eurasian landmass, the Germanic Teutons and Asiatic Russians. The stakes were immeasurably higher than those in the west European campaign. This wasn't about revenge for the humiliations of the First World War or a dominant position at the heart of the Continent; it was Nazism's war, not just Germany's, and it would be to the death. From the smoking ruins of an obliterated Soviet Union would rise the Nazi utopia that Hitler could see so clearly. It was a two-pronged campaign: first military, then cultural.

The Wehrmacht would conquer the Soviet Union, but the SS would Nazify it. The Soviet Union would become a racial laboratory where the SS would show the world what National Socialism really stood for, in a way they had not been able to in France, Scandinavia, or the Netherlands. The war in the east would be not only Hitler's "moment of destiny"[14] but that of every Nazi, especially those who, like Bruno, had lived this dream their entire adult lives.

They justified this to themselves by whom they thought they were fighting. The Russians were the essence of everything that was most un-German in a racially defined world. The Red Army was the outer shell beneath which lurked the *real* enemy—the "Jewish Bolshevik," a deadly conflation of the three most hated figures in the National Socialist worldview: the Jew, the Marxist, and the Slav.

Hitler spelled it out very explicitly for his troops:

> The war against Russia is an important chapter in the struggle for existence of the German nation. It is the old battle of the Germanic peoples against the Slavic peoples, of the defense of European culture against Moscovite-Asiatic inundation, and the repelling of Jewish Bolshevism. . . . Every military action must be guided in planning and execution by an iron will to exterminate the enemy mercilessly and totally. . . . No adherents of the present Russian-Bolshevik system are to be spared.[15]

Hitler had no intention of turning Warsaw, Minsk, Kiev, Leningrad, or finally Moscow into a version of Amsterdam, Copenhagen, or Paris. The endgame was not amnesty, or even just defeat; it was annihilation.[16]

The SD would play a crucial role, first conceiving, and then putting into practice, the attitudes and the wherewithal required for the task at hand. Hitler could remain undecided about what, finally, to do with Britain; he could even live with the reality of France in a state of divided collusion. None of this was incompatible with his National Socialist obsessions. Not so with the east. As in Poland, it was a matter of erasing the elites: the notorious Commissar's Order of June 6, 1941, culminates with: "High-ranking political leaders are to be removed. The goal: 'The Germanization of the east by the introduction of Germans and the original inhabitants to be treated like Red Indians.'"[17]

The invasion, launched on June 22, 1941, appeared, at least initially, to be a repeat of earlier campaigns, a return to tried and tested methods, only writ infinitely larger. The priorities were speed and obliteration, blasting a path toward Moscow and overwhelming the Red Army, which blocked the way. Ethnically and ideologically, the Soviets may have been considered Nazism's most dangerous enemy, but politically they were regarded with contempt. After Stalin's purges had decimated the Red Army leadership, Hitler's generals considered it a house of cards ready to come tumbling down with one swift push. The Germans had been terrified that the war against France would degenerate into murderous stalemate—but it was over in a month and a half. The Soviet Union was confidently predicted to be the exact opposite, a campaign that would be over not even by Christmas, but by late autumn.

For the time being, Bruno had to make do with watching it all from the sidelines, ensconced in his SD and dental roles. But he could take consolation from the fact that at least Berlin was booming, as yet physically unscathed by the war. The gap between the eastern and the home front could hardly have been wider, despite the occasional air raid. For those, like the Langbehn family, who so eagerly supported the regime, life was very sweet. Bruno's job, and his SS rank, gave the family enviable kudos. For the girls, now at primary school, these were halcyon days, taken up with their favorite treats: visits to the Berlin Zoo (whose world-famous aquarium was a particular favorite), ice creams from the cafés on the Kurfürstendamm, swimming trips to the spectacular Olympic Stadium pool to the far west of the city, and outings on rowboats and paddleboats on the River Havel. They had no idea what job their father did, but they easily recognized the glamour of his black-and-silver SS tunic. For their mother and grandmother, nothing was more pleasurable than putting on their fur stoles and promenading the busy thoroughfares of the bustling capital. There was still coffee and cake and, for the time being, whipped cream to garnish them with.

I got a sense of this charmed life from an unlikely source. My cousin had been given a document, which he had passed on to me; it was a page from the 1942 Berlin telephone directory that offered a fascinating snapshot of everyday life at the heart of the Reich during these early stages of the war. There, sure enough, was Bruno:

Langbehn Bruno, Landesdienststellenleit, Chlb 1,
Berliner Str 86/87 34 25 00

The document's sheer ordinariness made it oddly compelling. By their very nature, phone books are as utilitarian as is possible for books to be. And yet how much information they contain. Bruno's entry shares the same elements as all the others—name, job title, area he lived in (Charlottenburg), address, and phone number. What is so striking reading the page is how pristine, modern, and untouched by war Berlin appears to be. A crisp list of names, addresses, and telephone numbers depicts a city completely at odds with the later burned-out husk destroyed by three years of bombing and Russian artillery shells.

The sheer range of professions on display across both pages presents a picture of Berlin that is both undamaged and resilient. There are publishing companies, casinos, agricultural institutes, and also a large number of single women with addresses and phone numbers of their own. There is a profusion of civilian jobs on display: "lawyer" (*lots* of those), "engineer," "doctor," "music publishers," "towel and linen purveyors," "car salesman," "university lecturer," and—my favorite—"bespoke shoemaker." Perhaps this isn't surprising: their six-digit numbers suggest that telephones were still relatively rare, so you would expect them to be owned by the professional middle classes. But the page yields another, darker clue about life in Nazi Berlin in 1941–1942.

There is only one (obviously) Jewish name I can see on a page containing two hundred entries: "Landsberger Kurt Israel, Dr. Med." I know that it's Jewish because, although "Landsberger" is ethnically vague, "Israel" is not. This was the name he would have been forced to include (alongside "Sarah" for Jewish women) precisely to remove the "camouflage" of his generic surname. As late as 1941, and even into 1942, it was still technically possible to be Jewish and have an entry in the Berlin phone book. But how on earth had Dr. Landsberger managed to survive so conspicuously for so long, here openly advertising his Jewish background and his address and phone number? Was it courageous obstinacy or terrifying shortsightedness? And what possible chance was there that his name appeared in the 1943 edition? Had Bruno, too, noticed this name, separated by just two columns from his own?

In fact, Dr. Landsberger's days really were numbered. Hardened Nazis were daily growing more incensed that Berlin was still home to a number of German Jews. Since the boycotts of 1933, the Nuremberg Laws of 1935, and the fire and destruction of *Kristallnacht* in 1938, the Nazis had targeted Germany's Jews with every type of persecution they could think of. Bruno had played a role in this, too, and not simply with his rowdy ex-SA comrades from Sturm 33.

A key part of his role as *Landesdienststellenleiter* in charge of Berlin's dentists was to list and keep tabs on any Jew still practicing in Berlin. In 1938, a few had been granted permission to carry on treating patients, but only Jewish ones. By 1942, even that was regarded as intolerable. Why were these Jews even living in Berlin *at all*, screamed the Nazi press. Especially now that bombing raids were becoming more frequent, which meant replacement apartments were needed for Aryan families whose homes had been destroyed. On top of that, Hitler had commissioned Albert Speer to start work on rebuilding Berlin as "Germania," a gargantuan project that required thousands of buildings to be leveled, adding even more pressure to the situation of available housing stock. It was time for the Jews to be removed, not just because they were considered a racial eyesore, but to free up valuable real estate. And that included Jewish dentists. The lists of names and address compiled by Bruno's office were handed over to the Gestapo, and the roundups began.

It was while researching Bruno's role as a Nazi dentist that I stumbled on a Ph.D. thesis written in the late 1990s by a Berlin orthodontist and part-time historian, Michael Kohn. It took a rather unusual form. Kohn had set out to discover the identity of every single one of Berlin's Jewish dentists: their ages, addresses, and, bleakest of all, their fate at the hands of the Nazis. It was a list that contained names such as R. Isidor Seligman, born April 3, 1867, in Berlin; practice based in Berlin Charlottenburg, Mommsenstrasse 39; declared *Zahnbehandler* (dental practitioner) for Jewish patients only, until 1942; "murdered, 1943 in Theresienstadt." Or Dr. Herbert Ritter, born October 6,

1887, in Preussisch-Friedland, West Prussia; practice located in Berlin SW, Charlottenstrasse 74; "deported to Auschwitz 06.03.1943 and never heard from again." Dr. Walter Oscher, born April 16, 1912, in Königsberg; practice, Neue Promenade 7; he was "sent to Auschwitz; fate unknown." Dr. Käthe Klein, born 1907; practice, Kurfürstendamm 50; because of her Jewish roots, her permission to work as a dentist was withdrawn; "fate unknown." Or Dr. Hermann Hirsekorn—he later called himself Hirst—born January 28, 1903, in Wronke; practice, Berlin NW 87, Levetzowstrasse 22; his right to work within the national health system was withdrawn on June 29, 1933, because of his Jewish roots; he emigrated, to Glasgow, and shortly afterward, on April 27, 1938, he was entered in the British dental registry. He died in Glasgow on October 23, 1982.

There was one particular entry, however, that leaped off the page: Hartmann Levy; born in Posen, in Poland, in 1882, who "committed suicide [*Freitod*] October 1942." It wasn't the name that really made me sit up; it was the address of his practice: Berlin Charlottenburg, Reichsstrasse 5. I recognized it instantly: this had been where Ida, my great-grandmother, had lived during the war and where her practice had been located. It wasn't hard to work out what must have happened. After Levy's suicide, Bruno, in his capacity as head of Berlin's *Dentisten*, was in prime position to spot that there were recently vacated dental offices in Charlottenburg. What could be more natural than simply expropriating it on behalf of his grateful mother-in-law and setting her up with a brand-new practice. It was just one more example, among thousands, of Jewish property, money, and assets being stolen and redistributed. By 1942, Bruno could have been under no illusion about what fate awaited all those who, like Levy, had been singled out for deportation. Berlin's Jews were being rounded up and put on trains bound first for Terezín (Theresienstadt in German), a large holding camp in Czechoslovakia, and thereafter sent to other camps, including Auschwitz, where they were either gassed on arrival or offered a temporary reprieve if "selected" to work as slave laborers in the surrounding factories.

Of course, all this was supposed to be kept secret from the general population. But not from Bruno. He must have known exactly where his Jewish dentists were going, because it was the SD (to which he belonged) that had conceived, shaped, and helped implement this next stage in the Nazi war against the Jews. By the time Hartmann Levy killed himself, indeed, even while Dr. Landsberger's phone entry was being printed, a threshold had been crossed. What had started as Operation Barbarossa—the invasion of the Soviet Union—was about to become the Holocaust. Dr. Levy's suicide had made him a victim not of the "Jewish Question," but of its "Final Solution." Bruno's SD had laid the ground for this transition from persecution to mass murder; by October 1942, the Holocaust was at last in full swing.

A year earlier, back in June 1941, the Germans had made two strategic decisions about the eastern front. First, that the enemy was going to include every living human being, not just those in uniform. All Slavs, especially Russian Slavs, were race enemies, whether they bore arms against the Wehrmacht or not. It was even more emphatically true of the millions of Jews who lived here. Second, they knew it was going to be fought over a landscape whose vast scale was beyond comprehension. Unlike France, Russia was huge, empty, and far away. Protecting the fast-advancing Wehrmacht from attack from behind was virtually a war in its own right. This wilderness—of steppes, woods, swamps, and isolated villages—was perfect partisan country, but as far as the SS was concerned, it was waiting to be stripped clean of native populations. The very act of removing them would, in their minds, appear to strengthen the ethnic "Germanness" of the conquered land. Hitler was elated that Stalin for his part had ordered a partisan war because "it gives us the opportunity to exterminate anyone who stands in our way [*was sich gegen uns stellt*]. Naturally, the vast area must be pacified as quickly as possible."[18]

The Wehrmacht was unable to advance rapidly deep into the Russian hinterland, and simultaneously consolidate its fast-expanding rear lines. A new force was required, to subjugate the newly conquered territory. It wouldn't need large numbers, certainly nothing close to the Wehrmacht's 3 million, because the victims would be immobilized and unarmed. The SD answered the call, creating special operations units, called *Einsatzgruppen*, led by SD intellectuals, many of whom had been Bruno's superiors from his days with Amt II. They included men like Dr. Otto Ohlendorf, Dr. Martin Sandberger, Prof. Dr. Franz Six, Dr. Walter Blume, and Dr. Erich Ehrlinger, all with doctorates, all previously employed in high-end paperwork at the SD. Their cerebral backgrounds proved little hindrance to their campaigns of mass murder and racial annihilation.

As far as the *Einsatzgruppen* were concerned, there was no difference between anti-partisan warfare and ethnic cleansing, because insurgents and Jews were considered to be identical. As Arthur Nebe, commander of Einsatzgruppe B, put it: "Where there are partisans, there are Jews and where there are Jews there are partisans."[19] His counterpart in Einsatzgruppe D, Dr. Otto Ohlendorf, summed it up just as forcefully: "The goal was to liberate the army's rear areas by killing Jews, Gypsies and Communist activists."[20] They had no intention of making nuanced distinctions.

Hitler was already ruminating about the future "garden of Eden" that he would build in the East. Himmler estimated, with cavalier offhandedness, that 31 million people would need to be removed to clear the way for their new paradise, probably to Siberia; as many again would undoubtedly die from "natural" causes. In the end, it proved much easier just to let the firing squads deal with the problem. The idea of Siberia was quietly dropped. In town after town, village after village, German units, both Wehrmacht and *Einsatzgruppen*, took Hitler's admonishment literally: "Pacification . . . will happen best by shooting anyone who even looks sideways at us."[21] Russian land could be Germanized, its people could not—especially its Jews.

At first, the *Einsatzgruppen* killed in the hundreds—but not for long. The body count soon rose into the thousands, and any pretense that this campaign was a preventive anti-partisan measure was dropped. Bruno's SD came into its own, emerging from relative obscurity within the wider SS, shedding its role as compiler of national data and, as Heydrich had always intended, taking on the job of executing the Nazis' Jewish policy to its extremes.

Worse was to come. By September/October 1941, the SD death squads had crossed yet another line. It was now standard practice to include *all* captured Jews in the executions—the women and children, too, not just the men. Mass executions routinely numbered in the tens of thousands. "In late September [1941], Jeckeln's, Blobel's, and Reichenau's men reached the peak of their genocidal cooperation with the murder of more than 33,000 Jews—men, women, and children—in the ravine of

Babi Yar near Kiev. For the month of August the units of the HSSPF South [Höhere Schutz Staffel- und Polizeiführer, or senior SS and police officers] reported a total death toll of 44,125; by mid-October this figure had surpassed 100,000 men, women, and children."[22]

This wasn't just about defending the Wehrmacht from potential counterinsurgents, the SS convinced themselves; it was about "protecting" the next generation from Jewish revenge. This was genocide. Women and children were no longer spared. They were regarded as "possible avengers of the future," and Himmler ordered them included in the massacres. During July, for example, among 4,239 Jews "executed," Einsatzkommando 3 shot 135 women. By September, the proportion had risen dramatically: of the 56,459 Jews murdered that month, there were 26,423 women and 15,112 children.[23] It wasn't quite the Final Solution, not yet, but it was well on its way to becoming one.

The brutality of the war of annihilation on the eastern front sent shock waves around Germany in late 1941, rousing Party fanatics to new heights of anti-Semitic rage. They were incensed by the inconsistency that seemed to exist between the eastern front, where mass murder of Jews was utterly unrestricted, and their own situation in the German homeland, where the Jewish Question was tied up in procedural knots. Berlin Party activists, including the SD, were furiously trying to use the killing momentum in the east to force through commensurately radical anti-Jewish actions throughout the rest of the Third Reich, particularly in Germany itself. What was the point of fighting this war, with all its sacrifices, if they couldn't use it as an opportunity for a final reckoning with the objects of their greatest hatred?

Far from distracting them, the fighting thousands of miles away in Russia only intensified their anti-Semitism.

Before the end of 1940, the presumed "solution" to the Jewish Question had always been envisaged as one form of forced emigration or another, first to countries that could be persuaded to take them, such as Britain, Switzerland, Argentina, or the United States—and then, when that proved impossible, to alternative dumping grounds. The tropical island of Madagascar, off the southeastern coast of Africa, had been the bizarre front runner for a short time. The war stopped all of that. The earlier escape routes were now plugged. So if the Jews couldn't stay in Germany, they would have to be shipped east—to Poland, regardless of the objections raised by local Nazi *Gauleiter*, convinced they had no room or food to accommodate them.

The *Gauleiter* began lobbying Hitler with demented fury, demanding he make a decision on what should be done. Hitler, for all his determination to ensure that Jews would have no future in his Europe, nevertheless prevaricated over what form their fate should take. But he was prepared to make a start with visual stigma. From September 1941, all Jews were required to wear a yellow star. The SD's surveys of public attitudes reported how warmly (non-Jewish) Germans greeted the measures, but others in the SD refused to give up their ambition to terminate the Jewish Question once and for all.

The SD had another problem to solve: Should the Führer be persuaded to allow the killing to spread over the entire extent of the Reich, not just on the eastern front, how would it actually be done? *Einsatzgruppen* tactics, even at their deadliest, couldn't offer the prospect of a Final Solution on their own. Not even the most fanatical Nazi thought it feasible to shoot tens of thousands of Jews on the outskirts of Paris, Amsterdam, Frankfurt, or Berlin. That may have been acceptable in the outer darkness of the distant east, but not in the civilized west, in the full glare of the rest of the world.

There was another issue. Spectacular as their statistics had been, shooting alone just didn't work. The killing squads had hit a ceiling of what a few thousand men could do with bullets and open graves, and it was a long way short of total extermination. The executioners' nerves too were shattered; not even the "comradely evenings" stipulated by Himmler to alleviate the trauma of shooting unarmed men, women, and children at close range worked, and it pained the solicitous Reichsführer to witness the anguish of his special units.

Once again, the SD came up with a potential remedy. Between 1939 and 1941, their work as part of the T4 "mercy-killing" program had developed techniques for killing large numbers of people using poison gas and lethal injections. These came to a halt in late 1941, but not before 70,000 men, women, and children had been killed in this more "hygienic" way. Many were poisoned by carbon monoxide, delivered in trucks with sealed passenger compartments into which was pumped the engine's exhaust fumes. Even more devastatingly effective was the fumigation agent, Zyklon, whose B variant (crystals turning into gas on exposure to the air) was patented, produced, and sold to the Nazis by Degesch, a subsidiary of metals and chemicals giant Degussa.

Yet by mid-1941, neither the SD in Berlin nor its counterparts on the eastern front had a viable Final Solution of their own. In the east, there was permission for the indiscriminate slaughter of all Jews, but the killing process was crude and limited. In the west, they had the killing process (at least in theory), but no official approval to use it. The brutality in the east acted as a spur to hesitations in the west. The Nazis had the poison gas and had inured themselves to the reality of mass murder. All they now needed were the camps in which to do it, and the trains to move the victims to where they could be killed quickly and discreetly.

The camps were straightforward. They had been building these since 1933. Modifying those already in existence to take gas chambers and crematoria, or building bespoke new "death" camps, presented few problems. T4 officials set up new extermination centers in the winter of 1941–1942 at Chełmno, Sobibór, Majdanek, Treblinka, and Bełżec, in addition to facilities installed at Auschwitz, "where millions of victims—for the most part Jews and Gypsies—were murdered to satisfy the imperatives of the regime's utopian biological vision."[24] Heydrich pleaded with Himmler to be allowed control of the camp system, but Himmler, anxious to curb his deputy's growing powers, refused him. No matter, because even more important than running the camps was getting the Jews *to* the camps, and that was a responsibility Heydrich would never allow to slip the grasp of the SD.

It was a huge job to organize the necessary infrastructure and logistics; the index cards; the detentions; the roundups; and, finally, the one-way rail journeys over thousands of miles of Europe, crossing many different frontiers. Heydrich had the perfect candidate in mind: SS Obersturmbannführer Adolf Eichmann, attached to SD Amt IV. Between the end of 1941 and the start of 1942, the last pieces of the murderous jigsaw puzzle were in place, and the Final Solution was no longer Nazi wishful thinking. In January 1942, Heydrich and Eichmann hosted their infamous Wannsee Conference, part of whose function was to acknowledge the SD for having laid the foundations for the Final Solution, and to assert the lead it would continue to play in its execution.

Once the procedural impasse was cleared, the Final Solution exploded into action. By 1943, it was so established as a Nazi strategy that it was being described in the heroic past tense. Europe's Jews, even those still alive, were history—in every sense. Though it was officially a secret, nobody who needed to know was allowed *not* to know. This was most infamously adumbrated by Himmler's much-quoted speech given to senior SS and Party officials, in Posen, Poland, on October 4, 1943.[25]

The SD had earned their place at the leading edge of what would become the Holocaust. They had run the *Einsatzgruppen*, devised the T4 killing processes, and coordinated the logistics of continental detention and transportation to a network of camps, adapted for industrialized killing. No wonder that all future death-camp activity would be named after the SD leader: Aktion Reinhard. At no point during this process did the entire SD comprise more than a few thousand personnel; its Berlin HQ was considerably smaller still, numbering only a few hundred. They were a tightly knit, highly focused elite who jealously protected both their own critical role in what they considered Nazism's most sacred battle and the exclusivity of their small number. Bruno would have known them all.

One question still hung over me: Had Bruno been involved in the Final Solution or not? Was it even possible to work for the SD and not be directly involved in it? In August 1961, Bruno was staying with my parents in Edinburgh (when the movie footage was shot of Bruno holding me as a baby by the Scottish beach).

It was a visit that coincided with the trial of Adolf Eichmann, which was taking place in Jerusalem, after Mossad agents had abducted the former SD lieutenant colonel from his hiding place in Argentina.

During a news bulletin about the day's proceedings in the courtroom, Bruno dropped a bombshell, turning around to my mother and proudly exclaiming, "I knew Eichmann," before adding: "He even offered me a job." She ran out of the room, white with anguish. The subject was never raised again. It's a boast I have thought about ceaselessly in the years since my mother first told me. Was it idle bragging? Was he enjoying being scandalous and provocative? Unfortunately, I rather doubt it. In 1961, he would have had nothing to gain by making it up. It was far more likely that he blurted it out because it was true. Why wouldn't he have known Eichmann? By the end of the war, they would have been SD colleagues for more than eight years, even though their offices were in different buildings. I think watching the sensational coverage from Israel had triggered an unguarded re-action in Bruno, when the significance of his SD career had spon-taneously risen to the surface, mixed, I am sure, by a hint of schadenfreude. Here he was, free to watch the trial on television, while his old SD colleague was caught in the glare of global in-famy, almost certainly on his way to a guilty verdict and a death sentence. I found it all too easy to picture the gruff familiarity with which Eichmann would have made his job offer, recogniz-ing in Bruno the agreeable profile of a fellow fanatic, a good drinking companion, and a man with an ideologically strong stomach.

Yet it appeared that Eichmann's offer was rebuffed. I could find no evidence linking Bruno directly to Eichmann's Office for Jewish Affairs, or even to Amt IV, which housed it. He must have weighed it up and decided that, for one reason or another, it just didn't appeal. How long did he think it over? Did he agonize? Working with Eichmann was simply "a job" to be offered, considered, and turned down (without any detrimental consequence), no different in the end from any other. Perhaps he preferred not to dirty his hands directly with all this Jewish business. It's hard to imagine a career this close to the center of the SD that nevertheless managed to evade direct involvement in T4, euthanasia, the *Einsatzgruppen*, or Eichmann's transport empire, but Bruno managed it.

So what *was* Bruno doing for the SD at this point in 1942? Did he, in fact, even have an active SD role? Scouring the records in Washington, we discovered on an index card his office room number, telephone extension, and the fact that he was attached to a new SD department—RSHA Amt VI. Alongside his Berlin *Inspekteur* role, he was involved now no longer in "ideological opposition," but with foreign intelligence. Bruno had become a spook. His new department head was another one of Heydrich's most able young` high flyers—Walter Schellenberg, four years younger than Bruno, but already a *Brigadeführer* (brigadier general).

Probably the most mentally acute of the young SD stars, Schellenberg was shrewd enough to cultivate both a sense of indispensability to the regime and a veneer of elegant detachment. Like Albert Speer, he used postwar memoirs to play down his Nazism (never ideological, only opportunist) while shamelessly talking up his own acumen and achievements (both quite exceptional, even if he says so himself). Both men would discover a huge market after the war for intimate, withering portraits of key Third Reich personalities, by those who had shared the inner circle with them (though not their guilt or their bloodshed). Just like Speer, Schellenberg repeatedly claimed that he could just as easily have risen to the top in *any* political context, not just that of the Third Reich. He was a technocrat first, and Nazi second, thanks only to the misfortune of having been born in 1910.

Schellenberg's description of why he joined the SS could not be more different from Bruno's. Instead of representing the culmination of more than twelve years of growing ideological ambition, for Schellenberg it was, so he claimed, little more than a way to mix in genteel, sophisticated company: "The SS was already considered an elite organization. . . . In the SS one found the 'better type of people,' and membership brought considerable prestige and social advantages, while the beer hall rowdies of the SA were beyond the pale. In those days they represented the most extreme, violent, and fanatical elements of the Nazi movement."[26]

Like so many other SD luminaries, Bruno's new boss was a lawyer by training, but had always been fascinated by the shadowy world of foreign intelligence. He was already responsible for a number of high-profile escapades, proudly described in his postwar memoirs: kidnapping, subterfuge, and, most infamously, coming within a whisker of abducting the Duke and Duchess of Windsor from Portugal. He would continue these high-wire acts of foreign intrigue until the end of the war.

According to the records, Bruno's first posting was on Amt VI's Britain and France desk (B4), collating intelligence information. In 1940, Schellenberg had written his magnum opus, an anatomy of the British state, intended not just to show off his alleged in-depth understanding of how the United Kingdom worked, but to give any future invasion the best blueprints with which to take over the running of the country, even identifying which British subjects to eliminate. Not everyone who has read it since has been as impressed with its insight as was its author: "Apparently assisted by information from two MI6 officers who had been kidnapped near the Dutch frontier . . . Schellenberg's classified *Informationsheft* GB offers a glimpse of Britain that is both oddly perceptive and utterly bizarre."[27] It was Schellenberg's job to turn Amt VI into something resembling British Intelligence, with which he was clearly mesmerized, convinced that Britain's ability to marry patrician effortlessness with imperial ruthlessness was best embodied by its spies.

It was a fascination that Bruno shared. I remember one rather unsettling conversation I had with him, around 1984. He was keen to know what I planned to do now that I had left university. I had been offered a job in a big London advertising agency, but couldn't resist blurting out that I had also just done the Foreign Office exam, which had culminated in an archetypal Oxbridge experience—the spy interview, conducted in a rather grand, sepulchral Pall Mall villa. I had always assumed this had been motivated by the fact that, with relatives in Berlin, I possessed the perfect pretext for travel behind the then Iron Curtain. "Ah!" he said, nodding. "The British Secret Service. The best in the world, but run by gentlemen."

He proceeded to offer me some typically brusque observations about the world, principal of which was that the world of geopolitics had no room for sentimentality. He cited the example of the Ayatollah Khomeini, who had, of course, returned to

Iran some five years before, having ousted the shah (whose half-German wife had made him the darling of the German right). Bruno's point was, *This* is what happens to political opponents you (foolishly) fail to eliminate. They come back. They topple you. The inference I was intended to draw was perfectly clear. If you let ideological enemies live, you simply create a rod for your own back. So the answer is: Don't let them live. Diplomacy, then, was finally no job for mere gentlemen. Bruno looked to me like someone who knew what he was talking about.

But there was another exchange that kept nagging away at me. My sister had once spoken to Gisela, Bruno's common-law wife, during one of her stays in their apartment. Vanessa had asked Gisela why she and Bruno were so scared of the Russians. Why was he still so convinced they would arrest him if he tried to drive through their Berlin checkpoints rather than fly out? Gisela had a pretty reliable nose for "questions about the war" and, like most of her generation, was very adept at swatting them away as unhelpful, uninformed, or just plain impertinent. But on this one, she volunteered an answer, distracted (I am convinced) by the fact the question addressed the Soviets and their notoriously vengeful attitudes. "Because in the war he helped get Russians to fight against their own side. It was all very secret, but the Russians will arrest anyone involved in it." I was reminded of this while finding out all I could about Amt VI and Schellenberg.

In 1942, Himmler and Schellenberg had hatched an extraordinary plan, later named Unternehmen Zeppelin (Operation Zeppelin). Was *this* what she had been talking about? It was a bizarre undertaking, a mix of lunacy and pragmatic common sense that appeared to fly in the face of standard SS procedure.

From the opening salvos of Barbarossa, the Germans viewed their new Soviet and "Asiatic" enemy as outright *Untermenschen*, but Schellenberg could see what price the Germans were paying for their indiscriminate violence:

> The Russians used the harshness with which the Germans were conducting the war as the ideological basis for their partisan activities. The so-called *Kommissar-Befehl* [order to shoot all commissars], the German propaganda about the "subhuman" nature of the Russian peoples, the mass shootings carried out by the *Einsatzgruppen*, the special security units operating with the army in and behind the combat zone—all constituted arguments which were psychologically effective in arousing a ruthless spirit among the partisans.[28]

What a waste of all that anti-Soviet feeling, in a campaign where the partisan/saboteur played such a major role. As the war ground on, month after month, and final victory started to look increasingly remote, the SS leadership realized they had fatally underestimated the Soviet Union. It was time to rethink their attitudes and their strategy.

Schellenberg's plan was to organize the recruitment of Soviet POWs held by the Germans as agents against their own Red Army. Who better to infiltrate the Red Army, organize acts of sabotage, and report back to the SD than disaffected Soviets? Thus Operation Zeppelin was born. "The main purpose of this operation was to drop mass formations of Russian prisoners by parachute deep inside Soviet territory. They were allowed the status of German soldiers; wore Wehrmacht uniforms; and were given the best food, clean quarters, lecture films, and trips through Germany," wrote Schellenberg in his memoirs.

Key to any chance of success, of course, was being confident about Soviet POW motives for joining: whether they had really turned against the terror of the Stalinist system or whether, racked by inner conflicts, they were hovering between the two ideologies of Nazism and Stalinism. This was a world of ciphers, codes, agent networks, radios, and black ops aimed at Germany's most dangerous enemy. Their biggest recruitment to the cause was a 20,000-strong army of Russian nationalists, under General Andrey Vlasov. There was even an SD think tank located in Wannsee, full of Russian experts, feeding a voracious appetite for accurate information about the Soviet war machine that Hitler now demanded. It all required a huge effort to analyze, write up, and distribute the reports now pouring in from Schellenberg's turncoat army of disaffected Russians, parachuted in behind enemy lines, with shortwave radios and bicycles to avoid the NKVD (Soviet secret police).

In the end, it was all to prove a damp squib. Once it was seen that the Germans were losing the war, incentive to help them against a resurgent Red Army quickly vanished. There were huge limitations to the training, and serious shortages of equipment, which made Zeppelin agents highly vulnerable to being captured and "turned" by the NKVD. Bruno's role is unclear. He didn't speak Russian, so he was probably in administration back in Berlin rather than on the front itself. But for all Bruno's desire to play the counterinsurgency game, it doesn't appear to have achieved very much.

That didn't stop 1943 from beginning rather well for Bruno. The Orders Manifest of the Chief of Security Police and SD, Number 5, dated Berlin, January 30,[29] listed him among that year's SS promotions; he was now a *Hauptsturmführer*, or captain, the highest rank that he achieved (and by far the most common rank among SD officers—Josef Mengele, Amon Goeth, and Klaus Barbie all ended the war as *Hauptsturmführer*, for example). It was scant consolation, however, for a deteriorating situation across the whole of occupied Europe.

There were staggering reversals in the Soviet Union, first at Stalingrad, then at Kursk. North Africa, too, was about to fall, making the prospect of an Allied Continental invasion all the more imminent. The imposition of total war was the only possible response. This was no longer about debating how victory might be achieved; it was a case of hammering home what the cost of defeat would be. Few Germans needed to be reminded. The whole country was being pulverized by bombs, dropped during the day by the Americans, and at night by the RAF. Even Berlin, at the limits of Allied aircraft range, was taking a terrible beating.

The Langbehn family were by now regularly sleeping in bomb shelters, but rather more auspicious ones than most. In 2005, I persuaded my mother to see the movie *Downfall*, the extraordinary dramatization of events in Hitler's bunker during the final days of the war, and it triggered a buried memory. The Reich Chancellery bunker was where Papa had used to take them when the raids were particularly heavy, she told me, after having seen the film. On one occasion, she had gone there with an earache, and a nurse had treated it with olive oil. The film had featured such a nurse, in uniform, and the memories flooded back:

the imposing building above, the tiled corridors full of soldiers and office workers below. She remembered being in no doubt that access was highly restricted; only very important people got to go there, clearly including an SD *Hauptsturmführer* like her father.

But in the end, even this proved inadequate. With the war now starting to close in on them, Bruno and Thusnelda made the decision to pack the girls off to a rural Catholic boarding school, out of harm's way. The building is still there, though all its records from the war years were long ago destroyed. Bruno and Thusnelda were on the move, too, quitting Berlin for their new home, in Prague, where they were to spend the final months of the war.

Nine

ENDGAME

1944–1946

By mid-1944, it was hard to imagine a more congenial place for an SS secret policeman to be assigned to than Prague, where the Bohemian beer flowed without obvious interruption. "A trip to Prague . . . was a trip to tranquillity. Surrounded by war, a truly worldwide conflagration, the Protectorate was the only central European land living in peace." The comment had been made more than a year earlier, but there was still a ring of truth to it. The legendary beauty of the city, a masterpiece of medieval and baroque design, was intact, having endured five years of war untouched by the ravages of bombing or shelling. A few hours' train journey away from Berlin, it was the gateway to Nazi *Lebensraum* fantasies to the east, but spared the charnel-house bestiality of Poland, the Baltic States, Hungary, and especially the Soviet Union. With the Red Army embarked on its inexorable march west, it didn't stay this way for long, but for the moment, it offered welcome respite from the endless bombing and the increasing squalor and privations of Berlin.

Bruno and Thusnelda arrived toward the middle of June (she

was eight months pregnant) and took possession of an apartment at number 15 on the street the Germans knew as Fleischmarkt ("Meat Market"; Masná Street today), a sturdy 1920s tenement, barely thirty seconds' walk from the twin spires of the great Týn Church and the Old Town Square, center of the city's historic quarter. It was a short motorcycle ride (Bruno's preferred means of transport, my mother recalls) to the SD office on Washington Street, near Wenceslas Square. The building was run by a concierge with a teenage son.

The Langbehns had been there barely a month, however, when disaster struck. Thusnelda was in the hospital giving birth to my mother's younger sister when the Gestapo hammered at the door with a warrant for Bruno's arrest. Versions of the story had circulated the family for years, but only after I had pieced together his activities with Walter Schellenberg's Amt VI did I deduce what must have happened. Bruno was accused of having been linked to the July 20 bomb plot, code-named Operation Valkyrie, which had taken place only a few days earlier, badly injuring but failing to kill Hitler in his East Prussian headquarters, the so-called Wolf's Lair. Bruno protested his innocence, dumbfounded by the charges. He was oblivious to the fact that his own boss, Walter Schellenberg, had been playing a very dangerous game since at least 1942, maybe even earlier, in which he now found himself lethally embroiled.

Schellenberg had been one of the first senior SS men to conclude that the Germans had little real chance of winning the war. A small handful of others among Bruno's SD superiors had started to form similar suspicions, but "none of them was capable of breaking loose from the still-compelling magic of Hitler and of acting to stave off catastrophe and ruin. But there was one SS leader who was both unscrupulous and clear-sighted enough to cast overboard all that he and his fellows had once worshipped—*Brigadeführer* Walter Schellenberg."[1]

By July 1944, the war was entering its last stages. Any thoughts of final victory were evaporating in all but the most fanatical minds at the top of the Nazi Reich. Not that that diminished their resolve. They might not be going to win, but they were determined not to lose, either. The talk now was about containment, holding back the Allied incursions, driving a wedge between the Americans and the Soviets, and unleashing a new generation of "wonder weapons" (the V-1 and the even more fearsome V-2 rockets). The Allied stipulation that only unconditional surrender could end the war made it clear there was no alternative but to fight to the death. That at least was the official version. Perhaps there was another way out for the besieged Nazi state. Maybe somebody just had to *ask* the Americans whether they were prepared to negotiate a separate peace. Nobody wanted this war to drag on longer than it had to. Surely they could listen to reason—especially if Hitler could be removed. Might that suffice?

Schellenberg was reckless enough to share this view with none other than Heinrich Himmler, head of the SS and Hitler's most fanatically trusted henchman. He was, in effect, asking the SS *Reichsführer*, the second most powerful man in the Third Reich, whether he had any contingency plans should Germany fail to win the war, plans that necessarily involved the forcible removal of the Führer. "Looking Himmler firmly in the eye, I went on, 'Well, you see, Herr *Reichsführer*, I have never been able to forget this advice given me by a very wise man. May I be so bold as to ask you this question: In which drawer of your desk have you got your alternative solution for ending this war?'"[2]

Incredibly, not only did Himmler fail to arrest him on the spot, he crumpled and *agreed*: there was a chance that Schellenberg was right; Himmler had recently encountered another trusted adviser who had been brave enough to tell him the same thing: Germany needed to have a plan B, a succession plan, for what was going to happen *after* Hitler had gone, to prevent the Allies from annihilating Germany in its entirety.

Even though the idea of going against his beloved Führer was so abhorrent to Himmler that it struck him down with vicious stomach cramps, he didn't dismiss it. Instead, he tentatively gave his approval for Schellenberg to proceed with what would have earned him an instant death sentence had Hitler ever found out, namely, a plan to put out feelers to the Allies. Having won his nod of approval, Schellenberg surreptitiously courted a circle of anti-Hitler resisters, the so-called Beck–Goerdeler group, who had secretly opened a line of communication with the Americans. They weren't hard for Schellenberg to identify, since most of these men were already familiar to the SD and, I assume, to Bruno, too, as part of his earlier activities monitoring opposition from the right wing.

Over the next two years, with Himmler's tacit consent, Schellenberg continued to probe the Americans for any sign they might negotiate. He knew they would insist on Hitler's removal from power—preferably handed over to them alive. Covert exchanges took place through 1943 and into 1944, some involving Schellenberg himself, others his proxies from the Beck–Goerdeler group. Meetings took place in Spain, Switzerland, and Sweden. Himmler was happy to let Schellenberg manage the details, while he agonized and equivocated over what his own role might be, should the plan show signs of actually working. He was torn between accepting that the war was indeed starting to appear unwinnable and self-loathing at his own implicit betrayal of his beloved Hitler.

And on July 20, 1944, it quite literally blew up in their faces. Claus Schenk von Stauffenberg's bomb ripped through Hitler's East Prussian headquarters in a coup attempt intended to kill the Führer, topple the Third Reich's leadership, and replace them both with a junta of senior army officers. It was a disaster for the reputation of the SS and the SD, who had so spectacularly failed to detect any sign of the conspiracy. Worse for Himmler and Schellenberg was the horrifying question: Were their own secret dealings with the Allies now going to emerge, as Germany's resistance circles were torn to shreds in the bomb's aftermath? Luckily for the two senior SS men, the Valkyrie conspirators, a circle of army officers and others built around the charismatic lead of Stauffenberg, a decorated army colonel, seemed completely unaware of their treasonous overtures. So for the time being, neither of them was under suspicion—assuming reports of their underhand dealings never came to light. Bruno appeared to have been less fortunate. But why?

A linchpin to both the July 20 plot *and* the joint Schellenberg–Himmler attempts to woo the Allies was a Berlin lawyer with strong contacts within the SS and senior army conspirators. Not only was he Himmler's next-door neighbor in Dahlem, their daughters were the same age and were classmates. Himmler had no hesitation supporting Schellenberg's plan to use him as their principal go-between in communicating with the Americans. Only now he was tangled up in the July 20 bomb plot. His name had been extracted under interrogation from other members of the Stauffenberg plot and was starting to circulate. Himmler was terrified; their conduit would have to be thrown to the wolves before he could divulge to any interrogator the full extent of what he had been doing on the *Reichsführer*'s behalf. The Gestapo might not have known fully who this man was, but they did know that his name was in some way linked to Schellenberg.

Unfortunately for Bruno, that name was the same as his; Himmler and Schellenberg's intermediary was also a Langbehn— Dr. Carl Langbehn. As I had already found out, Langbehn is a far from common name. In fact, in the 1942 Berlin telephone book, I could see there were only four Langbehns in the whole of Berlin. And there, sure enough, right below Bruno's entry, was Carl's:

> *Langbehn Carl Dr. Rechtsanw. und Notar . . .*
> *Wohn. Dahlem, In der Halde 5*[3]

The address is a handsome villa in the leafy district of Dahlem, still standing today, right next to Himmler's own. But in the chaos of the days after the July 20 explosion, the arrests, and the interrogations, the order to arrest Langbehn had gotten mangled; instead of simply picking up Carl (easy enough, given his Berlin address and the fact he was well known to Himmler himself), the Gestapo rushed around looking for *any* Langbehn associated with Schellenberg's Amt VI. Bruno fit the bill perfectly.

Carl Langbehn's cover had already been partially blown even before the bomb plot. An intercepted radio communication out of Spain had revealed his secret activities,[4] and without Himmler's knowledge, the name Langbehn had been fed directly to Hitler himself—though it hadn't at that point been connected to Himmler's neighbor. In the meantime, it didn't take the

Gestapo very long to track Bruno down to his new posting in Prague. Given how many senior Nazis had been involved in the plot, or appeared to be, the arrest of a fellow SS officer gave them little pause for thought.

Which was how the Gestapo came to be knocking on Bruno's new front door toward the end of July, his cases barely unpacked. The SD *Hauptsturmführer* and deeply committed Hitler fanatic now had to undergo the ultimate Nazi horror: of being arrested by his own colleagues from the security police and accused of plotting to kill the Führer he had idolized for nearly twenty years. Fortunately for Bruno, rather less so for Carl, the confusion was short-lived and quickly resolved. Bruno was the *wrong* Langbehn—and not just because it was a case of mistaken identity: somebody less likely to join an anti-Hitler conspiracy is hard to imagine. A couple of months later, on October 20, Carl Langbehn shared the fate of the rest of the conspirators and was executed at Plötzensee Prison. He died without implicating either Schellenberg or Himmler in their earlier scheming. They could now breathe a joint sigh of relief and plow on, unscathed. Bruno, too, was out of the woods, released, exonerated, and free to throw his weight into the last, desperate battle to stave off final disaster that loomed larger with every passing day.

Since being absorbed into the Reich in March 1938, Czechoslovakia had played little active part in the war. It was a backwater that had escaped the aerial bombing that was tearing Germany apart, and it would be one of the last countries to be breached by the incoming Allied armies, the Americans from the west and the Soviets from the east. The Protectorate of Bohemia and Moravia had been a Gestapo/SD showcase since 1938, the perfect example of how to manage an occupied country, especially after September 1941, when the prize of running it was handed over to the head of the SD, Reinhard Heydrich. The Nazi security services used all their black arts of coercion and collusion to keep the population in line. Heydrich prided himself on his ability to operate policies of carrot and stick and implemented them with a vengeance.

It helped Heydrich that the country enjoyed a level of prosperity found in very few other corners of the German empire, thanks to the country's renowned industrial infrastructure, especially its world-class armaments industry. Heydrich also had at his disposal the terrifyingly effective secret police, which created a pervasive atmosphere of bitter denunciation, colleague against colleague, family member against family member, Sudeten German against Czech. This was symbolized most horrifically by Pankrác Prison, its guillotine, its meat-hook gallows, and the ubiquitous posters that appeared each week throughout the city, listing those condemned to die.[5] Together they kept Czechoslovakia both subjugated and compliant.

Until 1942 that was, when the illusion that Czechoslovakia was nothing but an adjunct of the Third Reich was dispelled in the most spectacular fashion. On May 27, Czech agents, flown in secretly from Britain, succeeded in assassinating Heydrich. He had ruled the country as a personal fiefdom, deluding himself that ordinary Czechs harbored grudging admiration for their ruthless but fair German overlord. He ostentatiously dispensed with bodyguards or armored cars and refused to alternate his habitual routes around Prague. Edvard Beneš, the Czechoslovak president, living in exile in London, had begun to fear that Heydrich's complacency might be justified. His fellow Czechs were in danger of appearing rather too easily reconciled to Heydrich's rule. Killing him was the best way to provoke his compatriots into face-saving action: dispatching the "blond beast" would strike a blow to the heart of the Nazi leadership and would impress the Allies, who had formed rather a dim view of the Czech contribution to the war effort so far.

The overconfident Heydrich was ambushed in his unguarded, open-topped Mercedes as it slowed down at a hairpin bend on the outskirts of Prague. One of the assailants' Sten guns had jammed, leaving it to his accomplice to lob a grenade that rolled under the car and exploded, blowing splinters of horsehair seat upholstery deep into Heydrich's torso. He lay bleeding in his car for over an hour before a terrified van driver could be persuaded to carry him to the hospital. He took a week to die a slow and agonizing death, as sepsis spread through his body following an allegedly botched operation. The Nazi leadership reeled in disbelief at the audacity of the plot and at the casual recklessness of one of their most feared figures.

Prague erupted as the SS and Gestapo tore the city apart, looking for the assassins. Eventually they were tracked down to a hiding place in a church, where, after days of hiding in the basement crypt, repelling grenade attacks and fire hoses trying to flood them out, the survivors committed suicide to avoid capture. Retaliation was quick, indiscriminate, and brutal. An entire village, Lidice, northwest of Prague, was wiped out on June 10, on the pretext that partisans associated with the raid had been sheltered there (they hadn't); 192 men were killed, the women and some of the children sent to concentration camps. Of the remaining children, some were adopted by Germans, and some were gassed at Chełmno. The memory of both the assassination and the subsequent act of revenge haunted the Czechs from then on and helped seal the fate of many thousands of Germans caught stranded in Prague at the end of the war.

So, although it was in many ways a comfortable posting, Bruno knew that the issue of partisans and foreign agents was both important and urgent. They had already delivered one terrible body blow to the Germans and had to be prevented at all costs from ever doing so again. Order had been swiftly restored by Heydrich's successor in the Protectorate, SS Obergruppenführer Karl Hermann Frank, a Sudeten German ex-bookseller with a glass eye. And it appeared to be working. Sabotage was virtually nonexistent, and levels of industrial production rose every year—to the growing frustration of Czechoslovakia's government in exile, which was based in London. The anticipated upsurge in resistance had simply not happened. The exasperated President Beneš rounded on his fellow Czechs in a radio message:

> I don't want to lecture you today on where and how you should fight, where you should resist, where you should sabotage. Every one of us knows [the answer] quite well.... It would be a great mistake, it would be a national sin and crime, if it was said of us that we can or should wait while millions in the armies of the Allies bring about the ruin of Germany.... And therefore I repeat: To battle! Today, tomorrow, every day! Everyone as he can, purposefully and systematically, carefully, and persistently.[6]

The Germans suspected it was only a matter of time before more Czechs started acting on the exhortation.

By this point in the war, managing the protectorate was the

least of their problems. The reversals suffered by the Germans in 1943 (Stalingrad, North Africa, Sicily) had, by mid-1944, become catastrophic. The Western Allies now had a firm foothold in France to the west and Italy to the south; the Soviets had pushed the Wehrmacht out of Russia altogether, and were now bearing down on Germany itself. All thoughts of *Lebensraum* had long given way to the grim necessity of sacrifice and survival. The Germans consoled themselves with the ennobling idea that their war was no longer one of conquest but of holding back the tidal wave of Bolshevik barbarism, and it was they, not the Allies, who held the torch for Western civilization.

For those unconvinced by the high-minded appeal to culture, Goebbels was blunter—it wasn't just known Nazis who had the Soviets to fear: "No matter where individual Germans may stand on National Socialism, if we're defeated, everyone's throat will be slit," he warned them as early as January 1943. None of them was safe. The Soviets had lost millions, many of them unarmed civilians, so Goebbels knew what kind of revenge was heading their way. The whole of Germany now mobilized for total war. As he had confided to his diary back in June 1941, there was no way back: "The Führer says, right or wrong, we must win. It is the only way. And victory is right, moral, and necessary. And once we have won, who is going to question our methods? In any case we have so much to answer for already that we must win, because otherwise our entire nation—with us at its head—and all we hold dear will be eradicated."

Czechoslovakia, too, was driven to breaking point. Arms production was stepped up with every last able-bodied man and woman conscripted for factory work, both in the protectorate and farther afield in the Reich. The strategic value of Czechoslovakia could hardly have been higher. Shoe factories were converted to build V-1 and V-2 rocket components. The Škoda car factory began building tank and aircraft engines. It was more vital than ever to protect those factories, and the railways supporting them, from the risk of guerrilla attack and sabotage. Commandos could be flown in from both the west (the British SOE from their bases in Italy) and the east (Soviet NKVD, from bases in Hungary). Prague was to be defended at all costs. The former jewel of the Reich, untouched by war, was to be turned into a "fortress city," ready to stem the onward progress of the Red Army, no matter the sacrifice, before it could reach Berlin.

Amt VI of the Prague SD, to which Bruno now belonged, was bracing itself for the anti-partisan battles that the Germans knew were coming. Intercepted communications from the government in exile urged active resistance by the Czechs, in increasingly shrill terms. Jaroslav Stránský, the justice minister in exile, put it bluntly:

> A cornered rat is at its most dangerous. You have no other choice than to be the hammer or the anvil. Death awaits thousands of you and your children. We on the outside know [the situation], believe me, better than you in your prison. The freedom of our country, the future of our nation, the well-being of the republic—these are all great, noble, and things worth dying for.[7]

After all those years of irresistible domination, Bruno and his fellow army of German counterinsurgency officers had indeed been reduced to the status of "cornered rat"—and they had every intention of proving Stránský right; they would indeed be very, very dangerous.

By late 1944, the rest of Bruno's family was in the firing line, too. My mother, Frauke, and her sister, Gudrun, were no longer safe even in their Rhineland boarding school. In the months after the Normandy landings, the Wehrmacht had to reinforce its western periphery. They needed barracks and had started commandeering all suitable buildings, including schools. The girls, seven and nine years old, were brought back to live at home. Bruno set off from Prague to pick them up. Together they boarded the train bound for the east. At this point in the war, long-range American P-51 Mustang fighters, escorting B-17 and B-24 bombers to their targets deep in the Reich, were mounting ground-level attacks (called "rhubarbing") on the way back to their British bases. Trains were a favorite target, and the one the Langbehns were on was no exception. Allied fighters strafed them, riddling the locomotive with .50-caliber holes and forcing Bruno and the girls to flee over the fields in panic before diving into a ditch for cover.

No wonder Prague appeared such an oasis of calm by the time the two small girls finally reached it and saw their new home for the first time. There was another surprise in store for them: a baby sister. Thusnelda had given birth that July to a third girl, Heike, and the older girls were soon busily helping push the baby carriage up and down the streets of central Prague. Once established in their new apartment, they made friends with the Czech concierge's family, whose teenage son took them under his wing, playing with them and showing them around his native Prague. Both quickly fell in love with the fairy-tale beauty of its back streets and bridges, especially at Christmas, when a dusting of snow lit up by low, raking sunlight appeared to coat the city in icing. Oblivious to the nightmare that was heading their way, their memories of that Christmas in 1944 were of enchantment and hope. Their parents knew otherwise but played their part in maintaining the illusion that they were safe at last. Ida, their grandmother, had arrived from Berlin, and together the family made the five-minute walk to the Old Town Square, where, in front of the famous Astronomical Clock, they took part in the annual Christmas Eve celebrations, holding their candles and singing their favorite carols. It was to be the last such festive treat for quite some time.

The deteriorating military situation and gathering peril were no secret for Bruno, however. By early 1945 Czechoslovakia had become a refuge for the retreating Wehrmacht and SS units and tens of thousands of displaced Germans fleeing the Soviets. The eastern front was on the point of complete collapse. August 1944 had seen the fall of Nazi Poland and the systematic destruction of Warsaw. In October the Red Army and Tito's partisans had entered Belgrade. But the Nazis weren't finished yet, and could still inflict huge losses. Neighboring Slovakia witnessed the brutal suppression of an uprising, with nearly 20,000 killed. Ordinary Czechs were served notice; the price for opposition to the Reich remained lethally high—even in the war's dying stages. In January 1945, neighboring Hungary fell to the Soviets.

This was the moment of truth for Bruno. To this point, his war had been fought from a variety of desks in Berlin. His brief spell on the front line had taken place five years earlier, in circumstances unrecognizably different from these. This was the ultimate test for all those years he had spent playing at being a soldier, an intelligence officer, and a counterinsurgency specialist.

His ideological fanaticism had been enough to sustain him through the early stages of the war, but was it enough now?

I hoped the Prague archives might hold the answer. Apart from various listings and office affiliations (which was how we knew Bruno was still attached to Amt VI, working for the commander of the Security Police and the SS Security Service in Prague's secret police headquarters), we had yet to find any indication of what he had been doing. Many SS records from the protectorate were destroyed in the final days of the war, and those that survived were reportedly damaged by the calamitous floods that swept through central Europe in the winter of 2002, overflowing the banks of the Vltava, the river that bisects Prague, and deluging the cellars of the main archive.

My sister and I switched our attention to the immediate postwar period, going through the files compiled *after* the war, which recorded the many SD/Gestapo interrogations conducted later in 1945 and 1946. And, sure enough, Bruno's name appeared in three of them. The first was just a throwaway remark in the transcript taken from an ex–Gestapo man in January 1946. His testimony explained how he had been forced to evacuate Gestapo HQ in Bratislava (capital of Slovakia, to the protectorate's immediate east), and how he was then relocated, first to Brno, in Czechoslovakia, and then to Prague, bringing with him a number of his Slovakian agents. "After a short time [we] moved with them to Prague. The head of BdS (Dept VI) in Prague, Dr. Hammer,[8] referred us to SS Hauptsturmführer Langbehn . . . who ran the agents, and would know their names." This indicated that Bruno was running various teams of agents, as part of a campaign to prevent guerrillas, whose numbers were rising sharply toward the end of 1944 and into 1945, from attacking railways, Nazi officials, and Czech collaborators, or simply shooting up key buildings and vanishing back into the woods.

We then found an even fuller description of Bruno's activities. Most interesting of all was the illustration of his level of competence. Till this point, apart from the glowing platitudes of his CV, with their pro forma recommendations for promotion, I had no real indication of his aptitude as a soldier or intelligence operative. The interrogated man was another Gestapo officer, named Karel František Schnabl, born April 2, 1911. In his statement he recounted:

In March 1945 I was visited by SD Hauptsturmführer Langbehn. He told me that he wanted to put together an intelligence group [unit] that would be active behind the front line. The group would operate in Moravia, after its imminent loss to the Soviets. Langbehn said that the Germans would need an intelligence network even after the war, and that they would communicate via shortwave radio. He had been sent by SD, Amt VI, in Berlin to organize this network. He asked me to supply him with seven working shortwave radio apparatuses, but I could give him only five. Beyond that, I also gave him buzzers, cipher keys, and anode batteries, etc. He tested whether he could establish a radio connection between the Gestapo building [in Prague] and their main station in Brno, but he couldn't make it work. Probably because his people didn't know how to operate these radios. If I remember correctly, I gave him four Simandl radios and one English model "Mark 15." You need to be well trained to operate them. I also devised a further two cipher keys, but when he kept coming day after day, asking for more and more things, I said to him that, although I was interested in his work, unfortunately I didn't have time for it. As far as I know, Langbehn received from Berlin a few more radio sets (Soviet models). I believe all together he had about seven stations working for him.

But it was the next paragraph that really took me aback; for all his years of involvement in this kind of work, it turned out that SS Hauptsturmführer Bruno Langbehn had barely a clue about what he was doing.

Langbehn worked in Prague in the office of Amt VI. But I was very surprised he was given that task—he had neither technical knowledge nor coordinating abilities. He also was very conspicuous as he only had the use of one arm. Once I discussed Langbehn's activities with Commissar Leimer. Apart from that, it was only my secretary, Miss Hartmetz (who left for Austria in April 1945), who knew about the whole thing.

The business about the "one arm" was rather mystifying; Bruno had never lost a limb. I could only conclude that this was a reference to the aftermath of his earlier injuries to his left arm and wrist. The text is in Czech, though the interview had been conducted in German, which implied something may have been lost in translation. But there was no avoiding the main contention here, that as far as this Gestapo officer was concerned, Bruno clearly lacked both organizational authority and credible technical expertise. I hadn't been prepared for such a damning portrait of Bruno's incompetence, his manifest self-importance (having been "sent by Berlin"), and his blindness to the futility of the work itself. This painted a picture of a man gripped by the delusion that he really was some kind of secret-operations agent, capable of running a complex covert operation.

Vanessa and I then tracked down another reference to Bruno, buried deep in postwar interrogation transcripts, which gave an even clearer indication of the kind of end-of-war military fantasy my SS grandfather had now been sucked into. The interrogated Gestapo officer, referred to only by his surname, Schauschütz, was born in Yugoslavia in May 1912 and had been based in Brno. The subject of his interview related to the existence, purpose, and tactics of "specially trained and motivated men, agents and collaborators, [who were] to be trained for a range of special operations," as part of a team of agents operating behind the Soviet front, even after Germany lost the war. They were to form a secret network, known as a "Ri-Net," taking their orders from the SD/Gestapo. The most urgent requirement was for radio communications—not just equipment but also expertise and, above all, training. Once this was sorted, the agents were to "allow" the advancing Soviets to roll over them and then begin their covert operations from behind enemy lines. These were the so-called Werewolf divisions. Schauschütz recounted: "I first heard about the creation of the Werewolves, and their missions, in the German press and on the radio, around the time that British and American forces had first crossed over into the western part of the German Reich." But the plans were evidently real enough.

At the bottom of the second page of the transcript, Schauschütz mentions Bruno, yet again regarding radio communication. "I was made aware that one SS Ober- or Hauptsturmführer

Langbeen [*sic*], who was in charge of the radio station at SD headquarters in Prague, had been recruited for this 'Ri' [Werewolf] project. And that a radio operating team for the southeast, also based in Prague, had been ordered to carry out various radio feasibility tests." Schauschütz went on to describe the key people he worked with who were involved with setting up these units, but couldn't resist linking the evident self-importance these men exuded with the days of Operation Zeppelin. "It was Operation Zeppelin that first taught me the great secret feeling of self-satisfaction anyone who worked with the SD back in 1942 had; it was why the whole thing had ended so pathetically, because of the jealousy and backstabbing rife through German commando groups." Perhaps history was just repeating itself.

The Werewolf divisions were one of Himmler's most desperate ideas, forged in the face of imminent defeat. Rumors of their existence had spread across Germany and beyond. Allied intelligence was convinced that special squads of insurgents, fanatics incapable of accepting defeat, were indeed being set up to carry on the fighting after Germany's capitulation. Given how bitter the fighting had been, even at this late stage, the idea made sense, especially to the Americans, who were convinced that the war's final act was going to involve some kind of a last stand that would turn Hitler's Bavarian mountaintop retreat into a Nazi Alamo.

So this was the coda to Bruno's war: volunteering to become a Werewolf and fighting to the bitter end, if not beyond. How fitting it all seemed. The man who had joined the movement at the very first opportunity, still in his teens, more than twenty years previously, had enlisted in the Third Reich's last-ditch attempt to extend its reach from beyond the grave of total military collapse. His Nazi career was going to end, as it had begun, with unwavering ideological commitment, utterly untroubled by the fact that, in military terms, he was completely out of his depth. The idea that tiny bands of German partisans could have any impact whatsoever on an Allied force numbering in the millions, with radios not even he, the man who was supposed to do the training, fully knew how to work, was risible. But as a picture of what kind of man Bruno had always been, it is deeply revealing. If there was any hint of a struggle in his mind between the competing priorities of keeping his family safe and prolonging the existence of the Nazi regime, even if only for a few weeks, it was obvious which appeared to have the upper hand. But even Bruno and his SD/Gestapo colleagues must have sensed the wave of hatred and revenge heading their way.

While Bruno and his SD/Gestapo colleagues were hatching their counterinsurgency plans, the rest of Prague was busy, too, building antitank ditches and considering how best to fight what even they knew was going to be the war's final battle. The German Wehrmacht commander, newly promoted Feldmarschall Schörner, commanded a still-formidable force of nearly 800,000 men. But it was now caught in a pincer, between Patton's American 3rd Army to the west, about to breach the Czech border, and to the east two Soviet formations, the 1st and 2nd Ukrainian Fronts.

Cracks were also starting to appear in Bruno's resolve to "fight to the death." SS Obergruppenführer Karl Hermann Frank had placed his (dwindling) hopes on a political rather than purely military solution. Like Himmler before him, he was gambling that rifts might open up between the Americans and the Soviets, hardly the most natural of allies. That would make it possible to negotiate a peace treaty with the Americans alone and, who knows, maybe even join forces with them to fight the Soviets. The American and Red armies were by now virtually on top of each other, which gave Frank's desperate last roll of the dice at least the suggestion of plausibility.

In mid-April, Frank distributed evacuation plans to all his key German personnel, thereby appearing to place the Werewolf idea on hold. It was a change in strategy that seems to have had an impact on Bruno, too. Tucked away in the Prague files we found a bizarre document, dated April 24, 1945. It was a driver's license application form. Neatly filled in, there it was, radiating normality in every respect, except for its date—barely a fortnight before the German army's formal capitulation. The more I looked at it, the more absurd it appeared, evidence of a world turned upside down. How could anyone bother jumping through the bureaucratic hoops necessary to validate a driver's license at this final, fatal point of the war, with the entire Red Army barely a few miles away? And yet everything is present and correct; the rubric, the rubber stamps, the typed-in categories of vehicles Bruno was entitled to drive, even the name of the driving school that had approved him to hold a license (though revealingly, he cites his civilian job, not his SD one).

It seems to me that Bruno's last-minute application for this driver's license was more a demonstration that he had indeed changed his mind than an act of psychological denial, and that he was now thinking more about evacuation than Werewolf last stands—probably in response to Frank's plan. My guess is that, in the coming days, a German on the road would have needed such a license to avoid being accused of desertion. I will never know. But as I looked at the signature on the reverse of the form I could only wonder what could have been going through his mind at such a time. At home were his wife and three daughters (the third barely a year old), while surrounding Prague were two vast and unstoppable armies, bent only on the complete eradication of Nazi Germany and everyone associated with it.

In any case, there was one enormous problem with Frank's evacuation strategy, which was that it relied on the Americans, and the Americans *weren't* coming. The Germans didn't know it yet, but Eisenhower had explicitly forbidden Patton from going any deeper into the protectorate. This had enraged the general, whose trigger finger was itching for the chance to take Prague (which, after the end of April, was the last remaining major city in German hands—and therefore a mighty prize for a glory-seeking commander). Churchill urged Ike to relent and let Patton in, if only to help limit the Soviets' advance to the west. But Eisenhower stood firm. He had no intention of incurring more American casualties than necessary (not with war still raging in the Pacific) or of antagonizing the Soviets at this key final moment, and thereby jeopardizing the alliance still needed to achieve victory. So Patton was stuck at Plzeň, fuming with frustration. Perhaps Ike had correctly intuited that Stalin was never going to abandon the Czech capital to the Americans and that any confrontation would indeed have triggered violence. Either way, Frank was now stuck. It was the Soviets he and his forces would be dealing with—and they weren't about to negotiate, least of all for a safe passage back to Germany.

On April 30, Adolf Hitler, contemplating his own imminent rendezvous with the Red Army, chose an alternative escape route: at around three that afternoon, deep in his bunker below the Reich Chancellery, he shot himself. Incredibly, there was enough lingering "normality" in Prague even at this late stage for the event to be marked by full, black-bordered front pages of Czech-language newspapers. But German composure was crumbling fast.

The very next day, May 1, 1945, Marshal Koniev's 1st Ukrainian Front, on the outskirts of Berlin, was ordered to spin around and head west of Dresden, following the Elbe River all the way to Prague. On May 2, Marshal Malinovsky's 2nd Ukrainian Front, which had just captured Brno, was also ordered to move on Prague from the southeast. The Soviet offensive was to begin on May 7, and take the Czech capital within six days. Exiled president Edvard Beneš, having left London and now based in Slovakia, urged his countrymen into action: "When the day comes, our nation will take up the old battle cry again: Cut them! Beat them! Save nobody! Everyone has to find a useful weapon to hit the nearest German!"[9]

At eleven on the morning of Saturday, May 5, that day finally arrived. That morning, as they had every day for six years, Germans walked the streets of Prague, unmolested, even in uniform. German was still the official language, Reichsmarks the official currency, the Czechs a useful and tolerated population of second-class citizens. And then it all changed. Czech partisans seized the radio station and began transmitting, in Czech, the bloodcurdling call to arms: *"Smrt Němcům! Smrt všem Němcům! Smrt všem okupantům!"* ("Death to the Germans! Death to all Germans! Death to all occupiers!")[10]

Shielded by the Soviets, whose tanks were now idling on the outskirts of the city, the Czechs could at last rise up against their Nazi oppressors. Barricades were erected at key points around the historic center. German signs were pulled down. The banks stopped dealing in Reichsmarks. The Germans retaliated; dire warnings were screamed over the city's system of loudspeakers. There were reprisal shootings at Terezín's Small Fortress prison, and Messerschmitt 262 jet fighters strafed and bombed targets in and around Prague. But once triggered, the uprising could only grow. The question in all Czech minds was, How vindictive and destructive would the Germans' last stand be? Would they do to Prague what they had done to Warsaw, and dynamite it street by street, building by building? Outside the city were Schörner's Army Group Center of 800,000, but he was deliberating a safe escape to the west, not a street-by-street suicide attack on Prague. That left the city's large and fanatical SS contingent, with their police allies, who set out to stem, and if possible crush, the Czechs, even at the cost of their own lives.

Those German forces left in the city quickly surrounded the radio station and set up machine-gun nests in front of the National Museum, before surging up Wenceslas Square, forcing the assembled throngs of protesting Czechs off the concourse and into side streets. But it wasn't enough. Not only did the Czechs now hold the main radio station, they also managed to seize the citywide loudspeaker system, controlled from the Old Town Hall, as well as the main telephone exchange at Žižkov. By the evening of May 5, most of Prague east of the river was in Czech hands, with the exception of the Gestapo headquarters at the Petschek Palace, the main railway station, the tank school building in Žižkov, the barracks at Karlín, and the SS base in the former law faculty of Charles University, near the Mendel Bridge. SS Obergruppenführer von Pückler radioed his HQ with a desperate situation report: "Considerable casualties in action as we are under fire from every house. . . . Assessment of the situation only possible when we know the result of the planned advance of May 6. The insurgents are fighting unexpectedly well and spiritedly."[11] Bruno's boss, the head of the Prague security police, Oberführer Weinmann,[12] had no alternative but to open negotiations with the Czech leadership, the CNR, a committee hastily set up a few weeks earlier.

But this was intended only to buy time for SS Obergruppen-führer von Pückler to mount his counteroffensive. The Germans were still a long way from surrender. The SS plan was to clear, and then dominate, the heart of the old city. "Own troops will start attack at dawn on the southeastern and southern periphery of the city from the direction of Beneschau [Benešov] along the right bank, and from the direction of Konigsaal [Zbraslav], along the left bank of the Moldau [Vltava] toward the north. Note swastikas on houses and red crosses on buildings and visual mark-ing for the air force. . . . Many incendiary bombs. The whole nest must burn."[13]

Even at this late stage, with any realistic hope of evacuation to the west all but gone, there were some Germans who once again started talking about fighting to the death. Prague was not going to fall peacefully. *Where* were the Soviets, and *what* were they doing? To the consternation of General Patton, still stuck on the western fringes of the country ("You must not—I repeat *not*—reconnoiter to a greater depth than five miles northeast Pilsen [Plzeň]. Ike does not want any international complications at this late date"), three huge columns of Soviet armor rumbled into the city.

On May 6, 7, and 8, it finally turned *very* ugly. Rogue SS ele-ments rampaged through the city, shooting hostages if road-blocks were not cleared, setting fire to apartment buildings, and driving Czechs in front of their tanks. In Pankrác small children

were dragged out of air-raid shelters and bayoneted. In the suburb of Krč the SS committed its worst atrocities. Houses were
burned down, shops looted, civilians massacred indiscriminately.
"They included men, women, and even children from one to
three years of age, all killed in a terrible way. Their heads and ears
had been cut off, their eyes gouged out, and their bodies run
through and through with bayonets. There were pregnant women
among them whose bodies had been ripped open."[14]

The cruelty took on a surreal form: as well as looting shops
and firing on passersby, one SS group hunkered down in Olšany
Cemetery, holding out for several days and forcing funerals to
take place under the blanket of a heavy army guard. Czechs
responded in kind, lynching, shooting, and even burning alive
captured Germans, hanged upside down from lampposts. As one
witness recollected later:

> We had followed one crowd to a spot in the middle of
> Wenceslas Square around an arch (normally, I believe, used
> for advertising) at the entry point of Vodičková Street.
> There, several Soviet tankists were standing on their tanks
> and manipulating containers of . . . gasoline. . . . Today, after
> almost fifty years, I cannot recall precisely whether it was
> the Red Army soldiers atop the tanks, or some of our Czech
> civilians standing beside them, who poured combustible
> liquid onto two squirming victims in German uniform sus-
> pended heads-down from the arch and then set on fire.
> Fortunately, we had several rows of people in front of us
> and could not discern the details of the conflagration,
> though Milan observed that some degenerates were light-
> ing their cigarettes off the flaming bodies.[15]

Not even the total capitulation of the German army, signed in Reims on May 7, coming into force on the eighth, made any immediate difference to events in Prague. The Germans carried on fighting for three more days. Only on May 11 did the Soviets finally cut off the main German force as it attempted to flee westward, taking all 800,000 troops prisoner. The Germans had no alternative but to sign an armistice. In the uprising 1,694 Czechs had died; more than 3,000 had been badly wounded.

The immediate fighting may have been over, but the violence was not. When the backlash against the Germans came, it was truly terrible, a maelstrom of vengeance and torture, infinitely bloodier than anything that happened in other occupied countries like France. The Czechs wanted to show the world they were in charge and that they weren't the Allies' lackeys. The Germans had their disastrous Werewolves strategy partly to blame for the ruthlessness of future reprisals; its mere existence gave the Czechs unarguable incentive to fight to the bitter end.

However undistinguished Bruno's own earlier efforts to organize and run a Werewolf unit had been, the Czechs were convinced Werewolves existed and were going to go on fighting long after any armistice. One recent historian has explained:

> The memory of German power did not die easily, and many Czechs believed that Nazi Werewolves were mobilizing and preparing to attack. Remembering the vicious fighting that had accompanied the aftermath of the German defeat in the last war, they could not imagine the end of this one could possibly bring peace. . . . The Werewolf hysteria lived on there precisely because it was so difficult, especially in the west of the country, for the

Czechs to imagine a world in which the Germans were no longer dominant. . . . There was only one way to ensure the "the streets will not rule": that was to . . . "liquidate the Werewolves."[16]

Six years of occupation, repression, and national humiliation had to be atoned for. It wasn't enough that Bruno's family were now going to face the consequences of his years in the SS; his final Werewolf activities, for all their negligible strategic worth, nevertheless helped ensure that those consequences were going to be merciless.

It was no secret that Bruno and his family were in greater danger now than they had been before the cease-fire. Being identified as an SS officer, especially one who worked for the hated SD, was an automatic death sentence. Bruno's only hope lay in hoodwinking the Czechs that he was neither a Nazi nor a secret policeman. He was going to have to undo and dissemble every key aspect of his entire adult identity—and he needed to do it fast and convincingly. Just saving himself would require all of his cunning and a great deal of luck. His wife and daughters were going to have to fend for themselves.

My mother remembers Bruno leaving the apartment to attend one final military meeting, at which his unit was formally disbanded (I assume that this was Amt VI, in their Washington Street building). At some point after this, they stripped the family home of all incriminating evidence of SS membership, destroying uniforms, badges, and any documentation. Bruno urgently needed new civilian clothes if the ruse was to work. Where could he get them from? Amazingly, it was a Czech who stepped in at the crucial moment and provided them. It was the same concierge's son who had made friends with the girls who apparently took the stupendous step of helping Bruno get rid of his uniform, and then supplying him with an ordinary suit. At least that is how the story has always been recounted. It had always sounded fantastically self-serving to me, depicting Bruno as someone a Czech might have felt *worth* saving, especially at such huge personal risk. Perhaps it simply demonstrated the power of Bruno's charm, even in Nazi uniform. However, other recorded instances of Czechs aiding German occupiers do exist, so maybe he really was telling the truth, however implausible it may now appear.[17]

None of this was enough in itself to guarantee their safety. For the time being, the two older girls anxiously peered out of the apartment window, watching German soldiers crouch in the open doorways of the building opposite the apartment, firing their rifles until forced back by the arrival of Soviet tanks. Finally, central Prague was back in Czech hands, and armed militias began moving from apartment to apartment. Fortunately for Bruno, when at last they reached his front door, he was dressed as a civilian German and not an SS officer, which saved him from being shot on the spot. Instead they tore through the flat, searching it room by room. Extraordinarily, Bruno retained enough sangfroid to quip that not even the toilet cistern would be spared their attention. The humor was short-lived; he had forgotten about two hunting rifles he kept at home, whose discovery triggered an outburst of rage from the Czechs. Bruno was promptly arrested and marched away. Mother and daughters, too, were unceremoniously escorted out of the apartment and led off, forcibly separated from their father. Thusnelda and the girls were taken to one holding cell, and Bruno away to another. It would be many, many months before they saw one another again.

Prague had been home to nearly 200,000 German soldiers; in the area around Jihlava, commanders of the 4th Czech Brigade (mainly Slovaks) gave their soldiers free rein to terrorize the local German population. In preparation for a visit by President Beneš on May 12, local authorities rounded up the entire German population into the city's main stadium. Similar things happened in Brno. Lawlessness was everywhere. Many prominent Germans were summarily put to death. The killing widened. On the night of the fifth, there was a massacre of Germans at the Scharnhorst School: Germans were taken down into the cellars in groups of ten—men, women, and children—and shot. For those too squeamish to carry out the killings themselves, they handed over any captured Germans to the Soviets, who could be relied upon to do the beating and raping for them. The Czechs got to guard the camps set up to house the arrested Germans, in an act of glorious role reversal. This included the notorious Pankrác Prison, where so many of their countrymen and -women had been imprisoned, hanged, or guillotined.

An atmosphere of reprisal hung heavily over the city. The two main agencies of Czech retribution, the RG (Revoluční Garda) and the special police, or SNB (Sbor Národní Bezpečnostní), beat up and tortured captured and suspected Nazis. Surprisingly, many of them were wearing not only German military trousers but SA shirts, too. Bruno, veteran of the Berlin SA torture cellars of 1933 and 1934, knew what was coming. Even as an alleged civilian, he was still in real jeopardy. After being led away from the apartment, he was held in a cell with another group of around a dozen arrested German men, only too conscious of the chaos and bloodshed around them. Few had illusions about their likely fate.

Sure enough, the inevitable moment came when the whole group were led out of the building and made to kneel on the pavement outside. A Czech partisan drew a pistol and shot the first of them in the back of the head, before moving onto the second, and then the third, slowly working his way down the line, until it was Bruno's turn. Miraculously for Bruno, a Soviet officer stepped in, sickened by the bloodshed, and ordered the shooting to stop. Only Bruno and one other man survived. They were pulled to their feet and led around the still-bleeding bodies and back into detention. Extraordinary though it seems, even hardened members of the Red Army (occasionally) balked at the severity of Czech revenge. Had they known it was an SD officer they were sparing, I doubt they would have been so troubled.

One other surviving account bears a striking similarity to what happened to Bruno. A physics graduate identified as "K. F." was taken to the "death cellar," joining a group of other Germans who were about to be beaten to death. The partisans began dispatching them one by one. The graduate was the fourth in line. After the second killing a door opened, and a Czech man came in. He asked them who they were and led the graduate and a seventeen-year-old Hitler Youth outside, because they were the only two who could speak Czech. "[He] told them with a grin on his face that they were the only ones who had ever emerged from the cellar alive."[18]

Bruno was still under arrest, and soon after was subjected to one of the hastily assembled People's Court public tribunals, in which any Czech with a grievance could condemn an arrested German. Once again, Bruno's luck held: nobody stood up to denounce him. For the second time in as many weeks, Bruno had escaped with his life. At last he was handed over to the Soviets, who (according to my aunt) marched him off into internment near Budapest, in neighboring Hungary.

For Thusnelda and the three girls, meanwhile, the danger was every bit as grave. Crowds of Czechs, civilians and militia, were on the rampage, drunk on their deliverance from the Germans. The Germans were going to pay for what they had done; not just obvious, hard-line Nazis like Bruno. Likewise, their families would not be spared the Czechs' wrath. As late as June 1945, a Czech commander ordered his men: "The Germans [are] our irreconcilable enemy. Don't stop hating the Germans. . . . German women and Hitler Youth are also complicit in the crimes of the Germans. Be uncompromising in your dealings with them."[19] The Communists in particular were adamant that there was no gap between German and Nazi. They were all fascists, and every one of them was a war criminal. For many other Czechs, open and vengeful hatred toward all Germans was preferable to its alternative, a prevailing mood of self-recrimination and doubt, in the face of why they hadn't resisted more actively *during* the war.

This then was the vortex of violence and revenge into which the two girls, their mother, and their one-year-old baby sister had been plunged. All that has survived in any of their memories is a sequence of fragmentary, disjointed, but traumatically etched images. In particular, they recall with horror the large cellar where they were first taken. Here they were locked up with a large number of other German women. One by one, several of them were dragged out the door, returning hours later, badly beaten, with swastikas branded on their skin. Fortunately, Thusnelda managed to avoid these particular acts of revenge. Maybe my mother's version of events was right: her mother and father had managed to treat the Czechs they lived next to "decently" enough to avoid denunciation.

My mother and aunts' ordeal, however, was not over yet. They were loaded onto a train surrounded by large numbers of other Germans, before boarding yet another train, finally ending up in what even they knew was some kind of concentration camp. After a while they reached their final destination, a labor farm, where over the coming months they watched their mother hoeing and weeding all day long. Their only moments of pleasure in this picture of bleakness and terror came from some farmyard kittens they played with behind their sleeping quarters. After an indeterminate period (they had lost all sense of the passage of time) there was a final release. As they stood waiting for the train that took them out of Czechoslovakia, a bullet whistled just above their heads, a final reminder of the war that had brought them there in the first place.

The Terezín Initiative Institute[20] recommended a number of Prague-based experts on the period to help us piece together my mother's fragmented story. "Almost certainly," they explained, "after a period of initial incarceration, they, along with nearly 15,000 other German civilians, mostly women and children, would have been taken to a central holding—most likely the Strahov sport stadium." Descriptions of what took place here were grim enough: 5,000 Germans were forced to take part in races while being raked by machine guns; the dead were piled up in the latrines. Even after May 16, when order was meant to be restored, twelve to twenty people died daily and were taken away from the stadium on a dung wagon. From there, the majority of these people were then shipped off by rail to Terezín and put in the newly vacated ghetto–concentration camp. My aunt can recall overhearing (though not understanding at the time) a remark being made further along a Czech railway platform on first seeing the cattle trucks they were to board: "First we used them for the Jews, now they're using them for us."

From here, the great majority of women and children were distributed to a network of smaller camps and farms, where they were put to work in long, backbreaking labor. It fell to Thusnelda to keep her young family together. She was entirely on her own, with a ten-year-old, an eight-year-old, and a one-year-old toddler all looking to her for protection. Feeding the youngest was hardest of all; Thusnelda chewed stale bread and nursed her with small pieces of it. The girls were petrified and confused by everything going on around them, aware of immense danger, but with no understanding of its cause. They had been shielded from as much of the war as possible, but that was impossible now. All around them raged the violent aftermath of a dying war. As German children, they weren't just on the losing side; they were now bitterly hated, not for anything they themselves had done, but for who they were. For over a year, the girls clung to their mother, creating a bond of gratitude and closeness that would last till the end of Thusnelda's life. Thusnelda had cherished her Nazi husband and wholeheartedly supported his politics. Now she had only one priority, and that was her three daughters. She had no idea what fate had befallen the rest of the family or what awaited her and the girls.

Bruno meanwhile was languishing in circumstances no less

trying, surrounded by other German men, many of whom, like him, must have been working to conceal who they really were, especially any SS or Nazi party affiliations. The usual method was to take on the identity of someone one knew—but the authorities did not—was already dead. Again, Bruno had luck on his side. As he later boasted to my aunt, he had inadvertently missed receiving the giveaway SS tattoo, which took the form of a letter designating the bearer's blood group, and was usually located high up, under the left arm. This was of course the first thing the Soviets looked for. He didn't even have the cigarette-burn scar, with which many in the SS futilely tried to erase the incriminating mark. As for a plausible "civilian" story for what he had been doing in Prague this late in the war, my guess is that Bruno quickly reverted to his old profession and claimed simply to be a dentist. It wouldn't have been hard for him to prove it. Unlike so many others, he was neither shot nor taken back to the Soviet Union and imprisoned there, so he must have convinced them somehow that he wasn't what they were looking for.

We do know, thanks to a lone piece of documentation, his *Heimatkehrer Gesetz*, his home-return certificate, that Bruno was finally released on September 14, 1945. He later recalled how fellow prisoners had contrived their own releases. One had pretended to be blind; for months his Soviet captors had tried to catch him out, slamming doors in his face, jumping out from behind corners with rifles, but he had never faltered and was finally released alongside Bruno.

Though starving and ragged, Bruno was alive and, for the time being, free. He had to get back to Berlin. This was easier said than done in the ravaged landscape of central Europe in late 1945. He had no alternative but to join one of the endless marching columns full of displaced people, wending their way around the rubble and through the Allied checkpoints, heading for Germany. It took weeks, but finally, one winter's day, he arrived back at the apartment he had helped procure for his mother-in-law— at Reichstrasse 5. He was famished, emaciated, and under no illusions that, as an ex-SS officer, he needed to go straight into hiding at the back of the dental office/apartment, a semi-fugitive. He may have temporarily fooled his Soviet captors into thinking he was no war criminal, but he wasn't in the clear yet. At this point, neither he nor Ida had any idea what had befallen Thusnelda and the girls, or even if they were alive at all.

Awful though the fall of Prague had been, it was nothing compared with the fate that had befallen Berlin over the last months of the war. My great-grandmother, Ida, was the only member of the family who got to experience it firsthand. She was lucky to survive it at all; an estimated 100,000 Berliners—mostly women, children, and the elderly—did not. They were victims of Soviet shelling, and later the deadlier short-range destruction of streets and buildings suspected of housing snipers. They were also victims of rampaging SS units, scouring the ruins for any evidence of desertion, malingering, hoarding, or capitulation. The city lampposts were festooned with the putrefying corpses of the many scores of people who had, for one reason or another, fallen foul of the fanatic vigilantes.

Ida was one of nearly 3 million Berliners scavenging for food, water, and fuel in a city that now lived mostly underground, in cellars or U-Bahn stations, or huddled in the great flak towers in the center of the city. Those few who still had undamaged attics were considered the most privileged (it was an urban myth that the Soviets preferred looting only ground-floor properties). Ida was even luckier: her apartment had survived, and with it, her dental surgery. As the family later joked; not even the RAF or the Red Army had dared damage this formidable matriarch's building. Another family story celebrated her steely presence of mind on the day the Soviets finally arrived at her door. As they poured in, she faced them in full dentist uniform, her drill in hand. Apparently, they were so grateful to have their rotting teeth looked at, she was allowed to stay.

After the formal surrender of May 7 (repeated in Karlshorst, in eastern Berlin, to placate Stalin, who hated the idea that the Germans had surrendered to the Western Allies in France, at Reims), Ida made her way through streets that were by now unrecognizable. Everywhere were banners and posters in Russian Cyrillic text; gangs of loitering soldiers on the hunt for bicycles, watches, carpets, anything that caught their eye; bodies lying unburied that continued to do so for weeks; streets that had been ripped open, exposing U-Bahn railways beneath; buildings that had been disemboweled, while feral survivors endlessly prowled for scraps of food or firewood. For the moment Berlin was at the mercy of the Soviet empire, to which it had effectively been annexed.

Over the ensuing months, Ida became just one of thousands of "rubble women" press-ganged by the Soviets into clearing away the bomb damage (Berlin had a seventh of all Germany's rubble). She was woken day after day by Soviet work squads whose megaphones blared out the message "Come, women! Come, women!" and then she took her place in the long chains of grim-faced *Hausfrauen* who wound their way over the ruins. Slowly but inexorably, they worked through the mountains of rubble, piling the masonry and brickwork into salvageable heaps, clearing the streets, until, miraculously, first one bus, then more, began to navigate the city once again.

But the women of Berlin paid a different price for the loss of the war: mass sexual assault. If Ida was ever a victim of predatory Soviet soldiers, she never spoke of it. She would have been in a tiny minority had she managed to avoid it. Many in the Red Army regarded the rape of captive women not only as a legitimate prize of war, but as justifiable vengeance for the bloodshed and cruelty endured on the eastern front. Age wouldn't have protected her, either; though being in her early sixties would have spared her the fate of thousands of other women forced to have abortions (usually without anesthetic) during those first six months alone. Even worse, she was entirely on her own, having no idea if any of the rest of the family had survived.

Amazingly, they all had. Her son, Ewald, was still alive; the Wehrmacht motorbike dispatch rider had surrendered with the rest of his division in the west of the country and had been placed in an American POW camp, from which he was released a few months after capitulation. His son, a boy of seven (my mother's cousin), had been sent into the German countryside to avoid the worst of the bombing. The family looking after him had handed him over to the International Red Cross, who fed and housed him, before returning him to his mother's house in Berlin. But none of their stories could rival that of how Ida's husband Friedrich's war had ended.

The version handed down to me was that Paris-based Stabs-offizier Friedrich Pahnke had organized some kind of heroic stand against a Nazi plan to plunder the Louvre for its artworks, most notably the Bayeux Tapestry. Unfortunately for him, he then was caught up in a firefight inside the Louvre and suffered appalling machine-gun injuries at the hands of French partisans, just weeks before the Allies arrived to free the city, an episode that crops up in the classic account of the Nazi occupation of Paris *Is Paris Burning?* It describes what allegedly took place sometime during the summer of 1944. Four SS men from Berlin had arrived with orders to seize the tapestry:

> At just about that instant, a furious burst of firing which seemed to be coming from the Louvre itself tore apart the night. "The terrorists have apparently occupied the building," Choltitz [the German military governor of Paris] remarked. . . . Again the firing broke out around the building, and once again the SS men expressed doubts that the tapestry would be in the Louvre. . . . Choltitz never saw the four men again. The precious tapestry which they had been ordered to save from the Allies, and which represented a unique moment in history, remained in the Louvre. On its 84 square yards of fabric, the ladies of the court of William the Conqueror had, nine centuries earlier, embroidered a scene the cameramen of Adolf Hitler had often been promised but never filmed: the invasion of England.

This, apparently, was the "furious burst of firing" that so seriously wounded Friedrich, leaving him with injuries from which he never fully recovered. Whether this story is true I have never been able to establish. But it stuck to Friedrich for the rest of his life. He returned to Berlin a semi-invalid, after months spent recovering in a series of military hospitals in France and Germany.

But of her daughter, Thusnelda, and the girls, Ida knew nothing. Bruno had been the first to make it back, late in 1945, but he had no more idea than Ida of the fate of the rest of his family. There was neither any way of knowing nor even of making inquiries; who was there to ask? In any case, Bruno was preoccupied with maintaining and protecting his bogus civilian identity, especially from the Soviets. How many incriminating papers and files had survived the war? (In fact, it was the intervention of one lowly worker in a paper mill that had ensured the vast bulk of SS personnel records avoided being pulped.) Bruno had to assume that even now Allied intelligence officials were poring over Nazi documents, and that it was only a matter of time before the name Bruno Langbehn found its way onto a blacklist. The SS, the Gestapo, and the SD were all at the top of the list of Nazi organizations declared illegal. Any former member was to be automatically arrested. His only chance lay in Ida's ferocious strength of will to get them through. Exchanging dental work for scarce black market provisions, she managed it, eking out just enough food and fuel for them to get by, while Bruno cowered at the back of the apartment.

The two of them carried on their shared semi-fugitive existence through the winter of 1945 (one of the coldest on record) and into 1946. Still there was no news of Thusnelda and the girls. Berlin was a formally occupied city, with no prospect of the victorious forces' leaving anytime soon. More hopefully, it was also a magnet for millions of displaced, uprooted Germans who had been kicked out of formerly occupied territories to the east, who were slowly making their way back across the shattered remains of their German *Heimat*. Unbeknownst to Bruno, his wife and daughters were among them, having been released from their Czechoslovakian work camp toward the end of the year, and sent back to Germany. After eighteen months of detention, mother and daughters finally made it to Berlin, footsore, hungry, and exhausted. They had no idea if Bruno, or even Ida, was still alive, never mind if there was anywhere still standing that might serve as a roof over their heads. All they could do was hope that the apartment—and Ida—might be waiting for them as they made their way across Berlin, aghast at the levels of destruction, strangers in their old city, headed for Reichstrasse 5. To their relief and astonishment, not only had the block survived destruction, but their grandmother had as well.

So paranoid had Bruno become, however, that he wouldn't even let them back in until he had satisfied himself they were who they said they were. My mother still remembers shivering outside on the pavement, while Thusnelda went inside to convince him that he was not being deceived. She even had to show him a piece of baby blanket (it had a very distinctive pattern) before he was willing to let them in. At last, the family was together again. They had all survived, against astonishing odds. But they had little opportunity to celebrate their survival. They may have been alive, but they were still haunted by uncertainty. The war was over, but there would surely be a price to pay, not only for defeat, but also for the crimes committed by the Nazi regime that had started the war in the first place. What future could a defeated pariah state like Germany expect to face, guilty in the eyes of the world not only for starting two world wars within the space of twenty-five years, but also for the atrocity of genocide? The Langbehns may have been all back together, under one roof, yet it was a temporary respite.

Ten

AFTERMATH

1946–1992

Bruno's apprehension was fully justified. As the Allied grip on postwar Germany tightened, rooting out every last vestige of Nazism—especially the SS, Gestapo, and SD— became a widely declared priority. This wasn't just lip service, at least not to start with. Hard-core Nazis were going to be made to pay. Bruno knew staying put placed them in danger of detection and arrest. It was simply too dangerous for the family to stay in Berlin. The Soviets, alongside their erstwhile Western Allies, had begun to organize sweeps looking for key Nazis. They may have started off in an erratic and disorganized way, but that could change anytime. If Bruno was going to continue with his assumed name, it would be better to do it somewhere where nobody might recognize him. There were plenty of ex-Nazis being denounced by other Germans. It was clear, too, that, contrary to Stalin's hopes and expectations, the Western Allies *were* going to stay, and that Germany was going to be carved up into four zones, with Berlin lying deep in what would become the Soviet sphere, in effect a satellite of Moscow. The case for leaving Berlin and heading west was overwhelming.

The whole family, too, had to ditch their surname and adopt Bruno's new pseudonym. So, for the time being, the Langbehns ceased to exist; in their place, the family became the "Holms." It was a masquerade that they were forced to sustain for the next four years while the denazification process took its course. Like thousands of other Germans with questionable pasts, Bruno the former *überzeugt* Nazi was now forced to pretend that he had only ever been an apolitical, non-Nazi civilian, a dentist who had never been in the Party or, God forbid, a member of the SS or the Gestapo. He had to learn to protest his non-involvement as convincingly, and with as much gusto, as he had used to boast about his Party membership.

It must have stuck in his throat, but he knew he had no alternative. Unlike mere Nazi Party functionaries (who had been, at worst, nominal National Socialists) and who could offer the Allies significant help in the postwar administration, Bruno was doubly vulnerable. He was not just a compromised official, but an active Party member from the period well before Hitler's assumption of power. Worse, he had been an officer serving in an illegal organization—the SS. If his past did not situate him in the bull's-eye of hardened Nazi leaders/war criminals, it placed him in the next ring out. Bruno could not rely on taking refuge amid the postwar confusion. With a family to look after, going into active hiding was not feasible, either—he needed to appear legitimate to be able to claim rations and earn a living. That was no longer possible in Berlin.

Bruno lit upon a small, unremarkable town that fit the bill perfectly, a dormitory suburb to the northwest of Hamburg, in the British sector, called Wedel. It was everything that Berlin was not: off the beaten track, anonymous, and of no political significance—the perfect place to lie low. Once again, the family found themselves on a rattling, overcrowded train, wending its way out of Berlin toward their new home. It was a shrewd choice. Half of Wedel's entire population were refugees of one sort or another, so it was easy for the "Holms" to merge into the shapeless mass of so many thousands of other displaced Germans. Their new accommodation took the form of two cramped rooms at the back of a family house on the outskirts of the town. By extraordinary coincidence, their address now matched their fake family name: Holmerstrasse (which is still there). It was too late to change the surname yet again, so they stuck with it, hoping that the duplication of the name Holm did not draw attention to them.

For the time being, Bruno was safe. As "Herr Holm," he filled out his 131-paragraph denazification questionnaire, compulsory for all Germans of military age, and managed to avoid being placed in any of the incriminating categories. It wasn't hard for him to make his story stick. The sheer weight of numbers being processed by the understaffed Allied investigators made it impossible to mount genuinely rigorous interrogations. Bruno simply denied ever having been a Party member, never mind an SS officer, maintaining that he had spent his working life as a dentist and that he had fought only as a conscripted soldier. The name "Holm" did not appear on any of their (still woefully incomplete) SS or Party lists, and if challenged to prove that he was a qualified dentist, as with the Czechs, he would have had little trouble demonstrating the relevant skills. The whole family was soon well rehearsed in the new official version: The Third Reich had nothing to do with them; they were just a family trying to get by; they had been misled by liars and criminals. Survival had trumped ideology.

During the day, Bruno scratched together a subsistence income from cutting turf in local fields and, later, selling magazine subscriptions. It was an abject time, but no worse than for the great majority of his German compatriots. None of this stopped Bruno from tyrannizing the rest of the family with his frequent hangovers (when he could afford the drink) and the volatile temper that went with it, venting the larger frustrations that were eating him up. His filthy moods and raging censoriousness, exacerbated by the lack of space and dire shortage of food, dominated the tiny home. This was the price he made his family pay for the insufferable humiliation of the lies and the denials he was bitterly forced to tell. Of course, he knew he had no choice. But it didn't stop him from reacting to his shattered dreams of power and domination, never mind the degrading humiliation of having lost two world wars within his own lifetime, by becoming a monster to live with.

If he ever doubted the wisdom of his subterfuge, there was plenty to remind him of its wisdom. Nazism's major culprits were being hunted down, not as prisoners of war, but as criminals. The Nuremberg trials, in October 1946, had seen eleven senior members of the Nazi hierarchy sentenced to death. Others, like Speer, Dönitz, and Rudolf Hess, were given long sentences in Spandau Prison, Berlin. They could protest all they wanted that this was "victor's justice," whose legality had been compromised by the presence of a Soviet judge on the tribunal, hardly a stranger to the crimes of a brutal tyranny, but for most Germans it was hard to dispute the verdicts or deny the legitimacy of the charges. The Nazis had done more than just lose a war, they had run a criminal regime and been guilty of atrocities the whole world was still reeling from. Of course there would have to be some kind of reckoning.

"Successor" trials followed, focusing attention on the next rung down of alleged war criminals and, in so doing, inching closer toward men like Bruno. A number of his ex–SD bosses were prominent among them, including Naumann, Ohlendorf, and Daluege. This time, the Allies were indicting whole categories of war criminals, not just high-profile individuals. Many doctors, *Einsatzgruppen* personnel, camp officials, and men accused of executing unarmed Allied prisoners of war had their day in court. A number found themselves behind bars; some were condemned to death.

These trials offered the postwar world its first penetrating— and horrifying—picture of the extent of Nazi guilt; Allied barristers pieced together how the Nazi system had worked; they demonstrated the complicity of German administrators, German lawyers, German doctors; they revealed the nature of the war in the east; they unpicked the regime that had set up and run concentration camps and then turned them into death camps. It was the moment, too, when the rest of the world had its chance to peer inside organizations such as the SS and its subsets, the SD and the Gestapo. They had been familiar enough names, but only now were their internal structures, ethos, and murderous missions comprehensively (if still superficially) understood. Bruno must have been getting very nervous. It was true that these trials involved men further up the pecking order than he, men more clearly guilty of what even the Nazis knew were criminal and immoral acts. But the judicial process was working its way inexorably down the chain of command. The net would have to spread only one category wider and it would be hauling in men like Bruno.

And then, before this final stage of investigation and arrest had a chance to get fully started, it appeared to be all over. Other priorities and difficulties, not least the increasing tension between East and West, began to take precedence. By this point, too, there were enough Germans, including ex-SS men, in key positions in the judiciary and the administration to help convince the Allies that it was time to draw a line, rather than drag the judicial processes into the next decade. Lucky Bruno. It meant that for the first time since the war itself he was starting to feel safe—though he still took the precaution of having a friend discreetly probe the denazification lists to confirm whether his name was on them or not.

International politics had saved Bruno. A confrontation with the Soviets over Berlin was inevitable, and it had finally happened. Stalin was determined to try, one last time, to expel the Western Allies from "his" Berlin and had instituted a blockade designed to starve them into submission. The response was staggering—an Allied armada of aircraft,[1] the "Berlin Airlift," supplying the city with food, fuel, and medicines that at its peak had an aircraft landing every three minutes. Even Bruno later conceded that it had been a miracle of Allied courage, generosity, and daring. I remember, barely seven or eight years old, saying good-bye to my grandmother Thusnelda at Tempelhof Airport, about to fly home to Edinburgh, and her being almost in tears in front of the memorial outside, which commemorates the airlift. My father had to explain the story to me on the flight home. I was especially impressed when he told me how American planes had deliberately parachuted sweets and chocolates to crowds of children who gathered specially below the final approach.

Germany was changing under the weight of all these crises, and the slowly emerging world order that they signified. The deteriorating relationship with the Soviets presaged the Cold War. The British, too, had their own problems: rationing and near bankruptcy at home; crises in India, Palestine, and Korea abroad. Sooner or later the foundations for a new Germany had to be laid, one in which the "Bizonia" (as the twin British and American zones were called) of the Western Allies could provide the seed crystal for a future liberal democracy, from which all militarism had been purged. It looked like Germany could once again become a sovereign nation, with its own currency, capital city, and government, though it would need to be sustained by subsidies of millions of so-called Marshall aid dollars and suffer the presence of Allied forces for decades to come. For the Americans in particular, it was enough that onetime Nazis became good Germans, preferably democracy-supporting consumers. Apart from a handful of particularly appalling war criminals, there was nothing to be gained going after the millions of others. Bruno was hardly likely to argue. In the east, a similar process was unfolding, which would culminate in the formation of the German Democratic Republic, or East Germany, as it was better known. Against this background, the denazification trials simply petered out, and a general armistice was declared against alleged members of illegal Nazi organizations.

In 1949, Bruno discovered that his name, Bruno Langbehn, had been expunged from the Allied blacklist, the *Fahnungsbuch*.

He was in the clear, at last able to secure the document officially exonerating him of Nazi crimes, the so-called *Persilschein* (named after the famous washing powder), which declared its bearer to be whiter than white. With the removal of the threat of arrest, Bruno cast aside all his other remaining reticence.

It wasn't enough for Bruno simply to breathe a sigh of relief and carry on his low-profile life; instead, he did an extraordinary, but deeply typical, thing. He immediately proceeded to change his, and his family's, name *back* to its original, Langbehn, dumping "Holm" as fast as he could. It helped that, in an act of breathtaking cynicism, postwar German administrators had even created a procedure for it, with no attempt made to conceal what the only motivation for reverting to an old name must have been (as opposed to changing to an entirely new name). It wasn't their job to moralize.

Two simple forms, the first postmarked Wedel and dated April 18, 1950, the second from Berlin, dated February 23, 1951, officially confirmed the change; Bruno and family had taken formal repossession of their real, pre-1945 name. But few were fooled. My mother recalls the hollow sarcasm with which one particular schoolteacher greeted the news that she and her sister were Langbehns, not Holms. "A bunch of old Nazis," he had hissed in her face.

In little more than five years, the war, and the experiences of its aftermath, were over. A new era had begun, nationally and personally. Bruno could cross a line and enter his new life, unencumbered by the liabilities of the old. He intended to make full and conspicuous use of the opportunity. Wedel had served its purpose, and he hankered to be back on his old stomping ground as fast as possible. With their old name back, it was time to say good-bye to the cramped and depressing hostel town and return, at last, to what for both Bruno and Thusnelda had always been their home, Berlin, and not just any bit of Berlin, but their favorite area, Charlottenburg. It was a defiant homecoming.

Even after four years, the city's process of renewal was evident. There was no disguising the damage and the ruins, but the first clear signs of economic takeoff were already visible. Berlin had lost its dominant political role; it was no longer the capital even of western Germany (that had been switched to sleepy Bonn—later East Berlin would become capital of the GDR), but its combination of strategic importance, growing prosperity, and, of course, its resonant memories for Bruno made it impossible for him to consider living anywhere else.

Postwar Bruno was in a hurry to make up for lost time and put down roots in the new boom years, free to drink at will and lash out at everything about the postwar world that appalled him. Having his politics restricted to his armchair at home and the backrooms of his favorite pubs was a small price to pay. He had emerged from the denazification process completely unscathed. He had suffered no worse than most, and considerably less than many. And he felt entirely righteous; in common with thousands of other ex-Nazis, he considered six months in Soviet captivity and five years in a tiny two-room hostel as more than adequate redress for all that he had gained from the Nazi era. And who exactly was going to disapprove of him anyway? His own generation could be relied upon to let sleeping dogs lie, while the next generation was too traumatized and distracted to be in any position to criticize, at least for the time being. If the price he had to pay to be allowed to earn a very good living as a dentist and enjoy the fruits of the German economic miracle was to bury his two decades of ideological fanaticism and renounce the genocidal war it had spawned, then so be it.

But to do that, he needed to pick up his old profession once more and start practicing again as a dentist, even though it was over ten years since he had last done so. He would need to have a new license in order to be allowed to do so—one final bit of postwar bureaucracy to be endured. Special committees had been set up to vet doctors and dentists wishing to work again, and he would have to win their approval. It was easy enough to argue that the Berlin office of the Reichsverband Deutscher Dentisten that he had run throughout the time of Hitler proved nothing, because, technically speaking, it had predated the Nazis. His mother-in-law, Ida, had to do the same thing. Both were successful. Even better, they no longer had to accept inferior status as *Dentisten* rather than fully fledged *Zahnärzte*. The postwar German government abolished the distinction. Bruno also had the perfect place to regain his skills—working as assistant to Ida, which he duly did. She had by this time left her Reichstrasse surgery in favor of a new one on the Kaiserdamm. Two years later, in 1955, he decided he was ready to set up his own practice. But to do so required money. And he had none.

Yet help was at hand, in the form of grants from firms looking to furnish medical supplies to the newly burgeoning German health sector. The most generous was a particular German company, to which Bruno applied, called Degussa (the name a contraction of Deutsche Gold-und-Silber-Scheide Anstalt, German Gold and Silver Separation Works), a conglomerate that specialized in, among other things, valuable metals. Offering requalified

German dentists a helping hand was good business sense, especially as one of their most lucrative product lines was gold dental fillings. Luckily for Bruno, Degussa was sympathetic to old *Kameraden* like him. In response, he was happy to turn a blind eye to the fact that Degussa had been implicated in some of the most heinous crimes of the Third Reich—including the use of slave labor; the Aryanization of Jewish property; the acquisition, refining, and distribution of expropriated or murdered Jews' gold, platinum, and silver (in "Jew metal" or "pawnshop action" schemes), plundered from their stolen possessions or ripped from their corpses, especially their teeth. Degussa was also one of the principal suppliers of Zyklon-B poison gas pellets to the death camps, through its subsidiary Degesch (its name a similar contraction: German Society for Pest Control Ltd.).[2] All that was water under the bridge. A grant of 8,000 new Deutschmarks ensured that Bruno could set up his own private practice. In 1955, fifteen years since he had closed his first one, he once again had his own practice, at Rathenower Strasse 38. It was the third act of repatriation for the ex-Nazi: he was back in Berlin, back to his old family name, and now back with his chosen profession. It was hard to say that he had lost very much at all.

By the mid-1950s, relief gave way to self-congratulation. A number of photographs taken at the Dentists' Ball, January 1956, tell their own story. Bruno is still rather gaunt, but otherwise he is the very image of a beaming, opulent, postwar German, celebrating with others of his own age an almost Eisenhower-era degree of material comfort: food, drink, cigarettes, formal clothes. They had a lot to feel pleased about. Germany had become the powerhouse economy in Europe, enjoying levels of productivity and prosperity beyond the reach of most Britons. The broad and radiant smiles so visible in these pictures are testimony to the good fortune that had seen Germans of his generation not just survive the war, but thrive in its aftermath.

Behind his rather sharklike grin, however, the same old story was still playing out. Home life in the 1950s was hellish for Bruno's daughters. Success had done nothing to soften or deflect his dictatorial (and often hungover) moods. He was inflexible and grimly disapproving. My mother and aunts shudder when they remember it. Negotiating his temper, and his zero tolerance for anything that he considered unbecoming or in some way unacceptable—which pretty much covered the entire gamut of 1950s teenage behavior—was a daily battle. No wonder my mother fled its clutches the first moment she could, fetching up in Scotland, where she met my father, got married, and built a home as far away from him as possible.

Once Bruno was back in Berlin, there was no question that he was ever going to leave it. Not even the erection of the Berlin Wall in 1961 and the transformation of his city into a Cold War flashpoint, surrounded by tanks, mines, barbed wire, and an increasingly hostile Soviet-inclined GDR, was enough to make him rethink—despite the fact that staying in Berlin involved an element of genuine risk. Bruno knew the Americans and British had long since washed their hands of Nazis like him, but the Soviets had not. Berlin was surrounded by East Germany, which meant that Bruno could leave the city only by air. Any brush with East German border guards carried the real risk of arrest. They and their Soviet allies had had over ten years to scour the files and note every German name associated with the SD, especially those involved in the east. Both Amt VI and Operation Zeppelin would have attracted their attention. I am not sure if he didn't rather enjoy this frisson. Either way, he was a Berliner through and through, and would stay on for the rest of his life.

For all his bravado, his personality changed. The imperious and hard-drinking extrovert had become a much shadier, more apprehensive figure, who, my uncle recalls, frequently exuded a sense that he was in fear of something. He didn't shy away from danger, but appeared reluctant to court it too carelessly. Even with greater affluence, and middle age, he refused to move away from the suburban backstreets of his youth—North Charlottenburg, Moabit, and Tempelhof. He could easily have afforded to join the bourgeois flight to the leafy suburbs, groaning with lawyers, doctors, and dentists. And yet he forsook the flats and houses in the salubrious West Berlin suburbs of Zehlendorf or Dahlem and chose instead to inhabit a series of apartments that had grown increasingly modest, even grotty, especially after he had retired, in the late 1960s, surrounded by new generations of arrivals: Slavs and Turkish *Gastarbeiter*, or guest workers.

Though his name and profession were always emblazoned below his front doorbell, I couldn't help but think there was an element of conscious stratagem behind it all. This was the very part of Berlin where he had first fomented his Nazi politics, and its pull on him remained unbroken his whole life. The symmetry between the location of his prewar and postwar lives felt oddly deliberate. He seemed to draw a strange kind of comfort from the continuity. It was no accident that he ended up here, but why such nondescript, bleak apartments to live in? Though there was nothing furtive or defensive at all about his behavior in private, I couldn't help but think that this was paradoxically where he felt safest, most able to adopt a low profile and cover his tracks, while at the same time covertly surrounding himself with his memories. For a man so steeped in *völkisch* nationalism, he doesn't seem to have minded the racial melting pot bubbling away all around him, though he was always careful to keep two appointment books, one permanently "full," with which to ward off too many of the wrong kind of patients; and he made sure, too, to employ only Czech or Yugoslavian receptionists, never Poles, whom he claimed, consistent with his old Nazi worldview, to be thoroughly untrustworthy.

His past may have been out of sight, but it wasn't out of mind. He had made such a point of telling me how important his *Kriegskameraden* were to him that I sensed it was code for how vividly he could still recall his pre-1945 existence, and how much pride he still derived from it. It never occurred to me that this had any neo-Nazi overtones. I don't believe for a moment that he ever courted fantasies of any kind of Hitlerite revival. He didn't need to: the memories were a powerful enough supplement to the material well-being of the Federal Republic, animated by the sense that he hadn't done too badly after all.

There were plenty of consoling myths available. Soldiers—and even secret policemen—could take comfort in the fact that it was only overwhelming technological might, especially American, combined with "terror" bombing of their civilians (which made Allied claims to be appalled at German crimes appear mere cant), that had won the war, not German military failure. The war, too, could easily have stopped earlier had the Allies, so in thrall to the vindictive Soviets, not intransigently insisted on unconditional surrender. So those last millions of deaths should be on Allied consciences, not German.[3]

The rest of his time, as he so proudly told me, was spent at his

Stammtisch, at a pub near the Stuttgarter Platz, drinking with his *Kriegskameraden.* Only now it was reminiscences, not plans, that they hammered out between the cognacs and the tankards of Pils. He continued to mellow somewhat in older age, no longer quite the tyrannical malcontent who had made my mother's life so miserable. While driving around these streets, tracking down the addresses of the various apartments he had lived in, I was struck by the strange, full circle that characterized his life. He had painted me a vivid picture of the pleasure he got from drinking with his old *Kriegskameraden,* and I realized why. What had started life in the pubs on the backstreets of Charlottenburg, like the old Zur Altstadt, had come home again. The fact that these memory binges took place so deliberately close to the events they evoked reinforced their pleasure. How agreeable it must have been to have sat here, contemplating the way postwar events had unfurled, especially for the Nazi mind in search of consolation.

The war against Bolshevism had indeed engulfed the world in a long cold war, often just a step away from becoming all too hot. The West now mistrusted Stalin and his successors as vehemently as the Nazis had. The whole of West Berlin was testament to that. Maybe that was part of why Bruno had insisted in staying in Berlin. It was more than just an echo chamber, full of personal nostalgia. It was also a living reminder of the world order he had played his part in precipitating. There was a kind of self-redeeming schadenfreude in seeing the West now discover for themselves the truth of the old Nazi warnings about the Soviet threat. And then, over the Wall in the east, there was the living hypocrisy of Soviet-style totalitarianism, its institutions and apparatus so cynically modeled on Nazi precedents.

For the Gestapo, read the Stasi. Instead of the Hitler Youth, the Free Young Pioneers. Bruno and his cronies could point to other mass slaughters: the 20 million dead kulaks at Stalin's hand, the 30 million starved to death by Mao, fellow examples of genocide that were useful for a Nazi conscience looking to assuage itself. And doubtless, too, though carefully vetted should anyone be eavesdropping, a lot of muttering about the Jewish-controlled Western press endlessly reminding the world about the Holocaust. It was all just another swing of the extremist pendulum that had dominated his entire life.

In the mid-1960s, the family was torn in half by a new scandal. After thirty years of marriage, at age sixty, Bruno, suddenly and without warning, left Thusnelda; worse, he took up with another woman; and worst of all, that other woman was his wife's best friend, Gisela (the eurhythmics dancer at the 1936 Berlin Olympics). He had known her on and off for years and had even given her a job as a receptionist in his office. Thusnelda was completely devastated by the double betrayal. Who could blame her? After all those years of unreserved support for his political and professional career, never mind having given birth to, and having cared for, a family of three young girls through circumstances of unspeakable difficulty, she could hardly have foreseen that this would be her reward. Nobody had seen it coming. After decades of dominating his family with his abrasive moods, his tyrannical self-regard, it was Bruno who decided the time was ripe to find solace in the arms of a woman who was kind and benign, as though it was he, not Thusnelda, who deserved the respite. She sued for divorce, and he retaliated by severing all contact with the rest of the family. Communication shriveled overnight and was restored only intermittently after that. Things slowly calmed down in the middle to late 1970s; my mother's relationship with "Papa" blew hot and cold, but never fully escaped the memories of those early years, dominated by the war; the political egoism that he embodied; and his later, postwar domestic reign of terror. Eventually, they found a workable rhythm, and our encounters become more regular and less tempestuous, with any allusion to his early life utterly forbidden.

It was my sister who got to know him best; a frequent visitor to Berlin, she would occasionally stay in Bruno's apartment. Though he was still gruff and impatient, unable to resist contradicting everyone around him at every available opportunity, some of his more abrasive edges had smoothed out—thanks in part to Gisela's calming influence. By this point, he had retired and sold off his practice. Life quickly solidified around a set of routines. He owned shares in the Berlin Zoo and used to joke about owning "an eighth" of its most famous panda bear. Like most Germans of his vintage, he and Gisela would dress up every Saturday and go downtown, usually to the great KaDeWe department store, after which they would eat duck at their favorite Chinese restaurant. He indulged his passion for watches, clocks, and cameras, replacing his old Voigtländers with new Japanese SLRs. At home, he basked in front of wildlife documentaries and had a formidable stamp collection. He lost none of his taste for fine spirits, which he would serve from behind a lavish bar he had built in his apartment. He played skat (a German card game) expertly and knocked back formidable amounts of beer and cognac, smoking incessantly both cigarettes and cigars.

But behind this façade of normality, some of his old attitudes remained only too latent. In 1982, my sister, staying with him in his apartment, had been invited out by an old friend of hers, the lead violinist of the Berlin Opera, Giorgio Silzer. He had arrived at the apartment to pick her up. Bruno answered the doorbell, and his instinctive reaction to Giorgio's very obvious Jewish appearance was one of complete physical recoil. Vanessa remembers it vividly and could see that Giorgio had spotted it, too.

My grandmother, meanwhile, made the best of her now single life, carrying on living in her Charlottenburg apartment (in the same apartment building, she used to love telling us, as Maly Delschaft, an actress most famous for nearly landing the Marlene Dietrich role in *The Blue Angel*) with her series of fox terriers for company. She never fully recovered from the shock of Bruno's actions, or the abject unhappiness they provoked; she spent her time in the company of a group of other women her age, or else looking after her mother, Ida, now in her late eighties, and still running a dental practice a few minutes' walk away on the Kaiserdamm. Later, I gathered that she remained a touch too nostalgic about life in Hitler's Germany, which earned her a stern rebuke from my mother, but it never happened in front of the grandchildren. We used to visit her most years, and I can still picture every inch of the apartment, as well as the tug on the leash of her dogs, impatient for their walk.

My last encounter with Bruno, however, was marked only by absence. It came in 1992, when my mother, my sister, and I had turned up at his apartment, a low-rise building in a racially mixed corner of Tempelhof. I hadn't seen him for some years, but my mother had, having visited him a couple of years prior, in late 1989, after the collapse of the Berlin Wall. It had seemed an extraordinary milestone for the old Nazi to have reached, outliving the Iron Curtain and all that it entailed. On this occasion, the atmosphere was more somber.

The interior was dark and quiet. Gisela, now wheelchair-bound, was there to greet us, but there was no Bruno—he was in hospital, suffering from prostate cancer. What was I doing in Berlin, she asked me. I told her, in my hesitant German, that I was there making a film for the BBC about an extraordinary piece of cultural history taking place in the Altes Museum, on the Unter den Linden. It was a reconstruction of a 1937 Nazi art show, the "Degenerate Art" exhibition. The Nazis had mounted it to demonize the contemporary art they so execrated, guilty in their eyes of being obscenely modern and primitive at the same time. They had confiscated every offending painting from the walls of Germany's galleries and bundled the whole lot together for everyone to come see and scoff at. On display was the cream of German Expressionism, satirical realism, and, needless to say, anything painted by a Jew. As an insight into Nazi cultural madness, the exhibition had been painstakingly reconstructed, and I was in Berlin to make a documentary about it. In 1937, the exhibition had toured the whole of Germany, attracting the biggest crowds ever to have flocked to an art gallery up to that point, making it the most visited exhibition in modern history before Tutankhamen came to London in the early 1970s. Oh, yes, Gisela replied. She remembered it. She had visited it as a teenager. Everybody had. Even Bruno had been there! Yes, I thought. Bruno had been there. He really had been, hadn't he.

And absence would also mark his death. A few weeks later, Bruno died. His body vanished into an anonymous grave, without any funeral, as he had explicitly wished. There wasn't even a headstone. He had been thirty-nine at the end of the war, ten years younger than I am now, and had lived another forty-seven. Two years later, Gisela was also dead, having succumbed to chronic diabetes. She was the last of them. Thusnelda had died of stomach cancer in 1982, never having reconciled herself to losing Bruno, with whom she had remained infatuated her whole life. Friedrich had gone much earlier, in 1972, after a long illness exacerbated by those wounds he had received in Paris, which had never fully healed. Ewald had vanished into West Germany, banished as the black sheep of the family, a lifetime of disappointment and failure, culminating in his getting one of Ida's housemaids pregnant. He died, too, sometime in the 1970s. Ida lasted longest, and was well into her nineties when she passed away in 1984. The last of the older Langbehns had departed. And with them the final link to the Nazi era.

POSTSCRIPT

So that was that. I had fleshed out Bruno's Nazi career as fully as I could. Of course, I had merely touched the surface. There were still great holes in the record, and, even more tantalizing, a void beneath the physical events of his life, where once had lived the mind-set, the attitudes, and the reality of day-to-day participation in a regime like the Third Reich. For all that, there was no question that the effort had been worth it. My sister and I had discovered some startling secrets and, I think, we understood a little better who this man had been and what he had stood for. Mostly, I was overwhelmed by how quickly it had all happened. Bruno—an "old fighter"—was only thirty-nine when the war ended.

And what about Bruno himself? Where, along the spectrum of Nazi evil, could we locate him? It appeared to me that he had managed to avoid the worst category of obvious war criminal.[1] He hadn't been a "major offender," like a Himmler, an Eichmann, or a Mengele. I had failed to find any evidence of specific atrocities.

There was some consolation in discovering that his story hadn't ended up in the nightmare of an anonymous Polish quarry, or a Belorussian village, or, worse, in any of the camps (assuming no further evidence comes to light to refute this), and I don't think I am whitewashing him by saying that he doesn't appear to belong to the inner core of absolute Nazi atrocity, in either the war or the Holocaust. He had ended up an SD spook—and not even a very adept one. And yet it still felt as if he had gotten off on a technicality, a "not proven," as the Scottish courts say, rather than a not guilty.

His was a very *specific* Nazi trajectory. I couldn't fail to notice a pattern that cropped up time and time again in his life, one of complete proximity combined with last-minute career swerves, certainly not changes of heart, just fortuitous changes of direction. Again and again, he appeared to avoid working directly with the worst perpetrators, but still, how he loved being near them, as their colleague, but seemingly never as their accomplice: Hans Maikowski in SA Mördersturm 33; SD Amt II leaders Franz Six, Hermann Behrends, and Otto Ohlendorf in the *Einsatzgruppen*; and, of course, Adolf Eichmann in the Office for Jewish Affairs. Many of these men were executed after the war. It meant that, in the end, he succeeded in appearing guilty by association rather than by direct commission, though I can scarcely imagine an "association" more tangible than his.

Of course at one level he *had* been declared a war criminal—he had belonged to an organization declared to have been, by definition, illegal, guilty of crimes against humanity. But was that fair? I wondered. Was his part of the SD any worse than an equivalent job in the CIA or MI6, never mind the NKVD?

Yes, it was. Because the SD was more than just a secret police department. Anyone, especially a long-serving, twice promoted officer, working for the SD was inextricably linked to the bureaucratic machinery of genocide. The SD had led the way in articulating and defining the Jewish Question, as the think tank of the Final Solution. They had gone on to provide the impetus for the *Einsatzgruppen*, as well as its leadership. It was the SD that created the Office of Jewish Affairs to mastermind it all. And it was the SD that provided Eichmann, Heydrich, and Himmler with the means to run their nationwide system of deportations to the camps. Bruno had worked hard to join the SD and was attached to two of its most important divisions, internal surveillance of "enemies of the worldview" and, later, foreign intelligence. Neither of these roles was peripheral or merely administrative, even if they were separated from direct involvement in the Holocaust by the paper walls of departmental structure. Providing a "Final Solution" to the "Jewish Question" was the SD's most important (self-delegated) mission. Bruno's choice of a career path through the SD that avoided direct involvement in that Final Solution never involved questioning its morality, much less challenging it; and none of it made any real difference to the key legacy of his Nazi fanaticism, which was something far worse.

No matter how many lies and excuses he must have told both in his denazification papers and to himself, the final truth about Bruno is blunt and horrifying. He had worked all his early adult life to bequeath to his children, and his children's children, a world stripped bare of democracy and *Untermenschen*—and above all, a world without Jews. A Jew-free Europe was to have been the biggest Nazi gift to posterity. Later generations were expected to rise up in gratitude, not just for the satisfactions of their Aryan-only Utopia, but for the fact that they had been spared the unpleasant business of having to achieve it for themselves. If the plan were to have worked as intended, those next generations might never have known it had happened at all. They would have accepted it as a simple fait accompli. Blissful ignorance would have been the ultimate privilege, for which their grandparents had so burdened their consciences; this would have been the "glorious page in our history that must never be spoken about" about which Himmler had spoken to his SS leaders in Posen in 1943. Had the Nazis ever been able to finish their mission, the Final Solution would have been the regime's crowning achievement against which all others paled by comparison.

That was why both my sister and I felt that it was so important to understand *what* Bruno felt he believed. That is where the horror lay. The central abomination of Nazism wasn't just its militarism or its craving for war but its insistence that any values that put the *human* at their center were weak, corrupting, and irrelevant. All had to be downgraded in favor of the *Volk*, which, though made up of humanity, owed the idea of humanity nothing. The Nazi worldview used biology to undermine life itself. It used rationality to underwrite the irrational. And it made mass killing not just the only consequence, but the final validation, of all its views. Our grandfather spent twenty-five years of his life in thrall to these ideas, convinced of their irresistible truth.

So it was all very well for Bruno, having failed to achieve these goals after the small matter of losing the war, to have mellowed later into his agreeable old age. He had spent his life railing against democracy and humanism, but when it came to it, he proved only too willing to accommodate himself to their benefits. It's not about whether he (or they) should have suffered more. That isn't for me to judge. But we are allowed to question the very generous benefit of the doubt that former Nazis like Bruno lavished on themselves in the years after the war.

Of course, the deeper into this book I got, the more I came to recognize the dangers of Nazi *fascination,* how easily it can cross a line into the ghoulish and the voyeuristic. It was never my intention to become an Ancient Mariner, stopping one in three with the fruits of my obsession. In my own defense, I would argue that just because the subject exudes a dangerous veneer doesn't mean we don't have to keep on investigating it. Nazism represents the defining nadir of modern Western civilization. That is no less true today than it was in 1945. It is entirely right, in my view, that we continue to interrogate it as energetically as possible.

But I realize, too, that my own role raises questions. I now look back on those early conversations that I used to have with my grandfather in a more chastened light. I know that I found him fascinating and intriguing; that I let him mesmerize me with that aura of forbidden knowledge that he used to radiate. He had played with me, quietly milking the fact that, at some deep level, his adolescent grandson was in awe of him. I smoked those cigars he gave me, enjoyed the transgression of the underage drinking sessions, and duly rewarded him with a frisson that must have felt highly gratifying for the unrepentant egotist. I am sorry if I gave him the satisfaction, however slight, of being able to recall what an *important* man he had once been.

I could also see that my mother's tactic for dealing with him had been far more understandable than I had ever given her credit for. I had always been impatient with her lack of curiosity and couldn't understand why she, unlike me, had no appetite whatsoever to know more than she did already about what

Bruno had done. I realized now the reason was she didn't *need* to know. She may have been ignorant of the letter of his Nazi life, but she, far more than I, had known its spirit. She was the one who had lived through it, whose childhood and adolescence it had utterly blighted. She was lucky to have survived it at all. She and her sisters had reacted to the predicament in which his actions had placed them in the only way they could: they closed him down, froze him out, and made it completely impossible for him to glorify his past in their presence. They refused to reward him with their attention. Yes, I could now see that my own far more callow and impressionable appetite to know more was by no stretch of the imagination braver or more intellectually bracing than their refusal to let him off the hook. I realize that much in this book will cause them pain, but I take great reassurance from their quiet determination that this is nevertheless a book that needed to be written.

For me, however, not digging deeper into Bruno's Nazi life was never an option. The more I uncovered about him, the more I needed to know. To see a Nazi story as archetypal as Bruno's acted out in the flesh—flesh I was directly related to—was both uncomfortable and, in the end, irresistible. Two burning questions now felt answered in my mind. The first was the personal one. Most important of all, Bruno was no longer the only member of the family who knew what he had done. It had been our deliberately encouraged ignorance that had allowed him to relish the notoriety of his Nazi career, safe in the assumption that he could never be called to account for it—and he exploited it fully. I was glad that was no longer the case, even if it had not been possible to confront him while he was still alive.

The second question was wider: The rise of Nazism had relied on men like Bruno, more than I had ever previously realized. For the first time in my life, I felt I had been given, up close and personal, a long, hard look at the face of National Socialism, at least in one of its guises. My grandfather's story, so anonymous and ordinary in every other respect, might at least play one useful role—as a cautionary tale, a living example of the harm even little men can achieve, in times of historical madness. He was indeed the perfect Nazi—just not in the sense in which he would have used the term.

I will never know, of course, exactly what mixture of regret, repentance, and bloody-minded pride characterized his memories of that early life, but one thing I am certain about: The last word on the Third Reich belongs *not* to the perpetrators, but to those who come after, however limited our insights. The perpetrators long ago forfeited the right to be the ones who got to draw a line in the sand.

Notes

CHAPTER TWO. SS CURRICULUM VITAE

1. A collection of essays that were commissioned, collated, and studied by a 1930s American sociologist named Theodore Abel. Traveling across Nazi Germany in 1934, he had the idea of asking Germans themselves to help explain the appeal of National Socialism for those around the world who were utterly mystified by it. Abel organized a competition with a substantial cash prize for the most illuminating submission. The sole criterion for entry was that the writer had to have joined the Party voluntarily, before 1928, in other words, that he was, like Bruno, one of the "old fighters," men whose early conversion to Nazism set them apart from those who came later.

   Abel was soon inundated with replies—581 of them, some barely covering a single page, others the length of a thesis; they came from all over the country and embraced a wide variety of people (though all sharing the key characteristic of being early, and zealous, Nazi Party members). Stored now at Stanford University, they were studied by two main scholars: by Abel himself, in a book published in 1938, and then again later, in a more statistically systematic way, by Peter Merkl, in two books published in the 1980s.

   The date of their composition, 1934, saved them from the kind of self-exculpation that characterized later (especially, postwar) autobiographical accounts of life spent in the Nazi period. They exude the mind-set, opinions, and attitudes that must have driven men like Bruno, the men who discovered they were Nazis almost instinctively, years before others had even heard of the Party name. They are the perfect proxy for the thought processes that must have been at work inside Bruno during this early and formative period.

2. Awarded to those who could point to over a decade of unbroken Party membership, with years prior to 1928 counting double.

CHAPTER THREE. FATHERS AND SONS, 1906–1922

1. See, in particular, Michael Wildt, who coined the phrase in the title of his magisterial study of the SS Security Service, *Generation des Unbedingten*, translated into English as *An Uncompromising Generation: The Nazi Leadership of the Reich Security Main Office* (Madison, Wisc., 2010).
2. Peter Fritzsche, *Life and Death in the Third Reich*, p. 85.
3. Later, in the Weimar Republic, the post of *Wachtmeister* took on even greater significance in Prussian police training, maintaining a link between the military and the judiciary. Many *Wachtmeister* went on to join the early SS and inform its methods and culture. See George C. Browder, *Hitler's Enforcers: The Gestapo and the SS Security Service in the Nazi Revolution*, p. 19.
4. Sebastian Haffner, *Defying Hitler: A Memoir*, p. 15.
5. Hans Rosenthal, *Kurmärkisches Feldartillerie-Regiment Nr. 39 (Erinnerungsblätter deutscher Regimenter)* (Oldenburg i.O./Berlin), 1923.
6. The Abel testimonies are identified only by job description and their author's date of birth; no names are given. Peter Merkl, *Political Violence Under the Swastika: 581 Early Nazis*, p. 158.
7. The peace treaty signed in March 1918 between Germany and Russia, ceding land, and large reparations of gold, to the (temporarily) triumphant Germans. Its memory haunted later Nazis and helped drive their eastern ambitions.
8. John Keegan, *The First World War*, p. 433.
9. Merkl, *Political Violence*, p. 296.
10. Ibid., p. 158.
11. Count Harry Kessler, *Berlin in Light: The Diaries of Count Harry Kessler, 1918–1937*, p. 9.
12. Ibid., p. 4.
13. Abel, *Why Hitler Came into Power*, p. 24.
14. Ibid.
15. Ibid., p. 33.
16. The story goes that it was actually a British general who supplied the fateful phrase: "Ahh, you mean you were stabbed in the back?" he is supposed to have told the great German general Hindenburg. Once uttered, there was no retracting it, and it would become holy writ for the German right. Even national leaders subscribed to it; Friedrich Ebert, the provisional German leader, whose two sons had been casualties of the war, greeted troops returning to Berlin in December 1918 with the words "Your sacrifice and deeds are without parallel. No enemy defeated you!"
17. *Deutsche Zeitung*, October 12, 1918, quoted in Abel, *Why Hitler Came into Power*, p. 23.
18. The Treaty of Versailles was the punitive settlement brought by the Allies against the defeated Germans. As well as being made to forfeit huge tracts of territory, they would pay (what they considered to be) vast reparations. Even worse for an army town such as Perleberg was the news that the German army was to be decimated from its 11 million or so, and decimated again, down to a paltry 100,000 men. German papers were soon screaming in rage: "UNACCEPTABLE" ran one headline. Another turned prophetic: "Should we accept the conditions, a military furor for revenge will sound in Germany within a few years, and a militant nationalism will

engulf all." Hardest to swallow for German nationalists was the so-called war-guilt paragraph, which asserted Germany's sole culpability for the war.

19. David Redles, *Hitler's Millennial Reich: Apocalyptic Belief and the Search for Salvation*, p. 20.

20. See Nigel Jones, *The Birth of the Nazis: How the Freikorps Blazed a Trail for Hitler*. The Freikorps provided the vanguard of the later Nazi movement—men such as Ernst Röhm, Ernst von Salomon, Hermann Göring, and Reinhard Heydrich—with the perfect opportunity to prolong their active service and vent their nationalist resentments.

21. In von Salomon's words, "The war would not release them from its grip. The most active part of the Front marched simply because it had learned to march. It marched through the cities enveloped in a cloud of sullen rage—a cloud of vaulting, aimless fury—knowing only that it had to fight, to fight at any cost." Cited ibid., p. 122.

22. Many Freikorps men made no secret of the fact that this had been the reason that they joined it in the first place. Ernst von Salomon put it with lyrical abandon: "We were cut off from the world of bourgeois norms. The bonds were broken and we were free. The blood surging through our veins was full of a wild demand for revenge and action and adventure . . . we were a band of fighters drunk with all the passions of the world; full of lust, exultant in anger. What we wanted, we did not know, and what we knew we did not want! War and adventure, excitement and destruction. An indefinable surging force welled up from every part of our being and flayed us forward." Ibid., p. 126.

23. "Our patriotism and readiness for action won out. The separatists were beaten decisively and scattered in all directions. The bonds of blood and the ties to our native soil were stronger than weapons and alien bayonets," boasted a railway worker, born in 1898. Merkl, *Political Violence*, p. 195.

24. See in particular Paul Fussell, *The Great War and Modern Memory*.

25. The diary ends with the following piece of poetry:
By field and city
By any road and way
A march which angels pity
And none may stop or stay
Till the last head is rested
On the last crimson clay
So they go marching on.

26. If the dominant image of the First World War for the British is the head-bowed, melancholy figure, weighed down by his uniform and equipment, but most of all by the burden of so much loss, then his German counterpart could not be more different. Jünger created the defining German icon for the war, the "man of steel": "The immovable face half-rimmed by steel and the monotonous voice accompanied by the noise of the front made the impression of an uncanny gravity. One perceived the man had paid out every terror to the point of despair and then had learned contempt. Nothing seemed left but a great and manly indifference." It would be an image that would stalk German history for the next twenty-five years, embodying the strength of will that, in the eyes of the military fetishist, only war can produce. See Thomas Nevin, *Ernst Jünger and Germany: Into the Abyss, 1914–1945*, p. 51.

27. By the early 1920s, Jünger himself was starting to make the connection between his vision of war and the wider world of politics. The *Fronterlebnis*, or trench experience, was an elixir of *Germanness*: "[Despite belonging] to a generation predestined to death . . . the idea of the Fatherland had been distilled from all these afflictions in a clearer and brighter essence." He even revisited his novel *Storm of Steel* and rewrote its final lines; now, instead of ending on an ambiguous and traumatized note, it ends with a triumphalist tone: "Though force without and barbarity within conglomerate in somber clouds, yet so long as the blade of a sword will strike a spark in the night may it be said: Germany lives and Germany shall never go under!" See Niklaus Wachsmann, "Marching Under the Swastika? Ernst Jünger and National Socialism, 1918–1933," *Journal of Contemporary History* 33:4 (October 1998), pp. 573–89.

28. "Fascism was the major political innovation of the twentieth century, and source of much of its pain. The other major currents of modern Western political culture—conservatism, liberalism, socialism—all reached mature form between the late eighteenth century and the mid-nineteenth century. Fascism, however, was still unimagined as late as the 1890s." Robert Paxton, *The Anatomy of Fascism*, p. 3.

29. Kessler, *Berlin in Light*, p. 65.

30. "Trench fighting is the bloodiest, wildest, most brutal of all. . . . Of all war's excitements none is so powerful as the meeting of two storm troop leaders between narrow trench walls. There's no mercy here, no going back, the blood speaks from a shrill cry of recognition that tears itself from one's breast like a nightmare." Ernst Jünger, *The Storm of Steel*, trans. Basil Creighton.

31. As described by Heinrich Class, chairman of the Pan-German League: "We youngsters had moved on; we were nationalist pure and simple. We wanted nothing to do with tolerance if it sheltered the enemies of the *Volk* and the state. Humanity in the sense of that liberal idea we spurned." Jeremy Noakes and Geoffrey Pridham, *Nazism: A Documentary Reader.* Vol. 1: *The Rise to Power 1919–1945*, p. 4.

32. This anti-Semitism is graphically exemplified by another of Abel's essay writers, a retired infantry officer, born in 1878: "Returning home, we no longer found an honest German people, but a mob stirred up by its lowest instincts. Whatever virtues were once found among the Germans seemed to have sunk once and for all into the muddy flood. . . . Promiscuity, shamelessness, and corruption ruled supreme. German women seemed to have forgotten their German ways. German men seemed to have forgotten their sense of honor and honesty. Jewish writers and the Jewish press could 'go to town' with impunity, dragging everything into the dirt . . . while criminals and Jewish 'big-time operators' were wallowing in feasts and traitors were floating in champagne, the poorest of the poor hungered and suffered the most dire need." Merkl, *Political Violence*, p. 173.

33. Quoted in Saul Friedländer, *The Years of Persecution: Nazi Germany and the Jews, 1933–1939*, p. 74.

34. It wasn't just Nazi men who swallowed this wholesale, so too did Nazi women. In the words of a Silesian-born domestic servant, born in 1897, it hadn't taken her long to penetrate Communist propaganda and reveal the Jew within: "If you went with open eyes through all this chaos, you could tell that there was someone behind it all trying to pull our Fatherland into the abyss. . . . Then I went to Communist rallies where Karl Liebknecht and Rosa Luxemburg spoke. Again my innermost

feelings revolted. Those Communist rallies brought out the anti-Semite in me."
Merkl, *Political Violence,* p. 374.

35. Abel, *Why Hitler Came into Power,* p. 163.
36. Kessler, *Berlin in Light,* p. 53.
37. Merkl, *Political Violence,* p. 236.

CHAPTER FOUR. FULFILLMENT! 1922–1926

1. "Berlin was a working-class city. Of its total population of about four million in 1922, around 956,000 (twenty-four percent) were workers. There were around 25,000 businesses employing ten or more people, the German capital being a center of the metal, chemical, and clothing industries. Berlin was the most industrialized city on the European continent and the fourth most industrialized urban center in the world (trailing only London, New York and Chicago)." Russel Lemmons, *Goebbels and Der Angriff,* p. 89.
2. Peter Conrad, *Modern Times, Modern Places: Life and Art in the Twentieth Century,* p. 319.
3. As one particularly disillusioned bank clerk put it, "One government alternated with another. Marxist mass gatherings! The citizenry was splintered into smaller and smaller parties. Program upon program swirled through the air. A completely uniform and clear direction was lacking. It appeared impossible in this witch's temple to find one's way from one slogan to another. The *Volk* was fissured in interests and opinions, in classes and estates—a plaything of enemy powers and nations." Redles, *Hitler's Millennial Reich,* p. 20.
4. Sebastian Haffner, *Defying Hitler: A Memoir,* pp. 35–36.
5. Written by the son of a furniture factory owner, born in 1905, cited ibid., p. 133.
6. In alleged retaliation for the slow payment of Versailles reparations, but triggered bizarrely by Germany's default on a promise to hand over 140,000 telegraph poles. Nigel Jones, *The Birth of the Nazis: How the Freikorps Blazed a Trail for Hitler,* p. 246.
7. "Shortly thereafter, our town was heavily occupied. All private houses had to accept billets. Blacks, Moroccans, and Arabs were put up in schools and public buildings. . . . We had our fun with the colored troops. They were so stupid you could show them an old newspaper in place of a valid pass at the check-points. But it was dangerous at night for women and girls. Rape and miscegenation were unfortunately frequent," wrote a young civil engineer, born in 1906, quoted in Peter Merkl, *The Making of a Stormtrooper,* p. 136.
8. Koppel Pinson, quoted in Merkl, *The Making of a Stormtrooper,* p. 133.
9. Haffner, *Defying Hitler,* p. 53.
10. David Redles, *Hitler's Millennial Reich: Apocalyptic Belief and the Search for Salvation,* p. 24.
11. Peter Conrad, *Modern Times, Modern Places: Life and Art in the Twentieth Century,* p. 321.
12. As described by one of Abel's essay contributors: Abel, *Why Hitler Came into Power,* p. 69.
13. The attempted coup had culminated in a march through the center of Munich, with Hitler, Ludendorff, and Göring in the vanguard, before it was confronted by a battalion of a hundred troops blocking their way. Shots were exchanged, sixteen

Nazis were killed (Göring was wounded in the thigh), and the ringleaders were arrested. It wasn't the first right-wing "putsch," but it was the most serious, even if it had appeared to end in shambles. It would take on almost sacramental significance in later Nazi mythology.

14. Abel, *Why Hitler Came into Power*, p. 69.

15. Even the prosecuting counsel found himself mesmerized, describing Hitler's motives as "noble" in his summing up, later adding that Hitler's "honorable endeavor to reawaken faith in the German cause, in an oppressed and disarmed people, remains an honor."

16. An abbreviation for the terrifying-sounding "German National Freedom Party" (Deutschvölkische Freiheitspartei, or DVFP).

17. Many were attracted to it for reasons similar to this: "In my youth I was not much interested in politics, my nationalistic parents gave me a strictly patriotic education, and I sharply rejected Marxism. . . . I was strongly interested in the Jewish Question, but distrusted anti-Semitism at first because I was not aware of the Jewish role in politics and the economy. Only after hearing several lectures given by the DVFP did I realize the deleterious effect of the Jews in the political and economic area. In 1922 I became a member of the DVFP. . . . My political interest had now awakened." Merkl, *Political Violence Under the Swastika: 581 Early Nazis*, p. 353.

18. Ibid., p. 427.

19. J. K. Engelbrechten, *Eine Braune Armee Ensteht: Die Geschichte der Berlin-Brandenburger SA* [A Brown Army Arises: The Story of the Berlin-Brandenburger SA].

20. He enjoyed none of the support that his fellow First World War fellow commander of the entire German army, General Hindenburg, did. Kessler described him thus: "How shattering that from 1916 to 1918, the most frightful moment in German history, a man with such atrocious lack of political judgment should have been in dictatorial control of our destiny. . . . We have been the victims of political imbeciles and adventurers, not of great though unfortunate soldiers. This stunt of theirs stains our history retroactively. Ludendorff sinks to the level of an idiotic professional genius who was also a ruthless gambler." Count Harry von Kessler, *Berlin in Light: The Diaries of Count Harry Kessler, 1918–1937*, p. 121.

21. Ian Kershaw, *Hitler: 1889–1936: Hubris*, p. 269.

22. They stood on the left of the movement, Socialist first and nationalist second. Both were far more explicitly anti-bourgeois in their values, to the point where they appeared to be guilty of the ultimate heresy—being pro-Russian. Goebbels in particular was explicit in his awestruck admiration, if not for the politics of Bolshevism, then at least for its achievement in having overturned the rottenness of the Romanov ancien régime.

23. "I feel devastated. What sort of Hitler? A reactionary? Amazingly clumsy and uncertain; Russian question: completely by the way. Italy and England natural allies. Terrible! Our task is the smashing of Bolshevism. Bolshevism is a Jewish creation! We must be Russia's successor . . . short discussion, Strasser speaks. Hesitant, trembling, clumsy, the good, honest Strasser. God, how poor a match we are for those swine down there. . . . Probably one of the greatest disappointments of my life. I no longer believe fully in Hitler. That's the terrible thing: my inner support has been taken away." Ibid., p. 275.

24. As an East Prussian dental apprentice born in 1910 explained, "A non-Nazi who has not experienced the enormous elementary power of the idea of our *Führer* will never understand any of this. But let me tell these people as the deepest truth; whenever I worked for the movement and applied myself for our *Führer*, I always felt that there was nothing higher or nobler I could do for Adolf Hitler and thereby for Germany, our people and our fatherland . . . when I say so little in this vita about my external life, my job, etc., this is only because my *real life*, the real content of my life is my work for and commitment to Hitler and toward a national socialist Germany. . . . Hitler is the purest embodiment of the German character, the purest embodiment of a national socialist Germany." Merkl, *Political Violence*, p. 397.

25. As Kessler shrewdly observed as early as February 1919, "There are three main ideas and power structures which make for real international division and are in conflict with one another: clericalism, capitalism (including its offspring Militarism and Imperialism), and communism. The three protagonists of our day are the Pope, Wilson, and Lenin, each of them with enormous, elemental power and human potential behind him. . . . Germany is being stealthily entrapped into clericalism while Bolshevism tears at it, from within and without, and capitalism, through the mediation of Wilson, offers it a Cinderella role at its own table. Consequently the fight for Germany is on. For its soul, the inherent strength of its people, and its advantage as an area of maneuver. All parties sense that in this global catastrophe the decisive battle must occur here." Kessler, *Berlin in Light*, p. 65.

26. A railway engineer, born in 1876, put it: "My principle of action was always to break up the associations affected by the Social Democratic-Communist virus and to disturb their meetings with heckling. After the glorious days of the November Republic I joined the DNVP. After merely half a year, the Jewish question began to arise and I . . . ran . . . for the Charlottenburg city council. But I did not stay there either, because now the *völkisch* idea was spreading and so I joined the DNVP [Deutschnationale Volkspartei, the German National People's Party], of which I became a treasurer. I did this for two years until I saw the first signs of our *Führer* Adolf Hitler. Then one fine day, I and another person now in the party broke up the *völkisch* movement in Charlottenburg to make way for the NSDAP." Merkl, *Political Violence*, p. 354.

27. Abel, *Why Hitler Came into Power*, p. 240.

28. For Nazi anti-Semites, the Jew didn't just tell lies, the Jew *was* a lie, as Hitler spelled it out in one of *Mein Kampf*'s touchstone paragraphs: "The foremost connoisseurs of this truth regarding the possibilities in this use of falsehood and slander have always been the Jews; for after all, their whole existence is based on one single great lie, to wit, that they are a religious community while actually they are a race—and what a race! One of the greatest minds of humanity has nailed them forever as such in an eternally correct phrase of fundamental truth: he called them 'the great masters of the lie.' And anyone who does not recognize this or does not want to believe it will never in this world be able to help the truth to victory." Adolf Hitler, *Mein Kampf*, trans. Ralph Manheim, p. 211.

29. Hugh Trevor-Roper, *The Last Days of Adolf Hitler*, 2nd ed., p. 3.

30. Piers Brendon, *The Dark Valley: A Panorama of the 1930s*, p. 91.

31. Russel Lemmons, *Goebbels and Der Angriff*, p. 11.
32. Alexandra Richie, *Faust's Metropolis: A History of Berlin*, p. 225.
33. Brendon, *The Dark Valley*, p. 92.
34. Ibid.
35. No wonder those like Bruno would count this moment one of the most important in their Nazi careers, when they all came together for their first collective show of strength: "October 9–10, 1926: The first National Socialist Freedom Day of the Mark Brandenburg in Potsdam," wrote a gardening apprentice, born in 1905, "six hundred brownshirts under the command of SA leader Kurt Daluege, we are marching along the old army route followed by General Lützow into Potsdam. . . . That night in the festival hall of the airship port, Dr. Goebbels, the drummer of the Ruhr area, spoke to us. His speech made the meeting into a church service. The hall is no longer on the sands of Brandenburg, but a cathedral in the plains of Flanders. Young war volunteers now are the parishioners who are crowding closer and closer to the altar. . . . Dr. Goebbels no longer speaks as a party man, but as a *Führer* who has returned from the fire of the first front lines to inspire new reserves and lead them into battle." Merkl, *Political Violence*, p. 448.

CHAPTER FIVE. STREET-FIGHTING MAN, 1926–1933

1. "They called themselves 'political soldiers.' Élan and audacity were their dogmas . . . the destruction of all social connections had made them rootless. With many, going berserk was overcompensation for their measureless weakness, their camaraderie a product of their fear of being alone." Rudolf Diels, a senior Weimar police officer, quoted by Benjamin Carter Hett, *Crossing Hitler: The Man Who Put Hitler on the Witness Stand*, p. 70.
2. "Berlin! What wishes and hope, curses and threats are released at the sound of this name! Berlin—the magical destination which pulls in all those seeking adventure, the international meeting place of all the races and peoples of the earth, the breeding place for the worst kind of piracy. . . . And in the casemate of this red fortress are people [Nazis] who swim against the current and because of it receive the filthy hate of an overpowerful press. They are spit upon . . . and if they fall in the hands of the masses [they are] beaten, kicked, murdered. . . . In plain German: Berlin is red and Jewish at the same time. Each political occasion, each election proves it again." Quoted by Pamela Swett, *Neighbors and Enemies: The Culture of Radicalism in Berlin, 1929–1933*, p. 166.
3. Peter Merkl, *Political Violence Under the Swastika: 581 Early Nazis*, p. 349.
4. "What we need is not a hundred or two hundred daring conspirators, but a hundred thousand and hundreds of thousands more fanatical fighters for our *Weltanschauung*. . . . We have to teach Marxism that National Socialism is the future master of the streets, just as it will one day be master of the State." Jeremy Noakes and Geoffrey Pridham, *Nazism: A Documentary Reader.* Vol. 1: *The Rise to Power 1919–1945*, p. 56.
5. The *"Hauptstadt* of Vice" according to Wyndham Lewis. See David Clay Large, *Berlin*, p. 157.
6. Alexandra Richie, *Faust's Metropolis: A History of Berlin*, p. 156.
7. Peter Merkl, *The Making of a Stormtrooper*, p. 166.

8. Count Harry Kessler, *Berlin in Light: The Diaries of Count Harry Kessler, 1918–1937*, p. 265.

9. Merkl, *The Making of a Stormtrooper*, p. 169.

10. "One after the other, our four speakers had their say, interrupted by furious howling and catcalls. . . . There followed a battle with beer *tankards*, chairs, and the like, and in two minutes the hall was demolished and everyone cleared out. We had to take back seven heavily injured comrades that day and there were rocks thrown at us," reported one gleeful, bleeding SA man. Ibid., p. 400.

11. Russel Lemmons, *Goebbels and Der Angriff*, p. 15.

12. "The year proceeded with propaganda, "hall protection" [aka meeting brawls], and such like, as well as maintaining impressive military disposition, if not with weapons, then with the demeanor of our discipline and our organization." Hans Maikowski, *Sturm 33: Geschrieben von Kameraden des Toten*, p. 25.

13. Goebbels published a book with the portentous title *Kampf um Berlin* (*The Struggle for Berlin*), full of Homeric exaggeration about the scale and success of his engineered brawls. SA men looked back on this early period with the euphoric pride of evangelical martyrs: "Only a man who fought side by side with me at the time can understand what it meant to be a storm trooper in a Marxist stronghold. . . . Wherever we went we encountered resistance and I took home a smarting reminder." Merkl, *The Making of a Stormtrooper*, p. 398.

14. Like Johannes Rutgers's 1908 book *Rassenverbesserung* (Race Improvement), full of suggestions about how to "solve" the problem of "rebuilding" the state by deciding who should live and who not.

15. Veterans associations, and close allies of the Nazis.

16. Poets, too, were seduced by all things New York, as writer Gottfried Benn complained: "There is a group of poets who believe that they have written a poem if they write the word 'Manhattan.' . . . All German literature since 1918 has been trading on the slogans 'tempo,' or 'jazz,' or 'cinema,' or 'overseas.' . . . I myself am against Americanism. I am of the opinion that the philosophy . . . of the permanent grin—'keep smiling'—is not appropriate to western man and his history." Quoted in Richie, *Faust's Metropolis*, p. 213.

17. Her shows were "a mixture of jungle and skyscraper, [like] the tone and rhythm of their music, jazz. Ultramodern and ultraprimitive . . . In comparison, our own products hang like a limp bow string, lacking inner tension and therefore style, and with far too much of a 'cozy parlour' origin about them." Kessler, *Berlin in Light*, p. 282.

18. Pamela Swett, *Neighbors and Enemies: The Culture of Radicalism in Berlin, 1929–1933*, p. 107.

19. Richie, *Faust's Metropolis*, p. 391.

20. Large, *Berlin*, p. 249.

21. Swett, *Neighbors and Enemies*, p. 174.

22. Large, *Berlin*, p. 249.

23. Maikowski, *Sturm 33*, p. 32.

24. Much of the following detail of Sturm 33 activities comes from Sven Reichardt's definitive study, "Vergemeinschaftung durch Gewalt: Das Beispiel des SA-Mordersturms 33 in Berlin-Charlottenbug," in *Beiträge zur Geschichte der Nationalsozialistischen Verfolgung in Norddeutschland* (Bremen: Temmen, 2002).

25. Maikowski, *Sturm 33*, p. 77.
26. Ibid.
27. Ibid., p. 16.
28. Later, a political amnesty called by Chancellor Schleicher allowed him to return and resume his upward spiral through the ranks of the SA.
29. Maikowski, *Sturm 33*, p. 34
30. See Hett, *Crossing Hitler*.
31. Though there was no official court stenographer, Benjamin Hett reproduces as full a transcript as possible in an appendix to his book, and it makes truly fascinating reading:

Litten: Are you not aware for the terminology of the Freikorps, that the expression "Roll Kommando" has taken on the meaning: a commando for the elimination of disliked opponents under all circumstances?

Hitler: Among us National Socialists the concept of a Roll Kommando is a laughable one. Already seven years ago I wrote that our goals could not be reached with bombs, hand grenades, and pistols, but rather through setting masses in motion.

Litten: You said that no violent actions are carried out by the National Socialist Party. But didn't Goebbels come up with the slogan "the enemy must be beaten to a pulp"?

Hitler: That is not to be taken literally! It means that one must defeat and destroy the opponent organizations, not that one attacks and murders the opponent. (Ibid., p. 265.)

32. And in the cinemas: one of Goebbels's most successful displays of street muscle was his campaign to have the movie version of *All Quiet on the Western Front* banned from Berlin cinemas for being too pacifist, and too American.
33. The death of fifteen-year-old Hitler Youth Herbert Norkus is only too typical: "There in the bleak, grey twilight, yellowed, tortured eyes stare into the emptiness. His tender heart has been trampled into a bloody pulp. Long, deep wounds extend down the slender body, and a deadly laceration tears through his lungs and heart. . . . Yet it is as life stirs anew out of pale death. Look now, the slender, elegant body begins to move. Slowly, slowly, he rises as if conjured up by magic, until he stands tall in all his youthful glory right before my trembling eyes. And without moving his lips, a frail child's voice is heard as if speaking from all eternity: 'They killed me. . . . This happened only because I—still a child—wanted to serve my country. . . . *I am Germany.* . . . What is mortal in me will perish, but my spirit, which is immortal, will remain with you. And it . . . will show you the way. Until the Reich comes.'" Lemmons, *Goebbels and Der Angriff,* p. 78.
34. Jay Baird, "Goebbels, Horst Wessel, and the Myth of Resurrection and Return," *Journal of Contemporary History* 17:4 (October 1982), p. 635.
35. It also helped that Wessel took a month to die (having avoided getting critical early treatment because the only local doctor was Jewish), which allowed Goebbels to wring weeks of *Angriff* articles out of it, as Wessel slowly slipped away into the pantheon of Nazi saints: "As I stand at his deathbed, I can hardly believe that this was Horst Wessel. His face is waxen yellow, and his wounds are still covered with bandages. . . . His crumpled cold hands are adorned with flowers—white and red tulips, and violets. Horst Wessel has passed away. His earthly remains lie here

mute and silent. But I feel it in my bones—I am absolutely sure of it—his soul is resurrected, to live among us all. . . . He is marching in our columns!" Quoted ibid., p. 639.

36. Lemmons, *Goebbels and Der Angriff*, p. 81.

37. A further consequence of Stennes's outraged break with Party central was that he would appear as a key witness in the Hans Litten trial (alongside Fritz Hahn, Bruno's old boss from Sturm 33), aggressively cross-examined by Litten in pursuit of evidence that Hitler had indeed sanctioned SA violence.

38. The Untersuchungs- und Schlichtungsausschuss, or Committee for Investigation and Settlement, the NSDAP court.

39. Lemmons, *Goebbels and Der Angriff*, p. 85.

40. Ibid., p. 86.

41. Anthony Read, *The Devil's Disciples*, p. 211.

42. Officially subordinate to the much larger SA, the SS (Schutzstaffel, or "Protection Squad") had its origins in the early 1920s as a special battalion with the responsibility of providing Hitler with a bodyguard. After 1929, it was run by Heinrich Himmler and, in contrast to the SA, never intended to become a mass movement. Himmler saw the SS as an elite unit, the Party's "Praetorian Guard," with all SS personnel selected on the principles of "racial purity" and unconditional loyalty to the Nazi Party.

43. Quoted Richard J. Evans, *The Coming of the Third Reich*, p. 223.

44. Lemmons, *Goebbels and Der Angriff*, p. 81.

45. Ian Kershaw, *Hitler: 1889–1936: Hubris*, p. 349.

46. The SA were, needless to say, in the thick of it, as described by one driven to a state of elated exhaustion, outlining what for Bruno must have become a regular experience: "Prior to the elections we did not get to see our beds for two weeks. Every night we put up posters and guarded them and tore off those of the enemies; we painted slogans on streets, fences, and rock walls, painted over those of the enemies, or 'corrected' them with appropriate additions. Since there were not enough activists to do this, we could never afford to rest. When the days were not long enough to pass out leaflets, they had to be shoved under doors at night. Sometimes we spent whole nights making up flyers or painting posters because there was rarely enough money to have them made. Like criminals we used to sneak through the streets at night so as not to arouse the attention of the police and of the enemies. We were not motivated by hopes for a position or for the gratitude of posterity, but only by blind obedience to the Führer." Quoted by Merkl, *Political Violence*, p. 440.

47. Richie, *Faust's Metropolis*, p. 399.

48. Large, *Berlin*, p. 238.

49. Ibid., p. 232.

50. Sebastian Haffner, *The Meaning of Hitler*, 2nd ed., p. 26.

CHAPTER SIX. TRIUMPH OF THE WILL, 1933–1937

1. Theodore Abel, *Why Hitler Came into Power*, p. 112.

2. Peter Fritzsche, *Life and Death in the Third Reich*, p. 41.

3. Richard J. Evans, *The Coming of the Third Reich*, p. 313.

4. Ibid.

5. The following year, his SA comrades even published a hagiographical tribute to their deceased *Sturmführer*: "That was Hans Maikowski: comrade and officer, nature-rambler and politician, National Socialist revolutionary. He embodied the ideal of the new leadership that the National Socialist movement has given rise to. We knew him as West Berlin's Horst Wessel." Hans Maikowski, *Sturm 33: Geschrieben von Kameraden des Toten*, p. 76.

6. In the words of one SA man, what was about to be unleashed represented the climax to years of uninterrupted struggle: "The years 1930/1 passed with constant fighting and proselytizing. After many a successful meeting-hall and electoral battle we thought that now our Führer would come to power . . . but not yet. . . . We SA men . . . were almost all unemployed. With a wife and child, I got ten marks on the dole. We lived on that the whole week. . . . I went out every night to protect our propaganda and election rallies. We were laughed at and ridiculed and punished, but never lost our faith in Adolf Hitler and his mission. Even after his appointment as Chancellor . . . we lay in waiting many a night in case the Communists would rise up, which they would have done if our Führer had not gone after them with an iron fist." Peter Merkl, *Political Violence Under the Swastika: 581 Early Nazis*, p. 436.

7. Alexandra Richie, *Faust's Metropolis: A History of Berlin*, p. 410.

8. Evans, *The Coming of the Third Reich*, p. 334.

9. This is why, for years, the rumor persisted it had all been a Nazi ruse—almost certainly untrue; in the end, the fire was just one of a long list of random bits of luck that convinced later Nazis that Hitler was providentially blessed.

10. Evans, *The Coming of the Third Reich*, p. 337.

11. Richard Overy, *The Dictators: Hitler's Germany, Stalin's Russia*, p. 232.

12. "That which summons you, German *Volk*, can alone lead you on the right path . . . safely to the light—to freedom and honor—your *Volk*'s Führer, your Führer! All of this is no longer an image, but a reality, a miracle, God's hand above our Führer and our *Volk*!" Quoted by David Redles, *Hitler's Millennial Reich: Apocalyptic Belief and the Search for Salvation*, pp. 83–84.

13. The SA nevertheless remained a large-scale Nazi organization to the end: see Bruce Campbell, "The SA After the Röhm Purge," *Journal of Contemporary History* 28:4 (October 1993), pp. 659–74.

14. Eleanor Hancock, *Ernst Röhm: Hitler's SA Chief of Staff*, p. 165.

15. As another old Nazi put it: "One would never have believed that anyone could dare to disturb the peace in Germany. We expected the struggles in our souls caused by the fight of the foreign countries against us and the boycott of German goods by a Jewish campaign . . . but the whole German people, which stood solidly behind Adolf Hitler, simply could not believe the treason of the unfaithful of 30 June 1934. It was particularly incredible that some of the oldest fighting comrades of Adolf Hitler would break the faith. With his customary and heroic activism, the Führer intervened like a man and stopped the treason. Again the German people were freed from a danger so great it boggles the imagination." Merkl, *Political Violence*, p. 400.

16. Nuremberg was where Berlin storm troopers had found their spiritual replenishment since the late 1920s. One of them had sardonically noted in 1927 that they

had gone expecting to have flowerpots hurled at them, but had instead been garlanded with flowers. Maikowski, *Sturm* 33, p. 24.

17. "The organizing committee was expecting 500,000 people to attend the rally—
180,000 political leaders, 88,000 storm troopers, 12,000 SS men, 60,000 Hitler
Youths, 50,000 Labor Service men, 120,000 Party members, and 9,000 SS functionaries and special police to handle the traffic." Hamilton T. Burden, *The Nuremberg Rallies: 1923–39*, p. 79.

18. Richard J. Evans, *The Third Reich in Power*, p. 40.

19. Communing with caves full of mystical crystals, for example, as in *Das Blaue Licht*
(*The Blue Light*), which she made in 1932.

20. To use George Steiner's phrase, in an interview given for the BBC documentary,
transmitted December 12, 1992.

21. For example, the cheesy opening sequence (in which Hitler, in his shining silver
Junkers tri-motor, descends like a god, his aircraft prizing the clouds apart, its cru-
ciform shadow caressing the buildings and marching columns below, a mix of Nazi
eagle, heavenly benediction, and cross-hairs of a bomb sight) culminates in Hitler
emerging from his plane both completely out of focus and mostly out of frame.
Other sequences, too, are impossible to watch without cringing—none more so than
its celebration of German laborers, men in uniforms brandishing their autobahn-
building spades instead of rifles, who bark out in unconvincing close-ups from
which parts of Germany they hale (all parts, it turns out—this is the worker's paradise of the new *Volksgemeinschaft*, after all).

22. Apart from snatches of sync from the speeches and a few very badly inserted sound
bites (which had to be shot later in a specially reconstructed set in Berlin), most of
the film is music and image only.

23. All of this is recorded in a long affidavit attached to Bruno's personnel file and
backed up by other BDC documents we tracked down.

CHAPTER SEVEN. MEN IN BLACK, 1937–1939

1. KdF, Strength Through Joy; BDM, the Union of German Women; DAF, German
Labor Front—the list was endless.

2. "We felt the time of a new 'brown German' rise around us—words like *Einsatz*
(strike force), *Garant* (pledge), *fanatisch* (fanatical), *Volksgenosse* (race comrade),
Scholle (soil), *Artfremd* (race alien), *Untermensch* (subhuman)—a revolting jargon,
every word of which implied a world of violent stupidity." Sebastian Haffner, *Defying
Hitler: A Memoir*, p. 66.

3. The SA and the SS had their own rubric; their officer ranks were designated by the
title *Führer*, or leader, not, as in the army, *Offizier*, or officer.

4. Quoted by Richard Overy in *The Dictators: Hitler's Germany, Stalin's Russia*, p. 240.

5. Michael Burleigh, *The Third Reich: A New History*, p. 285.

6. Victor Klemperer, *I Shall Bear Witness: The Diaries of Victor Klemperer 1933–1941*,
p. 304.

7. See Bruce Campbell, "The SA After the Röhm Purge," *Journal of Contemporary
History* 28:4 (October 1993), pp. 659–74.

8. "Only policy, not administration, was effectively controlled at the center. . . . The
structure of German politics and administration, instead of being, as the Nazis

claimed, 'pyramidal' and 'monolithic,' was in fact a confusion of private empires, private armies and private intelligence services . . . every man whose position makes him either strong or vulnerable must protect himself against surprise by reserving from the common pool whatever power he has managed to acquire . . . politics become the politics of feudal anarchy, which the personal power of an undisputed despot may conceal, but cannot alter." Hugh Trevor-Roper, *The Last Days of Adolf Hitler*, p. 2.

9. Michael Geyer, "The Nazi State Reconsidered," in Richard Bessel, ed., *Life in the Third Reich*, p. 61.

10. "However repulsive, and whatever their irrational basis, they did constitute a circular, self-reinforcing argument, impenetrable by rational critique, something which we can genuinely call a *Weltanschauung*, or ideology. This ideology was formed no later than 1925. There were really no more than three core elements, each of them a long-term goal rather than a pragmatic middle-range political aim, resting on an underlying premise of human existence as racial struggle: 1) securing Germany's hegemony in Europe; 2) attainment of 'living space' (*Lebensraum*) to ensure the material basis for Germany's long-term future; and 3) removal of the Jews. It amounted to a vision of Germany's salvation—a glorious future in waiting. . . . From the beginning of his 'career' in 1919, Hitler fanatically pursued two interlinked goals: to restore Germany's greatness; and in so doing to avenge and make good the disgrace of the capitulation in 1918, punishing those responsible for the revolution that followed and the national humiliation that was fully revealed in the Treaty of Versailles of 1919." Ian Kershaw, *Hitler: The Germans and the Final Solution*, p. 90.

11. Klemperer, *I Shall Bear Witness*, p. 163.

12. Most famously his own namesake—the turn-of-the-century cultural critic Julius Langbehn, whose most influential work *Rembrandt als Erzieher* (Rembrandt as Educator) was a hugely best-selling, elegiac description of the withering of German culture. As a schoolchild, my mother grew sick of being pestered with wide-eyed inquiries: Was the family related to the great man? In fact they weren't, but Bruno always loved the coincidence, enhanced by the relative rarity of the surname Langbehn. The book is an increasingly familiar mix of one part idealism to two parts hatred, blending cultural despair and nationalist hope into a potent *völkisch* cocktail. Germany's genius was under attack, its *Geist* having the life drained out of it by an alien culture, identified as the Jewish, which Langbehn characterized as everything the German was not: deracinated, overintellectual, divisive, pornographic, internationalist. This style of thinking was soon an upscale cliché. See Fritz Stern, *The Politics of Cultural Despair: A Study in the Rise of the Germanic Ideology*, chapter 2.

13. "Certainly the Jews, German and non-German, were overwhelmingly attracted to the larger cities, where they engaged and excelled in such traditionally denigrated enterprises as journalism, finance, and commerce. Hence it became customary to identify Jews with all the hateful innovations of the new age. Paradoxically, this antimodern element in anti-Semitism modernized the ancient prejudice and gave it renewed impetus in industrial Germany." Ibid., p. 63.

14. Victor Klemperer, *I Shall Bear Witness*, p. 340.

15. Wibke Bruhns, *My Father's Country*, p. 210.

16. Sebastian Haffner, *Defying Hitler: A Memoir*, p. 117.

17. Friedrich Reck-Malleczewen, *Diary of a Man in Despair* (London, 2000), p. 42. Nothing commended Nazism to Unity more than its steadfast refusal to be taken in by the Jewish threat. She infamously told the *Stürmer* magazine: "The English have no notion of the Jewish danger. English Jews are always described as 'decent.' Perhaps the Jews in England are more clever with their propaganda than in other countries. . . . Our worst Jews work only behind the scenes. They never come into the open, and therefore we cannot show them to the British public in their true dreadfulness. We hope, however, that we will soon win against the world enemy, in spite of his cunning. . . . England for the English! Out with the Jews! With German greeting, Heil Hitler!"

18. On June 17, 1936, Hitler appointed Himmler chief of German police in the Ministry of the Interior; his mastery over the entire German penal system was complete.

19. Policing the "healthy instincts of the people" was a brutal and blunt affair, contemptuously hostile to the liberal pedantry of "mere" law. At the sharp end of the SS's new judicial machinery, with its Kripo detectives, Gestapo agents, its draconian (or merely cowed) judges, pliant lawyers, courts, prisons, and camps, stood Himmler's most cynical legal invention, "protective custody." Suspicion was now all that was required to warrant arrest and internment, and thousands found themselves picked up and behind bars without even a nod to due process. Prisoners whose sentences were regarded by the SS as too lenient were simply rearrested on being released and thrown into a camp. Their new sentences were kept deliberately, and demoralizingly, open-ended. See Burleigh, *The Third Reich*, chapter 2.

20. *Lebensunwertes Leben*—life not worth living.

21. This was addressed by defining the targeted group as an illness, against which strong new legislation was required, such as Himmler's law for the "Prevention of the Gypsy Plague."

22. Mario Dederichs, *Heydrich: The Face of Evil*, p. 80.

23. Though apparently Adolf Eichmann didn't know this, either, mistaking the SD as Himmler's personal bodyguard. David Cesarani, *Eichmann: His Life and Crimes*, p. 39. An older relative of mine made the same mistake regarding Bruno, claiming his SS career had been spent as part of Hitler's personal honor guard.

24. Yaacov Lozowick, *Hitler's Bureaucrats*, p. 20.

25. Burleigh, *The Third Reich*, p. 185.

26. Heydrich defined the SD's mandate as follows: "The overall purpose of the security police is to protect the German people as a complete entity, its vitality and its institutions, against every type of destruction and decay. It is a task that is both defensive and offensive in nature. Defensive, in beating back all the attacks of all other powers, which, in whatever way, could weaken or subvert either the People's—or the People's State's—health, vitality and ability to act. Offensive means proactively investigating and combating all that stands opposed, before it has the chance to undermine and subvert. Which enemies are these, then, who endanger the stock of the *Volksgemeinschaft* or the vitality of the German people. . . . First, it's individuals who from physical and spiritual degeneration have broken with the natural connections of the *völkisch*, and as sunken *Untermensch* service their unbridled urges and personal interests. Secondly, it's international worldview and spiritual powers, for which our people, in their racial foundation, and spiritual, sacred, and political

posture, stands in their way of their goals, and therefore is combated by them."
Quoted by Ulrich Herbert, in Hans Mommsen, ed., *The Third Reich: Between Vision
and Reality*, p. 103.

27. He was made head of the Inland-SD section in 1937, from where he propounded
his idea of *Weltanschauungskrieg*, or total ideology war.

28. This was the voice of the SD at its most self-servingly rational: "We simply recognize
that certain people and characteristics damage our nation and threaten its existence,
and we will resist this. Similarly, in the fight against the Jews our goal is freedom
from domination, a clear separation and specific rights for the foreigners. . . . It is
irrelevant to us whether a heavenly judge will deem Jewry valuable or worthless;
anti-Semitism is not a world-view but a political, economic and cultural defense.
The *völkisch* principle of recognition for each people and its right of existence
applies equally to the relationship with all other nations. In times of conflict we will
of course pursue the vital interests of our people even to the extent of annihilating
the opponent—but without the hatred and contempt of any value judgment."
Quoted by Ulrich Herbert, ibid., p. 105.

29. As an SD intellectual in Jonathan Littell's roman à clef *The Kindly Ones* puts it:
"The highest morality . . . consists in surmounting traditional inhibitions in the
search for the good of the *Volk*. In that, the *Kriegsjugendgeneration*, the 'war youth
generation,' to which he belonged along with Ohlendorf, Six . . . and also Heydrich,
was clearly distinct from the previous generation, the *junge Frontgeneration*, the
'youth of the front,' who had been in the war." Jonathan Littell, *The Kindly Ones*,
p. 471.

30. "[SD personnel] combined mindless assiduity of a familiar kind with what is better described as fertility rather than creativity. Whatever their love of chess or
pretensions to scientific objectivity, these men were driven by nihilism, paranoia
and resentment. . . . They were collectively marked by the experiences of their
generation, by a lost war, revolution, foreign occupation and economic turbulence,
which inclined them to elite forms of extreme right-wing politics." Burleigh, *The
Third Reich*, p. 185.

31. "Heydrich switched on a violet light and slowly there appeared all kinds of Masonic
cult objects in the shadows. Ghostly pale in the dimness, Heydrich moved around
the room explaining the whys and wherefores of the world conspiracy, the degrees
of initiation and, standing occult, naturally, at the head of the hierarchy, the Jews,
leading all humanity to its destruction. There were more low-ceilinged, narrow
rooms, equally dark, which one could only enter bent double, to be seized by the
shoulder by the bony hands of automatically operated skeletons." Count Berna-
dotte, quoted by Dederichs, *Heydrich: The Face of Evil*, p. 76.

32. Haffner, *Defying Hitler*, p. 71.

33. Sebastian Haffner, *The Meaning of Hitler*, 2nd ed., p. 59.

34. Such as the "Stahlhelm," the "Red-White-Black" association of German nationalists.

35. It was the SD that gave birth therefore to the new watchwords of the regime. Gone
was Front Generation *völkisch* bombast and anti-Communist rant. In their stead, as
one German historian has described it, "a combination of radicalism, ideology and
a specific form of reason—on the one hand an internal ideological rationality, on
the other hand an 'objectivity' (*Sachlichkeit*) combining efficiency and functionality

with ideological premises." Ulrich Herbert, in Mommsen, ed., *The Third Reich*, p. 96.

36. There are two words in German that have always struck me as particularly closely aligned: *Gewalt* (violence) and *Verwaltung* (administration). It was as though any process of administration that wasn't just paper pushing was, of its essence, violent—dynamic, resolute, utterly cold to the pain it caused. Violence, too, was not just shapeless aggression and gratuitous bloodshed, but an indispensable element in the shaping of anything of political value. As the Third Reich began to split into two parallel realms—that of ordinary administration and that of the secret Nazi state—the fusion of *Gewalt* and *Verwaltung* became closer and tighter.

37. The book's original English title is *Butcher's Broom*.

38. Quoted in Bruhns, *My Father's Country*, p. 240.

39. *Vierteljahreslagerbericht des Sicherheitshauptamtes.*

CHAPTER EIGHT. WAR! 1939–1944

1. Sebastian Haffner, *The Meaning of Hitler*, p. 33.

2. As Sebastian Haffner later put it: "Could one therefore still reject Hitler without rejecting all that he had accomplished? . . . Accomplished, moreover, on the whole not by demagogy but by achievement. . . . Anyone who, say, in 1938, uttered a critical remark about Hitler, in circles where that was still possible, would . . . have received the answer, 'But look at all the things the man has achieved!' Not, for instance, 'But isn't he an enthralling speaker!' . . . No, it was, 'But look at all the things the man has achieved!'" Ibid., p. 33.

3. "Where there are Germans, there is Germany," as the Nazi phrase had it.

4. Richard Bessel, *Nazism and War*, p. 73.

5. Territory that separated the East Prussian city of Danzig from the rest of Germany and provided Poland with access to the Baltic. Creating it had been one of the consequences of the Treaty of Versailles.

6. Now, God be thanked Who has matched us with His hour,
And caught our youth, and wakened us from sleeping,
With hand made sure, clear eye, and sharpened power,
To turn, as swimmers into cleanness leaping,
Glad from a world grown old and cold and weary,
Leave the sick hearts that honour could not move,
And half-men, and their dirty songs and dreary,
And all the little emptiness of love!

Oh! we, who have known shame, we have found release there,
Where there's no ill, no grief, but sleep has mending,
Naught broken save this body, lost but breath;
Nothing to shake the laughing heart's long peace there
But only agony, and that has ending;
And the worst friend and enemy is but Death.

7. Wibke Bruhns, *My Father's Country*, p. 254.

8. Haffner, *The Meaning of Hitler*, p. 68.

9. An SD report dated June 20 stated that "the recent enthusiasm gives the impression

every time that no greater enthusiasm is possible, and yet with every fresh event, the population gives its joy an even more intense expression." Quoted in Richard J. Evans, *The Third Reich at War*, p. 135.

10. Alexandra Richie, *Faust's Metropolis: A History of Berlin*, p. 493.

11. Ibid., p. 494.

12. Piers Brendon, *The Dark Valley: A Panorama of the 1930s*, p. 464.

13. As *Gaufachschaftswalter für Dentisten mit Praxis*, a DAF functionary responsible for the administration of dental policies, and *Landesdienststellenleiter*, head of regional administration in charge of Berlin's 2,000 practicing dentists.

14. Mark Mazower, *Hitler's Empire: Nazi Rule in Occupied Europe*, p. 139.

15. Ibid., p. 143.

16. Even the generals, who had previously demurred over questions of harsh treatment in Poland, had no hesitation explaining to their troops what was now required of them. The result is an "Armageddon of biblical dimensions," about which Franz Halder, general chief of staff of the army, writes in his diary: "This war is beginning to degenerate into a brawl far removed from all previous forms of war." Hitler writes on March 3, 1941: "This campaign is more than just a battle of arms. It's the battle between two opposed political systems, the clash of two world-views." Hitler on March 30: "We must withdraw from any viewpoint of soldierly comradeship. The Communist was no comrade before, and he will be no comrade afterward. It is a battle of destruction." Bruhns, *My Father's Country*, p. 267.

17. Ibid.

18. Christopher Browning, *The Origins of the Final Solution: The Evolution of Nazi Jewish Policy, 1939–42*, p. 309.

19. Mazower, *Hitler's Empire*, p. 171.

20. French L. MacLean, *The Field Men: The SS Officers Who Led the Einsatzkommandos— the Nazi Mobile Killing Units*, p. 13.

21. Browning, *The Origins of the Final Solution*, p. 309.

22. Ibid., p. 291.

23. Kershaw, *Hitler: Hubris*, p. 468.

24. Richard Overy, *The Dictators: Hitler's Germany, Stalin's Russia*, p. 253.

25. "I shall speak to you here with all frankness of a very serious subject. We shall now discuss it absolutely openly among ourselves, nevertheless we shall never speak of it in public. I mean the evacuation of the Jews, the extermination of the Jewish people. It is one of those things that is very easy to say. 'The Jewish people is to be exterminated,' says every Party member. 'That's clear, it's part of our program, elimination of the Jews, extermination, right, we'll do it.' And they all come along, the eighty million good Germans, and each one has his decent Jew. Of course, the others are all swine, but this one is a first-class Jew. Of all those who talk like this, not one has watched, not one has stood up to it. Most of you know what it means to see a hundred corpses lying together, five hundred, or a thousand. To have gone through this and yet—apart from a few exceptions, examples of human weakness—to have remained decent, this has made us hard. This is a glorious page in our history that has never been written and never shall be written."

To get an idea about the nature and the meaning of this speech, you need to *hear* it. Extraordinarily, you can, as a recording of it has survived. I used it in a film I made about Albert Speer (who was accused of having been in the audience for the speech, which would render his "I didn't know, but should have" null and void), and ended up having to listen to it a number of times. It's not just the words that shock, it's the tone of weary self-importance in which Himmler delivers them and, worst of all, the (audible) audience reaction to them. Himmler even cracks a joke; the lines "And they all come along, the eighty million good Germans, and each one has his *decent Jew*. Of course, the others are all swine, but this one is *a first-class Jew*" are a sardonic throwaway. A kind of eye-rolling levity forms in the timbre of his voice: those people with their *"prima Juden."* A flutter of jaded recognition goes around the room, a clearly audible polite snigger. It's not even funny enough for a proper laugh; it's a truism, enough for a shared shrug of recognition. The audience does him the courtesy of giving him their deepest deference and attention. But they are all colleagues here, so the tone needn't be all forbidding and solemn. His bon mot delivered, Himmler then raises his voice to its orotund conclusion, grasping the lectern, head up, eyes forward, a glint, and the overenunciated cadence of history being made. Nobody in this room is being told either what he doesn't already know or what hasn't started to bore him. Bruno wasn't there—he wasn't senior enough—but his superiors were, not one of whom would have had any more inhibition about discussing its content than Himmler had in drawing them into the SS's gravest secret in the first place.

26. Walter Schellenberg, *The Memoirs of Hitler's Spymaster*, p. 21.
27. Mazower, *Hitler's Empire*, p. 112.
28. Schellenberg, *Memoirs*, p. 308.
29. Befehlsblatt des Chefs der Sicherheitspolizei und des SD, no. 5, Berlin, January 30, 1943.

CHAPTER NINE. ENDGAME, 1944–1946

1. Heinz Höhne, *The Order of the Death's Head: The Story of Hitler's SS*, p. 515.
2. Walter Schellenberg, *The Memoirs of Hitler's Spymaster*, p. 351.
3. The name features in two famous accounts of wartime Berlin, one autobiographical, the other fictional. The first is Christabel Bielenberg's moving memoir *The Past Is Myself*, which charts her life in Berlin married to a German lawyer (she was British, and her book was later dramatized by Dennis Potter). The second is Len Deighton's epic family saga (and roman à clef) set between the years 1900 and 1945, called simply *Winter*, in which Carl's tragic story makes a cameo appearance.
4. "A radio message about Dr. Langbehn's negotiations with Allied representatives in Switzerland was intercepted, and the fact that Dr. Langbehn had my blessing in this completely unofficial undertaking was mentioned . . . but Kersten's [Himmler's masseur] influence over Himmler saved me from disaster." Schellenberg, *Memoirs*, p. 428.
5. See Callum MacDonald and Jan Kaplan, *Prague: In the Shadow of the Swastika*, pp. 95–105.
6. Chad Bryant, *Prague in Black: Nazi Rule and Czech Nationalism*, p. 184.
7. Ibid.
8. Dr. Walter Hammer, another SD *Einsatzgruppe* commander, who had been in charge of Bruno's unit back in Berlin, Amt VIE, and who was now head of Prague SD.
9. Bryant, *Prague in Black*, p. 230.
10. Giles MacDonogh, *After the Reich: From the Liberation of Vienna to the Berlin Airlift*, p. 132.

11. MacDonald and Kaplan, *Prague*, p. 180.
12. Dr. Erwin Weinmann, another SD officer with a degree (in his case, medicine) who had commanded an *Einsatzkommando* earlier in the war.
13. MacDonald and Kaplan, *Prague*, p. 180.
14. Ibid., p. 192.
15. Bryant, *Prague in Black*, p. 235.
16. Mark Mazower, *Hitler's Empire: Nazi Rule in Occupied Europe*, pp. 546–47.
17. Giles MacDonogh, *After the Reich*, p. 135.
18. Ibid., p. 136.
19. MacDonald and Kaplan, *Prague*, p. 202.
20. The institute's goal is to support and conduct historical research on the Final Solution in Bohemia and Moravia and on Terezín ghetto, and to offer its findings to the public.

10. AFTERMATH, 1946–1992

1. Nicknamed *"Rasinenbomber"* ("raisin bombers") by Berliners.
2. See Peter Hayes, *From Cooperation to Complicity: Degussa in the Third Reich*.
3. All of this is a standard part of a certain German veteran mind-set. I tracked down an issue from May 2000 of a German Waffen SS veterans' magazine, *Der Freiwillige* (The Volunteer), which commemorated the events around Prague, and whose main article reiterated all these opinions as received fact.

POSTSCRIPT

1. Yaacov Lozowick, the author of a particularly illuminating study of Eichmann and his fellow Nazi administrators (*Hitler's Bureaucrats*), proposes four separate levels of evil. The first kind can be called "indifference." This is the ability to live while ignoring the suffering of others, when the suffering is not the result of our own actions. More troubling is the second kind of evil, "selfishness, the ability to cause suffering without intending it, but also without being bothered by it. An example could be selling arms to a dictatorship in order to provide employment for our own citizens." Then comes "heartlessness." The "heartless cause suffering consciously in order to advance their own interests. There is a large measure of evil here, since we first encounter the active desire to cause suffering, [either] limited suffering to an entire community . . . [or] absolute suffering on a small scale, such as terrorist organizations that murder individuals in order to advance their goals." But after indifference, selfishness, heartlessness comes the worst of all, "malevolence." The "malevolent are those who devote all their powers to causing as much suffering as possible." They also work in a coordinated and committed way, even to their own short-term detriment, to do everything necessary to make the exercise of their malevolence possible, justifying it (though not thereby diluting it) with reference to some larger goal, which, in itself, may not be defined in an explicitly malevolent way. For Lozowick, however, it is misleading to regard this process as a "slippery slope," an incremental series of steps by which somebody ends up an inadvertent perpetrator. He disputes this image and replaces it with one quite different: "mountain climbing." Instead of working toward malevolence absentmindedly, it is

achieved by conscious effort: "Just as a man does not reach the peak of Mount Everest by accident, so Eichmann and his ilk did not come to murder Jews by accident, or in a fit of absentmindedness, nor by blindly obeying orders or by being small cogs in a big machine. They worked hard, thought hard, took the lead, over many years. They were the alpinists of evil." Yaacov Lozowick, *Hitler's Bureaucrats*, pp. 277–79.

Bibliography

Abel, Theodore. *Why Hitler Came into Power.* Cambridge, Mass.: Harvard University Press, 1986.

Adam, Peter. *The Arts of the Third Reich.* London: Thames & Hudson, 1992.

Ahamed, Liaquat. *Lords of Finance: 1929, The Great Depression and the Bankers Who Broke the West.* London: Heinemann, 2009.

Ailsby, Christopher. *The Third Reich Day by Day.* Staplehurst, England: MBI, 2005.

Aly, Götz, and Susanne Heim. *Architects of Annihilation: Auschwitz and the Logic of Destruction.* London: Weidenfeld & Nicolson, 2002.

Anonymous. *A Woman in Berlin.* London: Virago, 2005.

Arendt, Hannah. *Eichmann in Jerusalem: A Report on the Banality of Evil.* New York: Viking, 1963.

Arendt, Hannah, *The Origins of Totalitarianism.* London: Allen & Unwin, 1973.

Aronson, Shlomo. *Reinhard Heydrich und die Frühgeschichte von Gestapo und SD.* Stuttgart: Deutsche-Verlags Anstalt, 1971.

Baird, Jay W. "From Berlin to Neubabelsberg: Nazi Film Propaganda and Hitler Youth Quex." *Journal for Contemporary History* 18 (1983), pp. 495–515.

Baird, Jay W. "Goebbels, Horst Wessel, and the Myth of Resurrection and Return." *Journal of Contemporary History,* 17:4 (October 1982), pp. 633–50.

Baldwin, Peter. "Social Interpretations of Nazism: Renewing a Tradition." *Journal of Contemporary History* 25:1 (January 1990), pp. 5–37.

Barron, Stephanie, ed. *Degenerate Art: The Fate of the Avant-Garde in Nazi Germany.* Los Angeles: Los Angeles County Museum of Art/Harry N. Abrams, 1991.

Beevor, Antony. *Berlin: The Downfall.* London: Viking, 2002.

Berg, Manfred, and Geoffrey Cocks, eds. *Medicine and Modernity.* Cambridge, England: Cambridge University Press, 2002.

Bessel, Richard. *Germany After the First World War.* Oxford: Oxford University Press, 1993.

Bessel, Richard. *Nazism and War.* London: Weidenfeld & Nicolson, 2004.

Bessel, Richard. *Political Violence and the Rise of Nazism: The Storm Troopers in Eastern Germany 1925–1934.* London: Yale University Press, 1984.

Biddiscombe, Perry. *The Denazification of Germany.* Stroud, England: Tempus, 2007.

Biddiscombe, Perry. *The Last Nazis: SS Werewolf Guerrilla Resistance in Europe 1944–1947.* Stroud, England: Tempus, 2000.

Biddiscombe, Perry. "*Unternehmen* Zeppelin: The Deployment of SS Saboteurs and Spies in the Soviet Union, 1942–45." *Europe-Asia Studies* 52:6 (2000), pp. 1115–42.

Bielenberg, Christabel. *The Past Is Myself.* London: Chatto & Windus, 1968.

Black, Peter. "Ernst Kaltenbrunner: Chief of the Reich Security Main Office." In Ronald Smelser and Rainer Zitelmann, eds., *The Nazi Elite,* trans. Mary Fischer, pp. 133–43. New York: New York University Press, 1993.

Brendon, Piers. *The Dark Valley: A Panorama of the 1930s.* London: Jonathan Cape, 2000.

Broszat, Martin. *Hitler and the Collapse of Weimar Germany.* Leamington Spa, England, and New York: Berg, 1987.

Browder, George C. *Foundations of the Nazi Police State: The Formation of Sipo and SD.* Lexington: University Press of Kentucky, 1990.

Browder, George C. *Hitler's Enforcers: The Gestapo and the SS Security Service in the Nazi Revolution.* New York and Oxford: Oxford University Press, 1996.

Browning, Christopher R. *Ordinary Men: Reserve Police, Battalion 101, and the Final Solution in Poland.* New York: HarperCollins, 1993.

Browning, Christopher R. *The Origins of the Final Solution: The Evolution of Nazi Jewish Policy, 1939–42.* London: Heinemann, 2004.

Bruhns, Wibke. *My Father's Country.* London: Heinemann, 2008.

Bryant, Chad. *Prague in Black: Nazi Rule and Czech Nationalism.* Cambridge, Mass.: Harvard University Press, 2007.

Burden, Hamilton T. *The Nuremberg Rallies: 1923–39.* London: Praeger, 1967.

Burleigh, Michael. *The Third Reich: A New History.* London: Macmillan, 2000.

Burleigh, Michael, and Wolfgang Wippermann. *The Racial State: Germany 1933–1945.* Cambridge, England: Cambridge University Press, 1991.

Buruma, Ian. *Wages of Guilt.* London: Jonathan Cape, 1994.

Campbell, Bruce. "The SA After the Röhm Purge." *Journal of Contemporary History* 28:4 (October 1993), pp. 659–74.

Campbell, Bruce. *The SA Generals and the Rise of Nazism.* Lexington: University Press of Kentucky, 1998.

Cesarani, David. *Eichmann: His Life and Crimes.* London: Heinemann, 2004.

Childers, Thomas, and Eugene Weiss. "Voters and Violence: Political Violence and the Limits of National Socialist Mass Mobilisation." *German Studies Review* 13:3 (October 1990), pp. 481–98.

Clay, Catrine, and Michael Leapmahn. *Master Race: The Lebensborn Experiment in Nazi Germany.* London: Hodder & Stoughton, 1995.

Collins, Larry, and Dominique Lapierre. *Is Paris Burning?* New York: Gollancz, 1965.

Conrad, Peter. *Modern Times, Modern Places: Life and Art in the Twentieth Century.* London: Thames & Hudson, 1998.

Cvancara, Jaroslav. *Heydrich.* Prague: Gallery, 2004.

Dederichs, Mario. *Heydrich: The Face of Evil.* London: Greenhill, 2006.

Deighton, Len. *Winter: A Berlin Family, 1899–1945.* London: Hutchinson, 1987.

Döscher, Hans-Jürgen. *"Reichskristallnacht": Die November-Pogrome 1938.* Frankfurt: Ullstein, 1988.

Engelbrechten, J. K. *Eine Braune Armee Ensteht: Die Geschichte der Berlin-Brandenburger SA* [A Brown Army Arises: The Story of the Berlin-Brandenburger SA]. Berlin and Munich: Franz Eher, 1937.

Evans, Richard J. *The Coming of the Third Reich.* London: Allen Lane, 2003.

Evans, Richard J. *The Third Reich in Power.* London: Allen Lane, 2005.

Evans, Richard J. *The Third Reich at War.* London: Allen Lane, 2008.

Fallada, Hans. *Alone in Berlin.* London: Penguin, 2009.

Fallada, Hans. *Little Man, What Now?* London: Allen & Unwin, 1996.

Ferguson, Niall. *The War of the World: History's Age of Hatred.* London: Allen Lane, 2006.

Fest, Joachim. *The Face of the Third Reich.* London: Weidenfeld & Nicolson, 1979.

Fest, Joachim. *Hitler.* London: Weidenfeld & Nicolson, 1974.

Fest, Joachim. *Plotting Hitler's Death: The Story of the German Resistance.* London: Weidenfeld & Nicolson, 1996.

Feuchtwanger, E. J. *From Weimar to Hitler: Germany 1918–37.* London: Macmillan, 1993.

Friedländer, Saul. *The Years of Extermination: Nazi Germany and the Jews, 1939–1945.* London: Weidenfeld & Nicolson, 2007.

Friedländer, Saul. *The Years of Persecution: Nazi Germany and the Jews, 1933–1939.* London: Weidenfeld & Nicolson, 1997.

Friedrich, Otto. *Before the Deluge: A Portrait of Berlin in the 1920s.* London: Michael Joseph, 1974.

Fritzsche, Peter. *Germans into Nazis.* Cambridge, Mass.: Harvard University Press, 1998.

Fritzsche, Peter. *Life and Death in the Third Reich.* Cambridge, Mass.: Harvard University Press, 2008.

Frommer, Benjamin. *National Cleansing: Retribution Against Nazi Collaborators in Post-war Czechoslovakia.* Cambridge, England: Cambridge University Press, 2005.

Fussell, Paul. *The Great War and Modern Memory.* Oxford: Oxford University Press, 1975.

Gellately, Robert. *Backing Hitler: Consent and Coercion in Nazi Germany.* Oxford: Oxford University Press, 2001.

Geyer, Michael. "The Nazi State Reconsidered." In Richard Bessel, ed., *Life in the Third Reich*, pp. 57–67. Oxford: Oxford University Press, 1987.

Geyer, Michael. "The Stigma of Violence, Nationalism, and War in Twentieth-Century Germany." *German Studies Review* 15: *German Identity* (Winter 1992), pp. 75–110.

Glassheim, Eagle. "Ethnic Cleansing, Communism and Environmental Devastation in Czechoslovakia's Borderlands, 1945–1989." *Journal of Military History* 78 (March 2006), pp. 65–92.

Golomb, Jacob, and Robert S. Wistrich, eds. *Nietzsche, Godfather of Fascism?* Princeton, N.J.: Princeton University Press, 2002.

Grant, Thomas D. *Stormtroopers and Crisis in the Nazi Movement.* London: Routledge, 2004.

Gregor, Neil, ed. *Nazism, War, and Genocide.* Exeter, England: University of Exeter Press, 2005.

Grunberger, Richard. *A Social History of the Third Reich.* London: Weidenfeld & Nicolson, 1971.

Haar, Inge, and Michael Fahlbusch. *German Scholars and Ethnic Cleansing, 1919–1945.* New York and Oxford: Berghahn, 2007.

Haffner, Sebastian. *Defying Hitler: A Memoir*. London: Weidenfeld & Nicolson, 2002.

Haffner, Sebastian. *The Meaning of Hitler*. 2nd ed. London: Weidenfeld & Nicolson, 2000.

Halliday, R. J. "Social Darwinism: A Definition." *Victorian Studies* 14:4 (June 1971), pp. 389–405.

Hamann, Brigitte. *Hitler's Vienna*. New York and Oxford: Oxford University Press, 1999.

Hamilton, Richard F. "The Rise of Nazism: A Case Study and Review of Interpretations: Kiel, 1928–1933." *German Studies Review* 26:1 (February 2003), pp. 43–62.

Hancock, Eleanor. *Ernst Röhm: Hitler's SA Chief of Staff*. New York: Palgrave Macmillan, 2008.

Hancock, Eleanor. "Ernst Röhm and the Experience of World War I." *Journal of Military History* 60 (January 1996), pp. 39–60.

Haste, Cate. *Nazi Women*. London: Channel 4 Books, 2001.

Hayes, Peter. *From Cooperation to Complicity: Degussa in the Third Reich*. Cambridge, England: Cambridge University Press, 2004.

Herf, Jeffrey. *The Jewish Enemy: Nazi Propaganda During World War II and the Holocaust*. Cambridge, Mass.: Harvard University Press, 2006.

Hett, Benjamin Carter. *Crossing Hitler: The Man Who Put Hitler on the Witness Stand*. Oxford: Oxford University Press, 2008.

Himmler, Katrin. *The Himmler Brothers: A German Family History*. London: Macmillan, 2007.

Hitchcock, William I. *Liberation: The Bitter Road to Freedom, Europe 1944–45*. London: Faber & Faber, 2009.

Hitler, Adolf. *Mein Kampf*. Trans. Ralph Manheim. London: Hutchinson, 1969.

Höhne, Heinz. *The Order of the Death's Head: The Story of Hitler's SS*. London: Secker & Warburg, 2000.

Höss, Rudolf. *Commandant of Auschwitz: The Autobiography of Rudolf Höss*. London: Weidenfeld & Nicolson, 1959.

Hutton, Christopher M. *Race and the Third Reich*. Boston and Cambridge, England: Polity Press, 2005.

Jackson, Julian. *The Fall of France: The Nazi Invasion of 1940*. Oxford: Oxford University Press, 2003.

Jakl, Tomas. *May 1945 in the Czech Lands*. Prague: MBI, 2004.

Jarausch, Konrad. *After Hitler: Recivilising Germans, 1945–1995*. Oxford: Oxford University Press, 2006.

Johnson, Eric. *The Nazi Terror: Gestapo, Jews and Ordinary Germans*. London: John Murray, 2000.

Johnson, Eric, and Karl-Heinz Reuband, eds. *What We Knew: Terror, Mass Murder, and Everyday Life in Nazi Germany*. London: John Murray, 2005.

Jones, Nigel. *The Birth of the Nazis: How the Freikorps Blazed a Trail for Hitler*. London: John Murray, 1987.

Judt, Tony. *Post-War: A History of Europe Since 1945*. London: Heinemann, 2005.

Jünger, Ernst. *The Storm of Steel*. Trans. Basil Creighton. London: Chatto & Windus, 1929.

Keegan, John. *The First World War*. London: Hutchinson, 1998.

Kershaw, Ian. *Hitler: 1889–1936: Hubris*. London: Allen Lane, 2000.

Kershaw, Ian. *Hitler: 1936–1945: Nemesis.* London: Allen Lane, 2000.

Kershaw, Ian. *Hitler: The Germans and the Final Solution.* New Haven and London: Yale University Press, 2008.

Kershaw, Ian. *The "Hitler Myth": Image and Reality in the Third Reich.* Oxford: The Clarendon Press, 1987.

Kessler, Count Harry. *Berlin in Light: The Diaries of Count Harry Kessler, 1918–1937.* London: Weidenfeld & Nicolson, 1971.

Klemperer, Victor. *I Shall Bear Witness: The Diaries of Victor Klemperer, 1933–41.* London: Weidenfeld & Nicolson, 1998.

Klemperer, Victor. *To the Bitter End: The Diaries of Victor Klemperer, 1942–45.* London: Weidenfeld & Nicolson, 1999.

Koonz, Claudia. *The Nazi Conscience.* Cambridge, Mass.: Harvard University Press, 2005.

Krockow, Christian von. *The Hour of the Women.* London: Faber & Faber, 1992.

Large, David Clay. *Berlin.* London: Allen Lane, 2001.

Lemmons, Russel. *Goebbels and Der Angriff.* Lexington: University Press of Kentucky, 1994.

Lepenies, Wolf. *The Seduction of Culture in German History.* Princeton, N.J.: Princeton University Press, 2006.

Liang, His-Huey. "The Berlin Police and the Weimar Republic." *Journal of Contemporary History* 4:4: *The Great Depression* (October 1969), pp. 157–72.

Littell, Jonathan. *The Kindly Ones.* London: Chatto & Windus, 2009.

Longerich, Peter. *Geschichte der SA.* Munich: C. H. Beck, 2003.

Longerich, Peter. *The Unwritten Order: Hitler's Role in the Final Solution.* Stroud, England: Tempus, 2003.

Lozowick, Yaacov. *Hitler's Bureaucrats.* London: Continuum, 2002.

Lunn, Joe. "Male Identity and Martial Codes of Honor: A Comparison of the War Memoirs of Robert Graves, Ernst Jünger, and Kande Kamara." *Journal for Military History* 69:3 (July 2005), pp. 713–35.

MacDonald, Callum, and Jan Kaplan. *Prague: In the Shadow of the Swastika.* Prague: Melantrich, 1995.

MacDonogh, Giles. *After the Reich: From the Liberation of Vienna to the Berlin Airlift.* London: John Murray, 2007.

MacLean, French L. *The Field Men: The SS Officers Who Led the Einsatzkommandos—the Nazi Mobile Killing Units.* Philadelphia: Schiffer, 1999.

Maikowski, Hans. *Sturm 33: Geschrieben von Kameraden des Toten.* 9th ed. Berlin: Deutsch Kultur-Wacht Oscar Berger, 1940.

Mazower, Mark. *Hitler's Empire: Nazi Rule in Occupied Europe.* New York and London: Allen Lane, 2008.

Meehan, Patricia. *A Strange Enemy People: Germans Under the British, 1945–1950.* London: Peter Owen, 2001.

Merkl, Peter. *The Making of a Stormtrooper.* Princeton, N.J.: Princeton University Press, 1980.

Merkl, Peter. *Political Violence Under the Swastika: 581 Early Nazis.* Princeton, N.J.: Princeton University Press, 1975.

Merridale, Catherine. *Ivan's War: The Red Army, 1939–45.* London: Faber & Faber, 2005.

Mollo, Andrew. *Sicherheitsdienst und Sicherheitspolizei 1931–1945*. Vol. 5 of *Uniforms of the SS*. London: Historical Research Unit, 1971.

Mommsen, Hans. *The Rise and Fall of Weimar Democracy*. Chapel Hill: University of North Carolina Press, 1996.

Mommsen, Hans, ed. *The Third Reich: Between Vision and Reality*. Oxford: Berg, 2001.

Müller-Hill, Benno. *Murderous Science: Elimination by Scientific Selection of Jews, Gypsies, and Others in Germany, 1933–1945*. Oxford: Cold Spring Harbor Laboratory Press/ Oxford University Press, 1998.

Nevin, Thomas. *Ernst Jünger and Germany: Into the Abyss, 1914–1945*, London: Constable, 1997.

Noakes, Jeremy, and Geoffrey Pridham. *The Rise to Power, 1919–1945*. Vol. 1 of *Nazism: A Documentary Reader*. Exeter, England: University of Exeter Press, 1983.

Noakes, Jeremy, and Geoffrey Pridham. *State, Economics, and Society, 1933–1945*. Vol. 2 of *Nazism: A Documentary Reader*. Exeter, England: University of Exeter Press, 1984.

Noakes, Jeremy, and Geoffrey Pridham. *Foreign Policy, War and Racial Extermination*. Vol. 3 of *Nazism: A Documentary Reader*. Exeter, England: University of Exeter Press, 1988.

Overy, Richard. *The Dictators: Hitler's Germany, Stalin's Russia*. London: Allen Lane, 2004.

Padfield, Peter. *Himmler: Reichsführer SS*. London: Macmillan, 1990.

Parker, Peter. *Isherwood: A Life*. London: Picador, 2004.

Paxton, Robert. *The Anatomy of Fascism*. London: Allen Lane, 2004.

Read, Anthony. *The Devil's Disciples*. London: Jonathan Cape, 2003.

Reck-Malleczewen, Friedrich. *Diary of a Man in Despair*. London: Duckworth, 2000.

Redles, David. *Hitler's Millennial Reich: Apocalyptic Belief and the Search for Salvation*. New York: New York University Press, 2005.

Reichardt, Sven. "Vergemeinschaftung durch Gewalt: Das Beispiel des SA-Mordersturms 33 in Berlin-Charlottenburg." In *Beiträge zur Geschichte der Nationalsozialistischen Verfolgung in Norddeutschland*. Bremen: Temmen, 2002.

Reitlinger, Gerald. *The SS: Alibi of a Nation*. New York: Heinemann, 1957.

Rhodes, Richard. *Masters of Death: The SS-Einsatzgruppen and the Invention of the Holocaust*. New York: Alfred A. Knopf, 2002.

Richie, Alexandra. *Faust's Metropolis: A History of Berlin*. London: HarperCollins, 1998.

Rürup, Reinhard, ed. *Topography of Terror: Gestapo, SS and Reichssicherheitshauptamt on the "Prinz-Albrecht-Terrain": A Documentation*. Trans. Werner T. Angress. London: William Arenhovel, 1989.

Schellenberg, Walter. *The Memoirs of Hitler's Spymaster*. London: André Deutsch, 2006.

Schneider, Helga. *Let Me Go: My Mother and the SS*. London: Vintage, 2004.

Schuster, Martin. "Die SA in der Nationalsozialisten 'Machtergreifung.'" In "Berlin und Brandenburg, 1926–1934." Ph.D. dissertation, Freie Universität, Berlin, 2005.

Shirer, William L. *The Rise and Fall of the Third Reich*. London: Secker & Warburg, 1960.

Stargardt, Nicholas. *Witnesses of War: Children's Lives Under the Nazis*. London: Jonathan Cape, 2005.

Stern, Fritz. *The Politics of Cultural Despair: A Study in the Rise of the Germanic Ideology*. Berkeley: University of California Press, 1974.

Stokes, Lawrence D. "Professionals and National Socialism: The Case-Histories of a Small-Town Lawyer and Physician, 1918–1945." *German Studies Review* 8:3 (October 1985), pp. 449–80.

Swett, Pamela E. *Neighbors and Enemies: The Culture of Radicalism in Berlin, 1929–1933.* Cambridge, England: Cambridge University Press, 2004.

Taylor, Ronald. *Berlin and Its Culture.* New Haven and London: Yale University Press, 1997.

Theweleit, Klaus. *Women, Floods, Bodies, History.* Vol. 1 of *Male Fantasies.* Minneapolis: University of Minnesota Press, 1987.

Timm, Uwe. *In My Brother's Shadow.* London: Bloomsbury, 2005.

Tooze, Adam. *The Wages of Destruction.* London: Allen Lane, 2006.

Traverso, Enzo. *The Origins of Nazi Violence.* New York and London: The New Press, 2003.

Trevor-Roper, Hugh. *The Last Days of Adolf Hitler.* 2nd ed. London: Macmillan, 1995.

Vick, Brian. "The Origins of the German Volk: Cultural Purity and National Identity in Nineteenth-Century Germany." *German Studies Review* 26:2 (May 2003), pp. 241–56.

Wachsmann, Niklaus. "Marching Under the Swastika? Ernst Jünger and National Socialism, 1918–1933." *Journal of Contemporary History* 33:4 (October 1998), pp. 573–89.

Weikart, Richard. *From Darwin to Hitler: Evolutionary Ethics, Eugenics, and Racism in Germany.* New York and London: Palgrave Macmillan, 2004.

Weinberg, Gerhard L. *Germany, Hitler, and World War II: Essays in Modern German History.* Cambridge, England: Cambridge University Press, 1995.

Weingart, Peter. "German Eugenics Between Science and Politics." *Osiris,* 2nd series, vol. 5: *Science in German: The Intersection of Institutional and Intellectual Issues* (1989), pp. 260–82.

Welch, David. "Nazi Propaganda and the Volksgemeinschaft: Constructing a People's Community." *Journal of Contemporary History* 39:2: *Understanding Nazi Germany* (April 2004), pp. 213–38.

Wildt, Michael. *Uncompromising Generation: The Nazi Leadership of the Reich Security Main Office.* Madison: University of Wisconsin Press, 2010.

Wildt, Michael, ed. *Nachrichtendienst, Politische Elite und Mordenheit: Die Sicherheitsdienst des Reichsführers SS.* Hamburg: Hamburger Edition, 2003.

Index